The Ghosts of NASCAR

The Ghosts of NASCAR

The Harlan Boys and the First Daytona 500

JOHN HAVICK

University of Iowa Press, Iowa City

University of Iowa Press, Iowa City 52242
Copyright © 2013 by John Havick
www.uiowapress.org
Printed in the United States of America

All photographs not otherwise attributed are in the author's
personal collection.

The University of Iowa Press is a member of Green Press
Initiative and is committed to preserving natural resources.

Printed on acid-free paper

Library of Congress Cataloging-in-Publication Data
Havick, John, 1940–
The ghosts of NASCAR: the Harlan boys and the first
Daytona 500 / by John Havick.
    pages cm
Includes bibliographical references and index.
ISBN: 978-1-60938-197-4, 1-60938-197-1 (pbk.)
ISBN: 978-1-60938-211-7, 1-60938-211-0 (ebook)
1. Daytona 500 (Automobile race)—History. 2. Stock car
racing—United States—History. I. Title.
GV1033.5.D39H38 2013
796.720975921—dc23   2013010113

To the Harlan boys and their competitors and
to Barbara Havick, who discovered my racing
photos and scrapbooks in a forgotten corner of the attic.

CONTENTS

FOREWORD | by Rex White, 1960 NASCAR Champion

Stock car racing in the 1950s was vastly different than it is today. In the old days a mechanic, operating out of a small garage, using native intelligence and elbow grease, could build a competitive racing machine, and a person eager to get behind the wheel could begin learning to race on a small dirt track. The entry costs were modest and danger was minimal. Many took the route I have just described to begin racing. Drivers Johnny Beauchamp and Tiny Lund and mechanic Dale Swanson began on small, local Iowa tracks.

Although these three began their careers in Iowa, many miles from the East, where I began, I eventually came to know all three. One of my first encounters was when I came to their home track in Council Bluffs, Iowa. We had some car trouble and needed to change a transmission; Tiny Lund jumped in to help us with the work, and he befriended us with an invitation to his place for a shower and food. In 1957 Dale Swanson and I worked together at the Chevrolet race shop, the Southern Engineering Development Corporation (SEDCO), in Atlanta, preparing cars for the Daytona beach race in February. Johnny Beauchamp and I raced together in that big race, both of us trying to win for Chevrolet. Later in 1960, when Swanson and Beauchamp brought a car from the Midwest and raced NASCAR for a while, we renewed our friendship; once, before a contest, I had loaned them a part. Tiny Lund moved to the South and lived at a friend's garage, where I sometimes worked on his car with him. In fact it is interesting that as a NASCAR driver, I had as much contact with these three Iowans as I in fact did.

I can say that Dale Swanson was a top race mechanic, careful and creative. Tiny Lund was a good, ferocious competitor, particularly on dirt tracks, and Johnny Beauchamp in fewer than 30 races proved he could race and win against the top NASCAR drivers. This book describes how these three learned to compete on midwestern tracks, and how then as they matured, they spread out to compete across the United States. It is a story not to be missed.

As a boy I watched Johnny Beauchamp, "motor magician" mechanic Dale Swanson, and many others race. During Beauchamp's first five years (1950–1954) at the Playland Park track in Council Bluffs, Iowa, he was the only two-time champion, winning many more main events than any other competitor. Suddenly, one season Beauchamp was not racing at the Playland track. I left for high school, then the university, and on to a career as a college professor. Stock car racing was pushed far to the back of my daily concerns, but I always wondered what happened to these great racers who had captivated me in my youth.

Now, years later, I stood in the Harlan, Iowa, cemetery, with the headstones of my great-grandparents and grandparents nearby, my father's grave directly in front of me, and I reflected back over the past. I recalled that one Harlan resident, Johnny Beauchamp, had purchased my grandfather's passenger car in 1950 and converted it to a stock car. Once Beauchamp had the car on the track, I went to watch it race. I was hooked. In an era before there was a television in every home, racing offered intense competition, thrilling action, and excitement.

As I left the cemetery, I was overcome by all of the memories and found myself driving to the nearby garage of the great race mechanic Dale Swanson. Perhaps I wanted someone there to share a memory with me. At the garage I found that Dale Swanson's son, Dale Jr., was now running the business. Although Dale Jr. and I had never met, we talked for almost an hour about the old days of racing, and I left thinking about those exciting times and what I might write about them.

I investigated and learned that in 1956, Beauchamp won more races in the late model Midwest circuit (the International Motor Contest Association, or IMCA) than any driver before or after. To Midwesterners, Beauchamp was known as the national champion. I also learned he had placed second at the famed Daytona Beach race in 1957, and that he had won a demonstration race in 1960 against NASCAR drivers that landed him on the Today show, then hosted by Dave Garroway. But Beauchamp's most notable accomplishment was winning the first Daytona 500 in 1959, only to have the victory taken from him three days later. This was a career-changing event, and losing the title was a major setback for him. Beauchamp died many years later, always certain he had won at Daytona. I had to learn more about his story.

To find out what had happened, I interviewed about two hundred people and did extensive research in newspapers and other sources. I learned far more than what happened at the first Daytona 500. I discovered that Johnny Beauchamp's career, along with those of mechanic Dale Swanson and of other midwestern drivers, reveal a slice of racing history seldom recounted: how to negotiate the corners on a dirt track, how to pass or spin opponents, how cars were torn down after races to determine if their mechanical construction conformed to the track rules, how violent drivers sometimes were in response to on-track competition, and how common camaraderie was even among fierce competitors. The book provides one of the few accounts of what it was like to race stock cars in the Midwest in the 1950s. Along the way, I solve countless puzzles about racing and profile many well-known and lesser-known drivers, mechanics, and their families.

At the center of this story are Johnny Beauchamp and Dale Swanson, but they were just two of a host of drivers and mechanics who came out of Harlan, Iowa, and dominated midwestern car racing in the mid-twentieth century. Among the men who achieved a measure of success in this sport was the charismatic, larger-than-life Tiny Lund, who won a Daytona 500 and became a champion in the NASCAR pony division, which was directly below the circuit with the highest horsepower cars.

For a landlocked farm town to spawn two Daytona 500 winners and a top Chevrolet racing mechanic is extraordinary, but the racing bench coming out of Harlan was so deep that several other Harlan boys also rose to the top in the region. Most notable was Bobby Parker. Parker, a 1944 Harlan High School graduate, competed for season stock car championships, winning several. Doing double duty, he also won many contests with other types of vehicles. Another top Harlan wheel man, nearly forgotten now, was Vernon "Hooky" Christensen, who achieved his moniker by skipping school. Christensen won numerous races and in 1951, at the Council Bluffs track, was the first driver with four straight victories — a feat even Lund and Beauchamp had not then achieved. In one season, 1951, Hooky finished third in season points.

In addition to telling the stories of midwestern race car drivers and mechanics, the book makes important but usually overlooked connections between the people in racing and the organizations involved with the sport, such as the racing associations and the automobile manufacturers. For example, the Corvette racing program was critical to Beauchamp's 1956 record-breaking season, and Chevrolet Racing's efforts to build winning cars also aided his career. Master mechanic Dale Swanson and the Chevrolet "clandestine" race shop played a significant part in Beauchamp's exciting near win at the big Daytona Beach race in 1957.

The history of stock car racing is also about the gray area between right and wrong, black and white. In this no-man's-land, stock car competitors ply their trade seeking an advantage. Mechanics, when routine wrench work is not enough, hope for an ambiguity in a rule that fails to say "No, you can't do this." On the track, drivers bang, spin, and use any rough tactic to gain an edge. Johnny Beauchamp accepted the on-track battling, saying, "That's racing."[1] But when has a competitor gone too far? When has an opponent overstepped the boundary of honesty and tough competition and, instead, slunk into cheating and dishonesty that no one could condone?

This is the story of the Harlan boys and midwestern stock car racing. It's about how races were won and lost as the sport came of age in the middle of the twentieth century.

ACKNOWLEDGMENTS

Many individuals shared information with me for this book. Dale Swanson Jr. patiently gave considerable time along with access to his historical racing documents, which provided a broad outline of his father's part of the story. Gaylord Beauchamp, John's younger brother, who also raced and was close to the action, gave details of the early years. John's children, Sanda, Bob, and Bill, all generously offered information and details. Marlene Renfeld and her brother, Russell Leslie, relatives of John's first wife, supplied valuable help. Tiny Lund's relatives and close family friends, Violet Weiss, Opal Bertsch, cousin Tom Lund, and his second wife Wanda, provided excellent assistance. I am grateful to all of these family members for their significant help.

A number of people close to the racing scene provided generous amounts of their time and memories, including Bud Burdick, who raced with Beauchamp during much of the 1950s and drove motorcycles with Tiny Lund; Hooky Christensen, who was from Harlan and raced with Beauchamp, Lund, and Swanson during the earliest days and who contested Beauchamp for the championship in 1951; Sonny Morgan, who congenially provided considerable insight into IMCA racing and the operation of the Swanson garage; Norma Brix, the wife of one of John Beauchamp's best friends, Don Brix, who was tireless in her willingness to talk to me and work through some gaps in my information; and Bill "Speedy" Smith, a great sage and focal point of midwestern racing who was on the scene from the beginning of the story. Rex White, the 1960 NASCAR champion and a great elder statesman of racing, gave me considerable support, encouragement, and information, never failing to answer my phone calls and my questions. Bradley Dennis, a NASCAR racing mechanic from the fifties, also generously talked to me numerous times. My thanks to these people, most of whom I talked to several times.

Others I would like to thank helped me assemble or locate documents. Lee Ackerman, an expert writer on midwestern racing, generously shared IMCA newsletters that enabled me to construct a detailed chronology of

Beauchamp's IMCA late model racing. Linda Burger, a librarian at the Harlan Public Library, did extensive searching and copying of race coverage in the local paper. Jo Weiss of the public library at Council Bluffs, Iowa, bestowed considerable personal guidance, help, and support working with the Council Bluffs microfilm newspaper records, locating material in the vertical file, as well as being on the alert for additional information that came to her attention. Also, Darlene Vergamini voluntarily helped me gather information at the Council Bluffs library.

Many public libraries were also indispensable in providing photocopies of newspaper accounts. Among the libraries that assisted me were the Bassett Historical Center, Bassett, Virginia; the Cabarrus County Public Library, North Carolina; the Cedar Rapids Iowa Public Library; the Charlotte and Mecklenburg County public libraries, North Carolina; the Council Bluffs Iowa Public Library; the Davenport Iowa Public Library; the Darlington City Public Library, South Carolina; the DeKalb County Libraries, Georgia; the Harlan Community Library, Harlan, Iowa; the Kansas City Missouri Public Library; the Memphis Tennessee Public Library; the North Platte Nebraska Public Library; the Owatonna Minnesota Public Library; the Reading Pennsylvania Public Library; the St. Paul Minnesota Central Library; the Topeka and Shawnee County Public Library, Topeka, Kansas; and the Volusia County Library Center, Daytona Beach, Florida.

While writing the book I profited from several associations. I participated in a writing group led by retired lifelong writer and editor, Bard Lindeman. Lindeman offered valuable advice about how to structure the thematic core of the book. Later, I received writing advice and encouragement from the 600-member Atlanta Writers organization, which actively sponsors workshops, speakers, and critique subgroups. At several junctures, the author J. L. Miles gave me advice on how to proceed in the preparation of the manuscript, and author Anne B. Jones, who co-authored two books with Rex White, gave strategic advice about the writing business. Batten Communications, Inc., analyzed film of the 1959 Daytona 500 race. Several people commented on prior drafts of the manuscript. Susan Ralston and Susan Artz Okun examined several chapters, and Barbara Havick and Ann Fisher reviewed and commented on an entire draft of the manuscript, the latter making several important suggestions that I added in a new revision. The book is a composite of all of the information gathered from interviews, print materials, and my experience, as well as the analysis that I applied to it. No one person held the entire story, and in many cases, no single person possessed all of the information on any one segment of the story. The appendix contains a list of the people who were contacted or helped me in some manner.

I would like to add that these aging racing people are some of the nicest, most courteous, most tolerant, and kindest people I have come across. Moreover, the degree of bravery and brains necessary to drive and build these race cars is not the stuff of average people. Bud Burdick demonstrated his bravery as a machine gunner in the Second World War. Tiny Lund helped save a man from a burning and exploding car. Many of these people are exceptional, and I had a great time talking to them and piecing the story together.

Special thanks go to the University of Iowa Press and its great staff. I owe the utmost gratitude to its director, James McCoy, who recognized the possibilities of the story, and Charlotte Wright, who expertly managed the work and kept it on schedule. I thank Karen Copp for her helpful, faithful, and careful design work; Michael Levine for his insightful, expert help and editing; and I especially want to thank editor Catherine Cocks. Catherine congenially worked line by line and page by page, substantially improving the manuscript. Catherine deserves great credit. I thank the entire Iowa crew for its effort.

The Ghosts of NASCAR

1 | The Natural

The story begins in 1947 in the sleepy Iowa town of Harlan. Johnny Beauchamp's journey into stock car racing began on a warm August day in that year, when he was twenty-four years old. He stepped out of his parents' house, not bothering to lock the door—this was the nation's heartland. The shabby, small frame house on the north side of town only cost a few dollars a month, although the family labored to pay even this little amount.

The Beauchamps originally lived near Rich Hill, Missouri, where Johnny's grandparents are buried, and he was born in Clinton, Missouri, before the family resettled to a farm close to Irwin, Iowa, a small village a few miles from Harlan, the larger community. Later on, they moved into town.

On this day Beauchamp's destination was the local track. He was eager to test what he sensed about himself. He loved to go fast but wondered if he had a speed limit, particularly in a race. He slowly drove along a Harlan street, avoiding the ruts in the dusty dirt road. In this part of town, city water pipes and sewers were nonexistent. The paved streets, large houses, and indoor plumbing were on the south side of town inhabited by businessmen, prosperous retired farmers, and skilled tradesmen. Occasionally, for amusement, south Harlan residents attended a stock car race, but they generally believed racing was low class—better left to the folks who lived on the north side of town.

Beauchamp, a confident man with a happy-go-lucky attitude, ignored elite opinion and found his life with people who had interests similar to his. He had an urge to race and little promise for anything else. An even more pressing reason to go into auto racing was the need to support his family.

At six foot two, lean, and movie-star handsome, Beauchamp in tenth grade had captivated Nettie Belle Densmore, a local girl two years his senior. But Johnny also was smitten, so much so he told Nettie Belle he was eighteen, and she did not find out differently until they were married.[1]

He quit high school, and they moved in with Beauchamp's parents on the farm. In 1941 Nettie Belle and John became the parents of a baby boy, Robert Beauchamp, who was born at his Densmore grandparents' house in Harlan. The next year, William Beauchamp was born in the same house.

John Beauchamp struggled to earn money. At first, the scarcity of employment opportunities in rural southwest Iowa led him to a federal government project operated by the Civilian Conservation Corps, located in Melbourne, Iowa, 70 miles away from Nettie Belle and Harlan. Then, searching for a new life, he enlisted in the army and was issued a uniform, but the military soon released him after a physical exam discovered a heart blockage. He returned to Harlan. Still looking for a new direction, he packed up Nettie Belle and the kids, moved to Davenport Street in Omaha, and drove a Checker cab.

But the move to Omaha did not solve the young family's difficulties. On September 15, 1944, Beauchamp divorced Nettie Belle. His adventuresome spirit rejected life with a daily routine, scratching out an existence in monotonous work. A spontaneous force propelled him away from married, settled life. When his son, Robert, was a teenager, he recalled that his father had been driving down an unfamiliar highway and had said to him, "I wonder where that side road goes?"[2] And in an instant, Beauchamp wheeled the car around and turned off the main highway to explore. He was restless and carefree.

After the divorce, Nettie Belle's parents became more involved with their daughter's life. Adjacent to their house in Harlan on Fifth and Walnut Street was a lot they owned with a one-room house, which the family now expanded to two rooms. Nettie Belle slept in the back room and the two boys slept on fold-away beds in the front room. They hauled water into the house from a cistern.

When World War II ended, Beauchamp returned through an ocean of cornfields to the Harlan area. Now twenty-three, he became a used car salesman.[3] He bunked with his parents, whose house was just a few blocks from the race track on Harlan's northeastern perimeter.

In 1947, when Beauchamp made the short drive to the track, Harlan, Iowa, population 4,000,[4] was the Shelby County seat. Consequently, the county fairgrounds were located there, complete with a one-half-mile oval, surrounded by well-clipped grass and a freshly painted grandstand. It was a handsome venue for the annual county fair. In an era before television, local residents, eager for diversion, flocked to the fair.

Fair races had no single format or rules; the main goal at the Shelby County Fair was a good show. On the schedule the day Beauchamp first raced were 4- and 6-lappers billed as stock car races. In these events it was all about winning, and the vehicles could be in a variety of shapes and sizes. The race card also included less serious events for which driving skill was not the only factor, including two 6-lap novelty contests that combined skill with silly activities, such as drivers stopping midrace to drink a glass of water or enter the stands to scavenge articles from the spectators. A final contest, the 10-lap Australian pursuit race, required that after each lap, the last place car drop out.[5]

Aside from testing his potential as a race driver, Beauchamp entered these events in hopes of winning desperately needed cash. He was struggling to meet his responsibilities. At first, it seemed as if he'd made a good bet. With spectators cheering and hooting for their fellow citizens, he won the first 4-lap race and earned twenty dollars, the equivalent of several days' pay for a car salesman. Significantly, Beauchamp appeared to be a more talented driver than most of the other amateurs that day.

But one competitor was difficult to defeat. In the 6-lapper, Beauchamp pushed his car into the lead. Suddenly a car sped past him but slowed too much for the corner, hugging the inside position. Beauchamp jammed his foot on the accelerator and flung his auto high and wide into the turn, outside of the other car. Coming out of the corner he sped in front. Once again, the competitor gathered speed on the straightaway and accelerated around Beauchamp. In the end, Beauchamp lost the event. Worse, in the heat of competition for first place, Hooky Christensen slipped past him to finish second, but still Beauchamp had won thirty-five dollars for the day.

Even more important was that he became acquainted with the man who had beaten him: Dale Swanson, a local mechanic. Five years earlier, Swanson had lived with his mother on a farm a few miles north of Harlan. The family had originally resided 40 miles away from Harlan near Mondamin, Iowa. When Dale was thirteen his father died, and he juggled completing high school with helping his mother operate the farm. After graduation, he and his mother relocated to the farm near Harlan. Swanson married an attractive local girl, red-haired Phyllis Kohls, and she moved to the farm with Dale and his mother. Dale Jr. was born in September 1942.

Swanson, however, was not especially happy with the life of a farmer. One day while slogging through the mud and worse, he slipped, fell, and was covered in pig slop. Disgusted, he concluded, "I'm finished with farming." In 1942 he and his family moved to Harlan, and there he set up a shop in which he converted conventional brakes to hydraulic brakes.[6]

Swanson supplemented the repair and brake shop business by helping farmers with his custom hay baling service. At first, he lost valuable time shifting equipment from one farm job to the next because his tractor crawled along the highway. To solve the problem, he tinkered with the engine, and soon afterwards that tractor could zip along.[7] His magic with a tractor engine would soon transfer to a more competitive endeavor, making him a much-sought-after mechanic among midwestern racers.

On the day at the Shelby County Fair races that Beauchamp and Swanson met, Swanson entered a fast car and won two 6-lap events as well as garnering several other good finishes, netting a grand total of $105.[8] So the skinny Swanson looked at Beauchamp and said, "You turn the corners real good and my car goes fast. Maybe we should team up."[9]

Beauchamp, aware that Swanson had the fastest car, gave him a big friendly smile, and nodded. "I believe we should race together."[10]

Beauchamp and Swanson's partnership changed the direction of their lives.

S oon the partnership between Swanson and Beauchamp was thriving. The two men's personalities meshed. Beauchamp was slow to offend. He was an easygoing, congenial guy. Somewhat reserved, he was careful with words. A few people suspected his silence may have concealed a man with an agenda. A local contemporary once reflected that "Johnny was a sly son-of-a-gun."[1]

Swanson, on the other hand, was direct and more likely to voice his opinions. He had the demeanor of a man who was right—especially about automobiles. Swanson, in his white coveralls, could be mistaken for a physician about to perform a delicate operation.

Race driver and Swanson customer Junior Brunick recalls his mechanic once disagreeing with Swanson over the proper setup of the suspension system. Swanson ignored the advice of Brunick's mechanic. The mechanic persisted in doubting Swanson's approach, but Swanson's confidence was unshakeable. "Why don't you try it my way and see what happens?"[2] When the car took the track, Swanson's setup worked well and the issue was settled.

Beauchamp, not a mechanic, happily gave Swanson full rein to build the cars. Born on Washington's birthday in 1918 and five years Beauchamp's senior, the mechanic was a responsible married man and by 1947 the father of two sons, Dale Jr. and newly born Richard. Swanson did the worrying and provided the mature stability to their enterprise.[3]

Beauchamp and Swanson lived in a land of cornfields interrupted by small towns connected by narrow highways. Settled at a time when the first capital of Iowa had been determined by how far a horse could travel in a day from the Mississippi River, the rural towns of western Iowa were spaced far enough apart to support local farmers. Atlantic, Avoca, Denison, and Missouri Valley were within a 30-mile radius of Harlan. These isolated communities, linked together in an informal social network, spawned all kinds of amusement.

One unusual bit of entertainment was the Manning "catsup murder." A man was gunned down on the street, a pool of blood appeared, and two men jumped out of a car, threw the body in the car, and sped away. The gangland-style slaying flashed on national headlines. The police eventually discovered that several high school students from Audubon, a neighboring community, had staged the entire affair, complete with tomato juice and ketchup for blood.[4]

A more conventional amusement was the annual county fair, an event that was common in many regions and states. At the Shelby County Fair in which Beauchamp and Swanson competed, spectators could see horse and motorcycle contests in addition to auto races. Each county fairground served as a community entertainment center, not only during the fair, but for other events throughout the year. Auto racing on the county tracks, particularly on holidays, became an activity that connected the communities and made southwestern Iowa an incubator for motor sports.

One modest local racing venue not associated with any county fairground sprang up at Anita, Iowa, where Claus Behnken, local Ford dealer and farmer, carved a track out of his pastureland. Because the competition resulted in banged up, dented automobiles, scarcely anyone was foolhardy enough to risk a passenger car in a race. To encourage locals to participate in the fun, Behnken hauled old cars from Chicago for his contests. A rumor circulated that his cars were "special purchases" that departed Chicago in the middle of the night—in other words, they were stolen. His races entertained the local people and gave the serious drivers a chance to practice. Eventually, Behnken became one of the many race car owners involved with Johnny Beauchamp.

Dale Swanson and Johnny Beauchamp were not the only ones to gain experience and confidence on the local community tracks; Dewayne "Tiny" Lund also began his driving career there. He loved motorized competition of every kind and virtually banged and slammed and willed himself to be a success. "Lund lived to race,"[5] and like Beauchamp, he was to become a recognized champion and top competitor—but he also was to become a star, in part because of his dynamic personality.

In the end, no fewer than six Harlan daredevils discovered they had talent and seized the opportunity to improve their skills at these community contests. Swanson, Beauchamp, Lund, as well as Bobby Parker, Hooky Christensen, and Wayne Selser, all claiming Harlan as home, went on to test their skills in events for more money and more glory.

The Harlan Boys did not have far to go to find "serious" racing.

1. Beauchamp's first hot rod. (L-R) James Leslie, who owned the garage; Delbert Leslie, who helped work on the car; John Beauchamp; Leo (Duke) Olson, a close friend of John who helped with the car; Junior Monson, neighbor of John's who lived south of Irwin, Iowa. At this time, Avoca was on the side of car because the Leslies were based in Avoca. Courtesy of Russell Leslie.

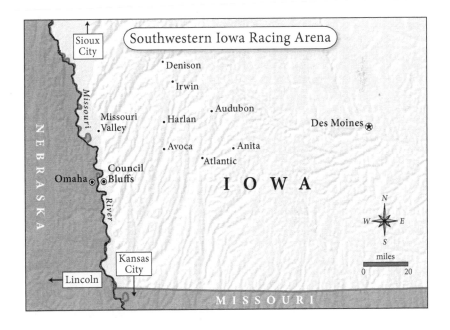

Southwestern Iowa Racing Arena

2. Tiny Lund and his hot rod, about 1949. Courtesy of Dale Swanson Jr.

3. The race track at Claus Behnken's farm in Anita, Iowa. Courtesy of Norma Brix.

4. The hot rod Beauchamp drove, with Swanson on the left and Beauchamp behind the wheel, in front of the Swanson one-door garage. Courtesy of Dale Swanson Jr.

5. Number 53, Beauchamp's first stock car, which he drove in the 1950 season.

6. Beauchamp and 55, in 1951.

7. Victory celebration party in Omaha's Peony Park, 1951. (L-R): Dale Swanson, Phyllis Swanson, Mrs. George Zenchuck, George Zenchuck (Playland track flagman), John Beauchamp, Donna Richter. Courtesy of Dale Swanson Jr.

8. John Beauchamp and Nettie Belle Beauchamp in front of 55, in 1951. Courtesy of Russell Leslie.

9. Beauchamp in the 55 and Lund in the 5, with Dale Swanson at the center, between the cars, in 1951. Photograph by John Sommers, courtesy of Dale Swanson.

10. The wrecked 55 in 1953 at an Avoca, Iowa, gas station. The car won Playland championships in 1950, 1951, and 1952.

11. The old model stock car, built by Holtz and Leslie, that Beauchamp drove in the 1952 and 1953 seasons.

12. The start of a race at Playland in May 1954. The 55 is at the back of the line.

14. Playland track action in 1954, showing Beauchamp's 55, Bud Burdick's V-8, and Bob Kosiski's 35. Courtesy of Russell Leslie.

13. Facing page: Victory celebration, Beauchamp and friends, 1954.

15. The late model car owned by George Short. (L-R): Dale Swanson, George Short, Mrs. George Short, and the Shorts' daughter, in 1955. Courtesy of Dale Swanson Jr.

17. Swanson (L) and Beauchamp at Daytona Beach in February 1957. The car with "Nalley" on side that is visible behind Swanson was the Black Widow that Beauchamp drove in this race. Courtesy of Norma Brix.

16. Facing page: Beauchamp and Norma Brix, a family friend, in 1955. Courtesy of Norma Brix.

18. A Black Widow in an IMCA event in 1957. Courtesy of Dale Swanson Jr.

19. The SEDCO banquet after the 1957 Daytona Beach race. Seated at the table, 8th from the left is Rex White; R seated at table from front, Possum Jones, 3rd, Hugh Babb, Bradley Dennis (top of head), Bob Cliff, unidentified woman, Vince Piggins; standing (L-R), an unidentified woman, Tom Jones, Bob Welborn, and last on left top, Betty Skelton, table center, John Beauchamp and Donna Richter; front row standing, Phyllis Swanson, Dale Swanson, Paul McGuffie, a Nalley Chevrolet representative, and two unidentified men; back row (L-R), two unidentified women, Buck Baker, another unidentified woman, Paul Goldsmith, and Jack Smith. Courtesy of Bradley Dennis.

20. Minneapolis Gopher 350, 1962 (L-R): Dale Swanson Jr., Dale Swanson, Sonny Morgan, Neil Larson (of Larson Chevrolet and a friend of Morgan). This was one of Swanson's last big wins; Morgan was the driver. Courtesy of Sonny Morgan.

3 | The Mafia Race Track

Wherever Meyer Lansky was, dead bodies turned up—a grand total of forty-three, according to one of his associates.[1] Lansky was an East Coast gangster, a New York Mafia mogul and Bugsy Siegel's pal. So what was he doing in 1941 on the streets of the Omaha–Council Bluffs metropolitan area?

Lansky, unwittingly, was about to build Beauchamp's "home track" and the biggest stock car venue between Chicago and Denver. Because the nationally known Ak-sar-ben (Nebraska spelled backwards) track had stopped horse racing during World War II, Lansky decided there was an opening for dog racing. Diminutive and easily mistaken for a businessman, Lansky settled in at the swankiest Omaha hotel, the Fontenelle, and signed a five-year lease for property on the Iowa side of the Missouri River. From the $50,000 track and grandstand that Lansky constructed in Council Bluffs, Iowa, spectators could see the river and the city of Omaha.

The Kennel Club, Lansky's name for his track, circumvented the Iowa law against gambling because fans bet on "options" to buy dogs. If the dog won, the option was sold back for a profit. Some 4,000 people packed the grandstand on July 11, 1941, for the first race. Dog racing boomed in Council Bluffs. In 1943 the eighty-six-night season netted the city $140,000 of tax revenue.

Although Lansky himself was a model citizen, the problem was that the races attracted criminals and gambling clubs. The Stork Club and the Riviera Club popped up on the less-traveled South Omaha Bridge River Road. The gambling was rough, wide open, and professional enough that participants knew how to avoid getting caught. When the police raided one night, all they found was 150 people quietly watching a floor show.

In 1944 Council Bluffs elected a reform mayor who shut down Lansky's operation. When a different mayor was elected two years later, the dog races again seemed possible, but the state government squelched them by closing legal loopholes.[2] Yet even today, signs of Meyer Lansky linger. A restaurant—Lanskys—adopted the notorious gangster's name even though its owners were no relation to the famous gangster, and it still operates in the Council Bluffs–Omaha area.

After the demise of dog racing, the old Kennel Club track and grandstand was managed in 1947 by the Council Bluffs government, which held a variety of activities at the venue. Then, however, the city was offered a proposal it could not refuse. The brothers Abe and Louis Slusky, operators of a concession stand in Omaha's Krug Park and an amusement park and race track in Houston, Texas, bought fourteen acres on the Iowa side near the approach to the Ak-sar-ben Bridge and leased the track and grandstand area from the city of Council Bluffs. The reported cost for the entire enterprise was $250,000, and the result was a huge, contiguous parcel.[3] Louis Slusky operated their Houston site.

Abe Slusky opened Playland, an amusement park, on May 30, 1948.[4] He experimented with different events at the track and grandstand. Omahan Jerome Givens recalls entering a vehicle in an antique auto race at the Playland track, but the owners of these cars quickly realized they were risking a precious possession in a frivolous moment of fun. The antique car races were short-lived.[5]

Motorcycle races also failed to draw big crowds, but the Sluskys found partial success with midget competition, which by this time had been organized into a circuit traveling to Missouri, Nebraska, and Iowa. In the decade before World War II, midget racing had become popular in California and quickly spread across the United States. The cars were built from scratch; they were not modifications of mass-market automobiles. The wheel base (the distance from the front to rear wheel) typically was 76 inches or less, the width was approximately 65 inches, and the weight about 900 pounds. By comparison, a 1939 Ford coupe, a vehicle frequently raced in the 1950s, weighed approximately 2,700 pounds and had a wheel base of 112 inches.

A carefully crafted racing machine, the midget car had open wheels without fenders for protection. The slightest tire contact with another car on the track could send a vehicle out of control.[6] Midget racing required more careful driving than stock car competition. One Harlan pilot, Bobby Parker, located a midget car driven by yet another Harlan resident, Wayne Selser. Selser, in the midst of changing to a new owner and a new midget to drive, helped Parker arrange to drive the old vehicle that he (Selser) had driven. Parker entered his first event in Sioux City and decided to keep racing midgets after finishing third.

Although midgets produced some fan interest, the stands were half empty. So Abe Slusky searched for events that would attract more spectators.

On July 9, 1949, Slusky introduced hot rods on the old Lansky dog track, and in doing so he gave Johnny Beauchamp and Dale Swanson an opportunity they had been looking for. Hot rods did not conform to a single look, but instead appeared to be the product of random parts bolted together. Although they gave the impression of a load of junk on wheels, they virtually flew on the highways and race tracks.[7] Concealed by the exterior, the engine could be loaded with such features as "a three-carburetor manifold, double springing ignition, reground ¾-race camshaft, high compression head"[8]—in short, a hot rod was assembled to go fast.[9]

Beauchamp had bought his younger brother Gaylord's 1932 Ford to convert into a hot rod.[10] Beauchamp's brother-in-law, Delbert Leslie, and Delbert's cousin, Jim Leslie, chipped in to help. Jim, who owned a farm implement business in nearby Avoca, provided mechanical assistance, and Delbert, employed by the railroad, supplied financial support.

John Beauchamp's plan to have a race car was not unusual in these early years after World War II. Many a young man, returned from the war eager for a thrill and some excitement, located an inexpensive old used car, parked it at a friend's gas station, tinkered with the engine by adding a few parts, and went racing. The cost of entry to the sport of car racing was minimal in those years. Race enthusiasts began small, little more than a hobby, with friends helping prepare the vehicle and wives and girlfriends bringing the mechanics lunch.

In 1949 Swanson worked on the Beauchamp hot rod engine and soon became half owner. A black-and-white paint combination finished the job, but a question remained: what number to paint on the hot rod?[11] An outsider might believe one number is as good as another, but certain numbers seem to propel a car to victory. Swanson believed he had such a number.

One night, after many hours of work on the car, Swanson decided to celebrate. Harlan had several "establishments," including the Chicken Hut, that not only offered food and drink, but gambling as well. He played the dice game. He rolled and the dice came up fifty-five. He rolled again: two fives. The dice seemed to keep turning up double fives. Finally Swanson concluded, "Fifty-five is the number for the car."[12] He and Beauchamp now had a vehicle to serve their ambitions.

For races at Playland, Abe Slusky hoped to lure hot rods from the large

Omaha–Council Bluffs metro area as well as from St. Louis, Kansas City (Missouri), Denver, and Chicago, and for this first event in 1949, he succeeded in attracting more than twenty, a larger number than in most other hot rod events. Over 4,000 spectators, almost a capacity crowd, paid to watch the first competition.

The program included preliminary contests called heat races. Drivers who finished poorly in the heat races next competed in a consolation contest; drivers who finished a heat in the middle of the pack found themselves in a semi-feature, sometimes called a semi-main event. Drivers who won or finished in a spot near the front in the heat entered the main event: the feature.

On this first night, Tiny Lund won the initial event, a heat race, but his win was the extent of the Harlan achievement for the night.[13] This win was an early glimmer of Lund's determination to be a great driver. He loved racing; his father, Chris, had been involved in racing and helped Lund build the hot rod. Often, Lund would caravan to a track with Swanson and Beauchamp. Upon arrival, the Harlan contingent appeared to be formidable competitors.

Later, Lund actually drove one season for Swanson and in other years drove in select races for him. Although Lund eventually became an important national stock car personality, his early years in Harlan have not been chronicled. His activities intersect with and are a part of the Beauchamp-Swanson story.

After the first night, Playland officials declared hot rods a success and promised another night of racing the following Saturday. Because the drivers and owners received a percentage of the gate receipts, big crowds resulted in a big purse, and a big purse attracted drivers. For the second set of events, competitors from St. Louis, Kansas City, Denver, and California announced they were coming.

The Harlan boys now had a big race venue 50 miles from their hometown, but the first night's results suggested they might not do so well against the competition. On July 16, the second night of racing, drivers from St. Joe, Kansas City, and Los Angeles captured the first three spots in the feature.[14] Lund managed to finish second in the second heat race and in the semi-main event. Beauchamp did badly in his heat race but finished third behind Lund in the semi-main.[15]

It's possible their mediocre performances were deliberate. The races were wild affairs with dangerous wrecks and cars skidding and slamming into one another. Drivers could easily lose control of their hot rods because they were open-wheeled. Beauchamp backed off, not wanting to wreck his car or injure himself, but the big races caused many drivers to take chances. They drove too fast into the corners and lost control, or they attempted to squeeze into a spot on the track already occupied by another car. And the hot rods were essentially convertibles with a roll bar. When they crashed and rolled over, drivers had no buffer to shield them. The formula for trouble was in place: an unstable vehicle, minimal protection for the driver, and high stakes racing.

Although Beauchamp struggled at Playland and Lund only did moderately well, in general Slusky's first two nights of racing were a great success. Suddenly, on the third night, there was a disastrous crash. Twenty-one-year-old Bill Pettit from Salt Lake City, Utah, had brought his hot rod and his new bride to Council Bluffs. He told her he would be careful and this night would be his last race—then he would sell the car.[16] On the last lap of the feature race, Pettit saw a slight opening between two cars in front of him, but the opening was not big enough, the cars' wheels locked, and Pettit's hot rod began barrel-rolling. When his car came to rest, his body hung out of the car, his head gone.

Abe Slusky pressed on with a fourth racing night, designating that profits from the night would go to the widow of the previous week's fallen driver. Unfortunately, Kansas City African American driver Curtis "Cyclone" Ross, originally from Columbus, Ohio, and the winner of a 1939 race in Chicago among exclusively black competitors, found himself in trouble on the track.[17] Ross, while attempting to move through the pack, ran up on the rear of the car in front of him. He lost control and began rolling end-over-end. The car landed upside down, crushing him. He, too, was decapitated.[18]

After this terrible event, officials immediately stopped the hot rod races,[19] and the Sluskys began hunting for a replacement attraction. Beauchamp and the other hot rod drivers had lost the biggest racing location in the region. But even though the Playland hot rod era lasted only a month, it demonstrated the popularity of racing. The track was well-positioned to become one of the hottest venues in the Midwest. Swanson, Beauchamp, Lund, and a host of competitors would soon see to that.

4 | Winning with a Hot Rod

With Playland racing slammed shut, Beauchamp and Swanson sifted through the forthcoming events in the region to find races with large prizes. Locating the more serious contests was critical, because many hot rod races attracted few cars and offered little money; however, several locations were promising.

One racing hot spot was in Des Moines, Iowa, where the Midwest Racing Association held a "championship" event. Beauchamp, leading by one-half lap as he sped into the final curve of the race, realized his hot rod's gas pedal was stuck. He recalled, "I went into a real tight fast spin and whirled completely around four times."[1] As the other competitors bore down on him, he straightened the car and accelerated toward the finish line, salvaging third place.[2] Another promising venue was in Nebraska, where in 1948 enthusiasts had revived the state's pre-war roadster racing and formed the Nebraska Hot Rod Racing Association (NHRRA), establishing a circuit of twelve communities that held events in 1949.[3]

Traveling to races did not prevent John Beauchamp from being with his kids. Occasionally, he would bring the boys and even Nettie Belle along to the races. Although spontaneous and unsettled, Beauchamp in his own way cared for his former wife and the children. Swanson's family also sometimes accompanied him, and the Beauchamps and Swansons bunked with friends. Robert Beauchamp recalls the great fun he had at one Nebraska event, where he enjoyed the camaraderie with the other children.

Johnny Beauchamp's driving exploits were etched in his son's memory. During one event, Robert recalled with amazement what his father did after leading the field coming out of the last turn. Suddenly he spun out, much as he had in the Des Moines championship, and found himself facing the onrushing vehicles. Without a moment of thought, Beauchamp jammed the car in reverse and backed across the finish line, winning by a few feet. Robert said, "I could not believe my father did that and managed to win that race."[4]

Most races were not that dramatic. In one typical day of hot rod races, at Beatrice, Nebraska, in August 1949, Beauchamp had possibly one of his first big successes in the Swanson car. He was one of fourteen drivers competing before 2,500 fans. The purse of $717.23, with other, nonpaying fans outside the fence donating an additional $40.53, gave Beauchamp considerable incentive.

Before the actual contests, the competing cars recorded a 1-lap time. These time trials gave officials a rationale to set the lineup for races. Normally, the driver with the fastest time trial starts in the front, and the slower cars stretch out behind according to their respective times.

At this event, Beauchamp won the time trials: he was five-tenths of a second faster than Gordon Shuck of Edgar, Nebraska. Beauchamp and Shuck, because they were the two fastest cars, then had a match race with no other competitors on the track, which Beauchamp won. He was not entered in the second event because it involved the seven slowest cars. But in the third event, Beauchamp won the "fast car heat race," comprising the six fastest hot rods.

These same six fastest cars competed in the fifth race, but for this event the order was reversed, with the fastest car in the back. Beauchamp, starting from the rear, had 5 laps to get to the front. He drove number 55 hard and fast into the corners, passing one car on the outside and then on the next lap ducking inside on the curve and passing another.

On each lap Beauchamp passed one car, but could he catch and pass Norman Shaffer, who had started in the front? Beauchamp, running in second with 1 lap remaining, edged into the lead at the finish line. The press reported that the Harlan boy gave the crowd "thrill after thrill."[5] Johnny Beauchamp could drive a race car.

To cap the day, Beauchamp finished second in the 10-lap feature, the details of which have been lost or were never recorded. For the day's competition, the black-and-white number 55 pulled in $200.81.[6]

The Swanson-Beauchamp hot rod next visited Missouri Valley, Iowa, on September 4, 1949. One thousand fans watched the thrills and spills, including three spectacular crashes. Beauchamp performed well again, winning the third heat and the main event. Harlan was such a powerhouse for racing that four other natives—Tiny Lund, Bobby Parker, Bernard McCord, and Chris Nelson—all well practiced at local fairground tracks, also placed. But it was Beauchamp, in the Swanson-tuned hot rod, who swept the big events.[7]

Missouri Valley races lacked the stiff competition of Nebraska, but Beauchamp's success on tracks in both states made mechanic and driver optimistic for the contests the following day. Four thousand spectators turned out on Labor Day weekend to watch twenty-seven hot rods compete in Sioux Falls, South Dakota. This was a big test for Beauchamp—the $1,000 purse had lured drivers from several states and as far away as Minneapolis.

Beauchamp won a "preliminary" or heat race, a trophy dash comprising top cars from the heat races and the Australian pursuit race. He finished second in the 20-lap feature, losing to a car driven by Vern Kolb, a top driver from Austin, Minnesota, who had been 4.4 seconds faster than Beauchamp in the time trials.[8] In the end, the Iowan captured three firsts and one second that day.

The only snag in the Sioux Falls invasion was that the local newspaper reporter credited Beauchamp's wins to "Johnnie Viewcamp." This reporter became an early leader in a long parade of announcers, journalists, and even fellow drivers who mangled and mispronounced the Beauchamp name. The family pronounced the name "Byou Kamp," but others pronounced it Bow Champ, Bow Kamp, Bow Shamp, and other ways as well. Beauchamp paid no attention to how his name was pronounced—he simply collected his prize money.

By the fall of 1949, the Harlan native was rapidly becoming a regional racing star, but Dale Swanson, in his own way, also gave a performance. After lighting up a cigarette and positioning it between his lips, he would ignore it. As the cigarette burned, the ash became longer and longer, but he never lifted it from his lips. Observers marveled that he could grow such a cigarette until it ultimately consisted of all ash. Was Swanson too preoccupied to give his cigarette attention, or was he simply neglectful? Not that it mattered—everyone thought it was amazing.

Beauchamp and Swanson's success that summer happened far from Harlan. In fact, the notoriety and money could never have been achieved within the Harlan city limits. And so the two men continued to take their talents on the road. But Swanson, ever the entrepreneur, also tried to boost his prosperity in Harlan by promoting hot rod races at the Shelby County fairgrounds.

In late October 1949, 1,400 spectators, about one-fourth of Harlan's population, flocked to Swanson's races. Fifteen competitors arrived from such places as Beatrice and Blair, Nebraska; Kansas City, Missouri; and

Des Moines, Iowa. The hot rods came because Swanson promised that the drivers would receive two-thirds of the gate receipts.

Beauchamp placed second in the first heat, but then his fortunes changed. Before the races began, several teenagers had taken up positions near the southwest curve, outside the track. The announcer and officials, including Swanson, repeatedly told the kids to move away because they might be injured. They did not move. One boy argued back, claiming he was not standing on track property, so they couldn't make him move. Then what everyone feared took place. During the race, a wheel flew off the Swanson-Beauchamp car and rolled toward the kids. The argumentative boy, rather than moving out of the way of the speeding tire as soon as he saw it, attempted to dodge it only at the last instant. He failed, and the accident broke his neck and paralyzed him from the chest down.[9]

Dale Swanson felt terrible about what happened, but everyone present had witnessed the officials' pleas and demands for the kids to move. Most people did not believe the promoter was to blame; however, for a year or so there were not many automobile races at the fairgrounds.[10]

Hot rod racing was notoriously dangerous. The Harlan injury was not Swanson's fault or that of any official, but it was yet another of the large number of horrible injuries associated with hot rods. Promoters were now searching for a safe vehicle that average mechanics could afford to build. In the meantime, Swanson and Beauchamp hunkered down for a cold, snowy winter, having no clear plan for the 1950 season. They now had racing in their blood, and somehow they would be back competing on the track.

n May 1950, big, gregarious DeWayne Lund lumbered into Dale Swanson's brake shop, a small building reached by entering an alley south of the town square. Lund was itching to compete again, and he had an idea. He wanted a partnership with Swanson to race a stock car. His name was DeWayne, but everyone called him "Tiny." At 6 foot five and 250 pounds, Tiny radiated a boisterous, fun loving, and wild presence. Mass alone was not what attracted people to him. His magnetism demanded attention. Constantly on the move, playing pranks, and showing off—no one ever said Tiny was quiet. His energy thrust him center stage.

Born November 14, 1929, he was six years younger than Johnny Beauchamp. A daredevil ready to attempt any type of motorized competition or stunt, he began racing while still in school. His first contest was competing on a motorcycle at the small hamlet of Yetter, Iowa, in 1946.[1]

Swanson and Lund knew each other; most everyone knew each other in Harlan, or at least knew about each other. But the two men were well acquainted because they had raced against each other at the fairground tracks and had caravaned to more distant hot rod races. Swanson had also helped Lund with his race car engine.

The mechanic was aware that Lund had a passion for motorcycles. He and other Harlan boys, including Ron Jensen, Ollie Pash, Bobby Parker, Vernon "Hooky" Christensen, John Kamp, and Lowell Jensen, found excitement in hill climbing—an event in which the motorcyclists competed to see who could go the farthest up a steep hill. Ollie Pash by all accounts was the best of the motorcycle competitors, but Tiny Lund was good. One might imagine that a huge man's weight would slow a motorcycle, making it unable to scale a hill; however, Lund's weight kept the front wheel of the cycle on the ground, preventing it from literally doing a cartwheel on the slope and falling on the rider.

As this risk suggests, hill climbing was a wild affair. The boys would talk a farmer into letting them use a field. Then they would mark off several different distances away from the base of a hill, and from these markers riders would get a running start. The farther back from the incline, the faster the cycle could speed ahead and up the hill.

Cyclists would attack the hill one at a time. In one climbing event, Bobby Parker, a beer in one hand and his cycle handle in the other, was certain he could get to the top. He managed not only to reach the top, but to fly right over it, narrowly escaping serious injury.[2]

For a time, the Harlan riders joined up with riders from nearby Denison, home of actress Donna Reed, and they formed the "Handlebar Jockeys." Ollie Pash recalls a Denison member of the Jockeys club saying, "Some of you Harlan guys would run through a brick wall if you had a crowd to watch you."[3]

Eventually, a promoter came along and offered each motorcyclist $50 each time he performed tricks and races.[4] The boys would go on ramps and fly over obstacles, they would go through flames, and they would perform about any stunt that would thrill the crowd. One time, the promoter had the boys go through flaming wood frames two at a time, side-by-side. The frames shattered, the one rider's frame striking the other rider. Ron Jensen incurred injuries that needed medical attention.

The "show" traveled to Nebraska, South Dakota, Missouri, and Kansas. Tiny and his teammates also entered numerous county fair motorcycle races. Several of the cyclists, such as Bud Burdick, Bobby Parker, and Hooky Christensen, later became winning race drivers.

Lund raced motorcycles on most Sundays from 1947 to 1949, breaking his leg once and his arm three times.[5] One of those breaks came when he fell off his motorcycle while showing off for neighborhood grade school girls. As his high school friend and fellow Handlebar Jockey Ron Jensen observed, "Tiny was not afraid of the devil himself."[6]

There was a downside to Tiny's devil-may-care attitude, though, and it appeared early in his life. Opal Bertsch, a close family friend who babysat Tiny, recalled that when he was nine years old, he led her out of the house and asked her to get into the passenger side of the family car while he climbed behind the wheel. Before she realized what was happening, he drove off.[7] Tiny, when most boys were still playing with blocks, was eager to get behind the wheel of an automobile, and he found a way to do just that. In later years, neighbors suspected Tiny of incessantly revving his motorcycle engine to annoy them. One day, while Tiny, about eighteen years old at the time, was in the front yard making repairs on the motor-cycle, it burst into flames. His mother, Hazel Lund, bought him another motorcycle the following day.[8]

Legend has it that one day Lund drove his motorcycle into the high school and up the stairs. Finally, he was expelled permanently from high school for socking a teacher. The teacher had lightly touched Tiny, but Lund, with little respect for authority or rules, jumped up from his chair and knocked the man across the room.[9] Once again, Hazel Lund inter-vened on her son's behalf, arranging for him to finish school and gradu-ate,[10] although Tiny did not graduate immediately. In fact, he had to wait several years before the high school allowed him to complete his last semester of courses. His photo appears in the Harlan High School year-book for 1950, when Tiny was about twenty-one years old.

Tiny's stock car racing began with his parents' automobile, probably in 1948. Various versions of this story have been told, but Ollie Pash, who rented an apartment on the upper floor of Chris and Hazel Lund's home and was a friend of Tiny, witnessed what actually happened: "Tiny was in the kitchen begging his father to let him enter the family car in the fair-ground stock car races." Chris Lund, who in his youth had done some race driving and who was a mechanic, said "No," but Tiny's mother entered the room and said he could race the car.[11] So Tiny rolled the family car at the races.[12]

Knowing what he knew about Tiny, Swanson was not certain what to say to his proposal in 1950 to team up to build a stock car. He already had a hot rod partnership with Beauchamp, but he understood that the future of the hot rod—and therefore the 1950 season in general—was in doubt. In contrast, old model stock car racing was just beginning. At this time an "old model" car was one manufactured before World War II. After the war, people were eagerly trading in the cars built in the 1930s, and so these old models were plentiful. The 1939 and 1940 Ford coupes were among the best suited to be made into race cars. The coupe was light weight and had a peppy engine.

The possibilities for racing, however, were wide open, and it was unclear how great any one opportunity was. Clearly, the hot rod had problems, and who was to say that some other vehicle might also not live up to ex-pectations in the heat of competition. On the other hand, Tiny and Swan-son were aware that the Playland track was going to race old model cars.

Tiny sweetened his proposal: he had already located a car, a 39 Ford coupe, in Audubon, a 15-minute drive from Harlan, and he promised to help convert the auto to a race car. Swanson could weigh the proposal and see that the race car in a week could earn enough money to pay for itself.

Tiny had more persuading to do, but Speedy Bill Smith, who knew him well, reflected years later that "Tiny had charisma." Smith was a man who would know. He was at the Playland hot rod races, and he actually competed as a driver against Beauchamp and Lund in the Nebraska hot rod races. Smith did not stay behind the wheel long, instead becoming a race mechanic. He eventually built his small speed shop in Lincoln, a place Lund frequently visited, into a multimillion-dollar worldwide auto and race parts supply business, complete with a massive museum. Smith is well recognized as one of the best race mechanics of this early post–World War II era.[13] Years later, Swanson said: "Tiny would give you his last dime. But he expected you to do the same for him."[14]

Although it was difficult to say no to Tiny, Swanson was intelligent and strong-willed enough not to let himself be talked into anything. He most likely reasoned that building a stock car for Tiny Lund to drive was not a big deal. Playland had not yet become established as a major magnet for racing, and even though hot rod racing had problems, its decline was not definite.

Also, Swanson still had the hot rod partnership with Beauchamp, but that was looking a bit shaky in May 1950 because Beauchamp's life was in turmoil. During the latter part of the 1940s, he had married Nettie Belle for a second time. This marriage was no less tumultuous than the first. According to Beauchamp's daughter, "They simply disagreed about almost everything."[15] Now once again they desired to be free from each other. So in March 1950, Beauchamp was in the middle of a second divorce, but the judge had postponed the proceedings because Nettie Belle was expecting a third child. There would be no divorce until after the child's birth. Sanda Beauchamp was born on March 18, 1950, and so Beauchamp's divorce occurred at the moment when competitors were organizing for the 1950 racing season.

Swanson, a no-nonsense man, may have decided Beauchamp was too preoccupied with personal matters to focus on racing. Also, the mechanic liked the idea of having several good drivers nearby. He built the fast engines, and if he had more than one driver available to him, it was all so much the better. Beauchamp could drive the hot rod and Tiny could drive the stock car.

Tiny, nevertheless, had provoked an undercurrent of tension between himself and Beauchamp. They were on friendly terms, but they were competitors. Swanson usually gave most of his attention to one car, but Harlan had two outstanding drivers. And now guileless Tiny had managed to talk his way into driving a Swanson-built stock car.

On May 12, Lund and Swanson drove the 27 miles from Harlan to Audubon, Iowa, and paid $112 for a barnyard 1939 Ford coupe, its rear compartment full of corn, oats, and dirt. Together, the pair worked on the body, finally painting it black and white.[16] The number of the stock car was never in doubt—another 55, the magic number of the Swanson garage.

Swanson's engine work was not extensive because the cars at Playland were to be strictly stock, that is, they could only have parts sold by the manufacturer. This meant the vehicles on the track were essentially the same kind one could find on the streets and highways. The race cars merely had a number on the side and the engine had a good tune-up. The cost barrier to purchase a decade-old car to compete was minimal, and almost any gas station attendant could do the engine work.

Beauchamp, meanwhile, raced the hot rod. Despite his personal troubles, one Sunday in early May 1950, he snared a first, second, and third in highly competitive races at Kansas City Olympic Stadium.[17] And Swanson would soon discover he had grabbed a tiger's tail when he formed his partnership with Tiny Lund.

On a sunny day in May 1950, Swanson and Lund drove a spiffy 1939 Ford coupe to Playland, the track Meyer Lansky had built.[1] The Swanson race car traveled from the east edge of Council Bluffs west onto the main artery, Broadway, which led to the Missouri River. Before coming to the river, they turned right onto a narrow street that passed under one of the three 60-foot humps of the roller coaster that paralleled Broadway and that formed a southern boundary of the amusement park.[2]

Swanson then turned west and drove along the edge of the amusement park to a pit gate. Fans arriving for the races walked a slightly different path, passing a bumper car ride, a Ferris wheel, a merry-go-round, and games of skill. Where the path of amusement park visitors and race spectators intersected with the road to the pits, Swanson and Lund may have stopped to permit a few people to cross.

A total of 1,907 spectators, half the number that attended the hot rod events, watched twenty-two cars initiate the first stock car racing at the Playland track. Swanson and Lund were, for the most part, not familiar with the mechanical and driving skill of their competitors because many of them lived in the Omaha–Council Bluffs metropolitan area—but these Harlan boys were eager for the competition.

From a standing start—the usual method to begin a race at Playland—Lund won the second heat, but he ran poorly in the trophy dash against other top finishers from the heat contests. He claimed second in the main event—the feature race.[3] Lund did well, but he did not dominate. Missing from the races was Johnny Beauchamp.

In subsequent weeks, more fans came to the track, and the field of cars grew to between fifty and ninety. The news back in Harlan was that Playland was a hot spot for racing, not just an experiment, but a thrilling and exciting success, great fun for participants and spectators.

Beauchamp, enjoying the hot rod, was slow to stop racing in it. By late

June he had competed in hot rod races at Avoca, but only nine cars showed up. The day of the hot rod was almost over,[4] and he decided to join the stock car party. First, he had to locate a race car. At a used car lot in Harlan, he bought a black 1939 Ford sedan, the former passenger car of my grandfather, Minor William Havick. Delbert and Jim Leslie then helped prepare the car, including a paint job with a white top, black bottom, and the number 53 on the sides. With a roll bar inside and a triangular crash bar in front to protect the radiator, the car was ready to race. Since it, like many race cars of the time, was still licensed, Beauchamp planned to drive it on the highway to the track.

As late as June 16, 1950, the printed program sold to the fans did not show Beauchamp's name. He entered his first contest on Saturday, June 24, and made a grand entrance. He won his heat race and led every lap of the 25-lap feature.[5] Beauchamp had arrived.

Despite the immediate success of his Harlan rival, Lund still was the top gun. He had won three of the first five feature races and had finished with a second and third in the two he had not won. By July 14, Lund had reeled off an additional three straight feature wins.

As Beauchamp transitioned to stock cars, Swanson struggled with the irrepressible Lund. After the mechanic drove 55 to the track, he disconnected the headlights, since they wouldn't be needed. He did not disconnect the back brake lights, but he never saw them come on during the race. Mystified, he asked Lund about it. Tiny replied, "I don't use the brakes."[6]

By mid-July, Playland stock car racing was a proven success. Because the drivers received a third of the gate receipts—promoter Abe Slusky raised their take to 40 percent later in the season after the drivers threatened to strike—the purse was substantial. The large purse attracted more cars. More cars attracted additional fans. The crowds often ballooned to more than 4,000 spectators. Eventually, Slusky had to build bleachers on the side of the grandstand to seat several hundred additional fans.

Like many promoters, Playland's owner also ramped up the thrills with special events. One such spectacle was the "powder-puff" race—a contest featuring female drivers. Women brave enough to enter the fray of the banging, spinning, male-dominated sport of racing were given their own competition. Those women eager to compete first had to find a stock car to drive. Most of the top point leaders would not loan their cars for a powder-puff contest. However, one driver with a reasonably good car, Glenn Robey, loaned his vehicle to Roxine Wyatt, a young lady from Council Bluffs, and by the end of the 6-lap race that she won, the reporters had dubbed her "Socky" Wyatt—a new star at the track.

The powder-puff races did not occur every week, but "Socky" usually was a strong entrant, winning occasionally. Driver Carl Lilienthal's wife, June, a fierce competitor, brought her own car and managed to finish near the top on several occasions. The women's driving was, in general, not as fast, less accomplished, and more erratic than the men's, and one had the sense the women were one corner away from wrecking their cars.

Several of the women drivers did have previous experience. Other venues, such as Claus Behnken's Anita track, had also held powder-puff races. On at least one occasion at Anita, there was a wreck in which a female driver was injured, not fatally, but seriously. In any case, powder-puff races did not become anything other than an occasional special event in a regular night race card.

The greatest success stories were Tiny Lund and Dale Swanson. Nothing, not even Beauchamp, could challenge the dominance of the Lund and Swanson team.[7] The big man's success was even more remarkable because Playland started the cars in reverse order. The drivers with more season points lined up behind drivers with fewer points. Newcomers with no points started in the front. Even if a driver was experienced, if he was new to Playland, he had no points and would start in front. Lund, who had been driving at Playland all summer, had more points than anyone.

Therefore, Lund's skill—and lack of interest in braking—couldn't always overcome the point system. Hooky Christensen, a veteran of the Harlan auto and motorcycle races and a scrappy, tough competitor unafraid of speed, arrived at Playland with few points on July 21, 1950.[8] Starting near the front, he jumped into a big lead while the drivers in the back struggled to work their way through the field of cars. A veteran of World War II and a welder, Christensen became the third Harlan driver to win a feature.

But Lund won a lot, and so on the track he became a marked man. Drivers fed up with losing formed the "Stop Tiny Lund Club." During races, club members blocked, banged, and attempted to "spin-out" Tiny.

The spin-out was a basic maneuver of the drivers with violence in mind. The move was typically executed when one vehicle followed another closely into a curve. If the front car took the curve wide enough to allow another car to duck inside, the back car could gently tap the front car's side rear fender, spinning the front car around. If the tap wasn't gentle enough, the front car might roll over or go out of control and crash. The competitors in the Stop Tiny Lund Club had no concern about being gentle, because Lund was one of the roughest drivers on the track.

That roughness came in part out of his driving technique. As Lund eagerly explained, "Actually I drive a square corner. I skid into a curve, throw the car and cut across the curve, then throw the car again and come out straight."[9] He claimed the square corner better maintained speed and control of the car than sliding all the way around the corner.

If he was following another car entering a corner, he might squarely smash into the car's back bumper, causing it to swing wide on the curve. He would then cut tight on the inside of the turn and gain the advantage. Tiny explained his strategy of passing cars on the corners this way: "If I can beat another car to the turn, I throw on the brakes instead and just stay even with him if I'm on the inside. This way I can ride him around, or use him for a bangboard, and then put him on the outside as I come out of the turn."[10]

Too often for many of the drivers, Lund's tactic of bumping cars out of the way turned out badly for the other car. Driver Fred Miller complained: "Tiny deliberately spun me into the fence, wrecking my car for no reason. He was a bully, too rough and too mean."[11]

To avoid just the kind of tangle he used so effectively, Lund rarely positioned his car outside another car on the turns. "If he's beating me to the turn, I slow up and let him go wide while I square up. You don't want to get spun on a turn, and that's what will happen if the car behind hits you."[12] But thanks to the Stop Tiny Lund Club, he didn't always avoid getting hit. One evening Lund was spun out in a heat race and failed to qualify for the feature. In the semi-feature he was again spun out, but recovered to win anyway. On July 11, he started last in the feature, was spun out four times, and still won.

Lund struck back against the Stop Tiny Lund Club by roughing up several of the offenders.[13] For his actions, he was disqualified. Beauchamp, solidly in second place in the season point standings, took full advantage of Lund's trouble and won his second feature of the season.

In less than two months and in spite of the best the Stop Tiny Lund Club could do, the big Harlan driver had become a regional star, and his fame was spreading to neighboring states. It was all about Lund. Tiny's mother could scarcely cope with his sudden fame. "So many people keep telephoning for him these days, and he's gone all the time," she said. "Then when I go to the races, car owners come up to me and ask about him driving their car. I don't know them, but they know me."[14]

Lund's appetite to race anything on wheels led to an opportunity to drive a midget car. He had not driven a midget before because he was too big to fit into one. Then Turko Motors, based in Omaha, gave him the chance. They had built a midget for another large driver, Tiny Wainwright from Kansas City, but he wasn't available to drive it. In fact, the Turko brothers wanted Lund to drive all three of their cars: the midget, the Indy car, and a stock car. Turko motors lined up twenty-seven races for August, and they wanted Tiny for all of them.[15]

Lund also began competing in late model, sometimes known as new car, races, driving a 1949 Mercury owned by Eddie Anderson of Grinnell, Iowa. Anderson drove late model cars all over the Midwest, usually in the IMCA circuit that operated mainly in the midsection of the nation (see chapter 13). In 1950, Speed Age magazine chose him as the top late model driver in the Midwest.

Lund's frenetic schedule took him all over Iowa and into neighboring states. He was traveling hundreds of miles from race to race, sometimes competing at two locations in one day. In late June, he won new car features at Sioux City and Algona.[16] On July 4, 1950, he raced the late model Mercury in Des Moines, finishing third in the time trials but crashing on lap 71. He finished twelfth.[17] That evening he raced the Swanson stock car, 55, at the Playland track, halfway across the state from Des Moines. Saturday he was in Milwaukee racing the late model Mercury. Sunday he was in Sioux City for a midget race that was rained out, and on Tuesday he was back at Playland again.

On a Sunday afternoon in nearby Atlantic, Iowa, a small venue of mainly local drivers, Lund steered Swanson's number 55 into the lead of the feature. Lund figured he was doing all right. Suddenly, he hit a deep mudhole. His car spun around, then did a full flip, landing back on all four tires. He started the car, moved back through the field, and won the race. He concluded, "I've had my share of bad luck for the day" and left for a midget race.[18]

In Sioux City, never having raced a midget before, he was in fourth place in the feature when he hit a rough spot on the turn, and the midget rolled over three times. According to Lund, "The car was quite badly wrecked." Later, he conceded, "I received quite a banging around." Although the spill looked serious, and he spent the night in the hospital, Lund minimized what happened: "I just got a burned arm and a slightly sprained neck." Back in Harlan, when someone asked him how he came out in the midget races, he replied, "On my head."[19]

Not surprisingly, the press reported a Lund win as normal, while his few losses were important news. After his loss in late July, the headline the day of the next race was, "Tiny Lund Will Seek Revenge," and the first sentence extended the point: "Tiny Lund of Harlan, who was temporarily dethroned. . ."[20] The press also was quick to notice that when Lund was unsuccessful, often another Harlan driver was winning. After Lund's loss on July 28, the press story begins, "Knock down one Harlan driver and up pops another one. . . . The Harlan monopoly on the feature firsts continued Friday."[21]

The press hyped the Harlan dominance—Harlan drivers had won ten of the fifteen feature races: Lund seven, Beauchamp two, and Christensen one.[22] When Christensen won on July 21, the headline was, "Christensen Leads Harlan Invasion at Playland Races," and the story began, "Harlan drivers again hogged the limelight."[23] Then, two weeks later, the Council Bluffs Nonpareil printed a story titled "Harlan Drivers Corner Cash at Playland Stadium," accompanied by a photo of three smiling Harlan Leadfoots: Hooky, Tiny, and Johnny.[24] The small Iowa community was overpowering the metropolitan area of Omaha–Council Bluffs.

But from Beauchamp's point of view, the season was not a great success. He was having car problems. The sedan he had bought was not the best vehicle for racing. Most drivers, including Lund, were driving coupe 39 Fords. On the small tracks, such as Playland's one-fifth of a mile oval, a coupe negotiated the corners better than a sedan. Beauchamp lost control of his sedan while sliding into the corner in Atlantic, Iowa, on July 23. Number 53 rolled over five times. Afterward, he complained of a "stiff neck and a sad looking car."[25]

He nevertheless managed to get the car ready for a Tuesday race at Playland, where he won the semi-feature, and he raced it again Wednesday in Sioux City. He then scrapped the sedan and began racing a Ford coupe.[26]

Meanwhile, Lund's relationship with Swanson was becoming strained. Tiny was almost too busy to drive the Swanson car. When asked if he would be driving in the August 21–24 Shelby County Fair races, he replied,

"I'd sure like to drive at home, but I don't know whether I can make it or not."[27] Making the situation worse, Lund had agreed to drive race cars, including a 1950 Ford, for the Corky Motor Company of Omaha.[28]

If Swanson wanted to enter number 55 at the Shelby County Fair races and Lund wasn't driving, then Swanson needed a new driver. The mechanic firmly believed that at least half of Lund's success was because number 55 was one of the fastest cars. Moreover, Dale Swanson was not the type of man to put up with people who made things difficult for him. He was already fed up with Lund's rough driving. The big man lacked patience on the track and took chances that resulted in busted radiators, broken axles, flat tires, and a banged-up race car. Swanson was frustrated with all the repairs he had to make.

The tipping point came in mid-August, during a Tuesday night feature race. The 55 car, with Lund behind the wheel, went out on lap 18 with a damaged radiator hose. Beauchamp won.[29] Friendly, low-key Johnny Beauchamp was performing at a steady, respectable pace with a car not as fast as number 55. Soon after this race, Lund was no longer driving the Swanson car. Stunned reporters and fans wondered why.

The Shelby County Fair, on August 23 and 24, became a convention of champions, all Harlan boys. Not only were Lund, Swanson, and Beauchamp present, but also Playland feature winners Christensen and Selser, as well as midget car winner Bobby Parker. This was an unprecedented group of stars for a small county fair track. The Shelby County Fair most likely had more expert drivers than any location in the state or, for that matter, in several states combined.

Chris Nelson drove the Swanson 55. Nelson, who worked in a Harlan auto garage, had racing experience, but no one believed he was of the same caliber as Lund or Beauchamp, or even Hooky Christensen. Lund, while he had announced earlier he might not be able to fit the fair into his busy schedule, did find time, but driving the Omaha garage Corky Motors' car,[30] he only managed a second behind Beauchamp in the trophy dash. Beauchamp won a heat race and the trophy dash, and he finished second to Nelson in the feature event.[31]

A few days after the Shelby County Fair races, Beauchamp was out on the Playland track warming up 55 before the Friday night, August 25, events while the sound system blared "Cry of the Wild Goose." Playland fans could not understand why Lund wasn't driving 55. Beauchamp won his heat race and finished second in the feature with the Swanson car. Lund, driving a different car, failed to qualify for the feature and finished sixth in the semi-feature.[32]

Swanson had proved his point. With Nelson, a second-rate driver, his car could still win at the local fair. At Playland, Beauchamp, a top-flight driver, did well with the Swanson car. Lund, on the other hand, had trouble winning when he wasn't behind the wheel of a Swanson vehicle. The mechanic had a good option with Beauchamp—who was far more than merely capable and who was in second place at Playland. One person close to the Harlan drivers said that Swanson pitted Lund and Beauchamp off each other. Without a doubt, Swanson was aware he did not have to tolerate Lund's antics, particularly if Beauchamp was available.

Yanking Lund out of 55 in August did not have much practical impact because the racing season was almost over. In Iowa, cold weather could arrive as early as September. In fact, on August 29 Lund was again behind the wheel of 55, and on September 8 the Harlan Tribune reported him winning the Playland feature, claiming that "his differences with owner Dale Swanson were patched up."[33]

Tiny finished the season in the Swanson car and with the highest point tally. By the second week in September he had 2,807 season points, while second-place Beauchamp had a mere 1,558 points.[34] Lund and number 55 won eleven features of the twenty-seven held at Playland during the 1950 season.[35] Lund, Beauchamp, and Christensen combined to put Harlan, Iowa, on the map as an improbable racing capital of the Midwest.

Dale Swanson was the only owner/mechanic widely covered by the press. Swanson's reputation among the competitors enabled him to have a lucrative side business building engines for hot rod enthusiasts, drag racers, and drivers at distant venues. No other car dominated the races, and it was evident that Lund's success was not all driver skill. After the season, Swanson reported that the car had been entered in sixty races and had mechanical failures in four. The car earned $4,800, which Swanson claimed proudly "was probably the highest amount in a four-state area."[36] Swanson's meticulous record keeping suggests a far more systematic, careful approach to racing than that of the average mechanic and driver.

At the close of the 1950 season, Tiny Lund announced he was enlisting in the Air Force for four years. His dominance was so complete that fans wondered if any other driver could be such a star. They did not have long to wait.

An informal poll of Playland drivers predicted Beauchamp was the man to beat. He had finished second in the 1950 season point standings, and now he was behind the wheel of the Swanson car. The big prize, the season championship, was within his grasp, yet could Johnny Beauchamp be as dominant as Tiny Lund?

On opening day in 1951 at Playland, Beauchamp battled eighty cars; however, in the feature, he could not go faster than the winner, the "roaring" Bud Aitkenhead, who piloted a car with an exceptionally loud exhaust muffler and modified parts. Track rules now permitted the use of such parts, but Swanson had gambled that the unmodified 55 was better than the "souped-up" cars.

Swanson understood how to install racing parts because he had done so in the hot rod Beauchamp had driven, but with hot rods there were few restrictions: any new racing part could be installed. At Playland, the rules for modified parts were more restrictive. A modified engine involved changes in the valves, pistons, and the cam that regulated the combustion. Also, a more powerful engine made by the manufacturer could be substituted for the showroom engine that originally was sold with the car.[1] Aitkenhead's win proved 55 needed modified parts to succeed. Faced with the evidence, Swanson returned to his cramped, alleyfront garage in Harlan and immediately began installing racing parts in the engine. The following week, at the second day of racing, Beauchamp—with a modified engine—pushed into first place in the point standings with a win in the feature. No sooner had he become the front-runner than Tiny Lund, stationed at Shepherd Air Force base in Wichita Falls, Texas, obtained a weekend pass. Tiny, anxious to race, phoned his mother and told her, "I don't care what car I drive just so I drive Sunday."[2]

Promoter Abe Slusky, who hoped to fill the stands, was delighted. Most likely with some incentives from Slusky, Swanson agreed to let Lund drive 55, so Beauchamp had to find another car. Giving up the car for Lund bothered Beauchamp, according to his son, but he remained friendly with his fellow Harlan driver. Beauchamp won a heat race with a stop-gap vehicle, but it broke down in the feature, a race Lund went on to win before returning to the Air Force.

Beauchamp climbed back into 55, and in subsequent weeks he won a semi-feature and feature. His victories made him a target of the previous season's Stop Tiny Lund Club.

One night early in June, as fans filtered into the stands, the cars were circling the track as drivers tested their equipment and practiced. The crackling sound system blared Guy Mitchell's "Truly, Truly Fair." One spectator, new to the races, looked over the cars on the track and wondered aloud, "Fifty-five is not on the track warming up with other cars?"[3]

When race time approached, officials signaled the warm-up period was over. The cars exited into the pits at the south end, leaving the oval empty. Suddenly, 55 sped onto the track, circled once, and returned to the pits—car and driver required little practice or warm-up. This kind of swagger on the part of Beauchamp and Swanson annoyed several of the other drivers as much as Beauchamp's many wins. The discontented men in the pits believed that these Harlan professionals needed a big lesson.

In the 10-lap qualifying heat race, starting from the back row, Beauchamp struggled to pass cars. He was locked in an intense battle with a competitor, soon to become Beauchamp's nemesis: Carl Lilienthal, "the Atlantic Arrow." Lilienthal drove the "2" with an arrow painted through the number. He blocked, banged, and boxed in Beauchamp, preventing him from advancing. With 10 laps to get to the front, Beauchamp decided not to let this inferior driver do any more damage. He went to his growing bag of tricks, one of which was "the tap."

Hooky Christensen explained that "John could delicately with his front bumper touch another car, so slightly that it was difficult to notice the contact, particularly on the south curve where the officials' view was not as good."[4] Beauchamp's surgeon-like tap could either cause a competitor to spin out or simply move out of the way.

This tap sent the "2" car spinning off the track, and Beauchamp surged ahead, winning the race. Lilienthal, enraged by what had happened, found Beauchamp in the pits talking to other drivers, and from behind tapped him on the shoulder. When Beauchamp turned around, Lilienthal slugged him in the eye.

There was more behind this blow than the outcome of that night's race. Lilienthal spent bushel baskets of money building cars, but all he could do was finish behind Beauchamp. Lilienthal, a man with large, rough features that betrayed his many hours working the fields of his farms, was obsessed with racing, and he mortgaged and eventually lost an entire farm to pay for the building of cars in the hope of winning. Competing at this time more widely than did Beauchamp, Lilienthal had raced at the state fairs of Nebraska and Iowa with only modest results.

Beauchamp's success was like salt in a wound for Carl, since Carl's persistent, substantial efforts were so much less successful. Johnny was better looking and more personable; females flocked to him. Even Lilienthal's wife, an excellent powder-puff driver, was rumored to have made moon-eyes at Beauchamp. And now, in this race, Beauchamp had deliberately knocked Lilienthal out of the way, as if he was simply one of the lesser drivers and his car a pile of junk in the wake of Beauchamp's exhaust. Lilienthal would remember and get even with this hotshot Beauchamp.

On this night, track officials disqualified Beauchamp for rough driving and banned him from the remainder of the events. They may have done so to quiet the discontent in the pits among the mechanics and drivers, his competitors; such minor actions as spinning a car out on the track were commonplace, and usually no punishment was meted out by officials. Beauchamp defiantly denied wrongdoing: "I have never raced dirty in my life."[5]

Although Beauchamp didn't agree with his penalty, in general Playland officials held fair races. Drivers could disagree about a ruling, yet there was a sense that the officials did their best to be honest brokers. Playland events, though rough and competitive, offered Beauchamp little preparation for the slippery ethical ambiguities he would later face.

Drivers and mechanics had a clear notion of what was fair and what was not. They did not—and do not—expect to lose a race because of a trivial detail, not dotting an "i," such as a minor brush during competition. On the track, flagrant and obvious attempts to wreck another car, although difficult to prove, could be sufficient cause to disqualify the perpetrator. Yet it was somewhat unfair for officials to disqualify Beauchamp for using tactics similar to those his competitors attempted to wield against him. Still, with the best vehicle and being the best driver, Beauchamp came to expect his competitors to plead with officials to disqualify him, and sometimes they were successful.

At the very least, drivers expect that the place they finished is the place the officials agree they finished. Manipulating the result after the completion of the contest would be equivalent to fixing a boxing or wrestling match.

Rarely, if ever, did anyone leave after the Playland events believing races had been stolen by the officials. Promoter Abe Slusky and his staff were never accused of deliberately manipulating outcomes of races. Occasionally, drivers might have considered a penalty too lenient or too harsh, but such matters were within the margin of error. In fact, Slusky was a model citizen. He allocated the profits of at least one race a season to charity. When his drivers rebelled one evening, refusing to put on the show unless they received more than the usual one-third of the profits, Slusky agreed to give the competitors 40 percent.

This one Beauchamp disqualification hardly satisfied the drivers jealous of his success. And the perplexing question remained: how did Swanson make his car faster than the other cars? The week after Beauchamp's disqualification, he fought through the field to win the $120 purse and the feature race. A contingent of disgruntled drivers then went on the offense.

Karl Barkdoll, Wally Thompson, and second-place finisher Lilienthal put up the $35 fee to have an official inspection of the Swanson car to determine if it was within the rules. The disgruntled drivers suspected 55 had a locked differential gear, otherwise called a locked rear end. The locked rear end, illegal according to track rules, allows power to turn both wheels on corners, giving a car greater speed.

After the race, 55 was immediately jacked up and tested, and the finding was "no locked rear end." The drivers after Swanson's scalp could not believe the result of the inspection; they demanded the test be done a second time. Now the rear end was locked. Swanson argued that the car was clear of any rule infraction because it passed the first test. He claimed that the "spider gear" used with the differential had frozen.

Mechanics understood that a spider gear was designed only to lock the rear end during the race. After the race, when stationary, it would not be locked upon inspection. Speedy Bill Smith, the wily owner of a Nebraska speed shop, pointed out that the spider gear could be used to cheat without getting caught. Swanson had a setup that was designed to break the rule while the car was racing on the track but to appear legal when checked after the race.[6] In this case, though, Swanson's spider gear had malfunctioned and locked up after the race. Official Bernie Kelly finally said that because the car originally passed the test, it was cleared, but in his next breath he added, "The car will be watched closely."[7]

Other competitors were unhappy with the outcome, but Swanson at least was exposed as operating a vehicle on the track that violated the rules. Bud Burdick, a competitor who was on good terms with Swanson and Beauchamp, laughed as he explained the nuances of the situation: "Well, usually when Swanson's car was torn down, Swanson was the only one at the track with tools and measuring devices to check. He came in with his tools and checked his car!" Of course, the officials and other competitors also observed the teardown, but "Swanson was difficult to get ahead of."[8]

This incident is the closest Dale Swanson ever came to being found guilty of fielding a car that was not within the rules. It would appear that with this spider gear episode, Swanson found a loophole in the rules that say a vehicle cannot have a locked rear end. He believed that if the car passed the test, it was legal to race. This illustrates the fine line Swanson walked with this spider gear between honest racing and illegal practices. This perhaps is a classic instance of how close a mechanic will come to breaking a rule without breaking it.

The legality of Swanson's vehicles was tested many times. With his cars and motors winning races, they were frequently torn down by officials. Competitors eagerly ponied up the cash for the official inspection, certain the 55 could not go that fast unless Swanson was cheating. During the 1950 Playland season, 55 was torn down twice, but officials uncovered nothing illegal.

One night Swanson encountered unusual trouble in Norfolk, Nebraska, when officials there inspected the motor of Junior Brunick's 1940 Ford. Brunick, a Sioux City–based driver, raced with a Swanson-built engine. As usual, the car was faster than any other on the track. Officials found no infractions, but they uncovered unfamiliar "heads." The cylinder heads, manufactured by Ford and duly marked as a Ford-numbered part, were legal according to the track guidelines. However, the local track mechanics did not recognize the part because it was not frequently installed in any car. Known as "Denver heads" or "Rocky Mountain heads," they were constructed with aluminum and so weighed less than other heads. They were sold especially in high altitudes and were intended to give the motor more pep.[9] Swanson had found an advantage that was within the rules, but even though the parts were legal, Norfolk officials then banned all Swanson motors from the track.[10]

The Harlan mechanic was incensed because he had broken no rule.

He considered hiring an attorney. Could the Norfolk officials ban a mechanic's cars for no good reason? They argued that their races were for local drivers and that Swanson brought in a level of professionalism that was unfair to other competitors. After more thought, Swanson concluded Norfolk was not a main arena for him and taking legal action was not worth the trouble.

With every win and every inspection, Swanson's fame grew. The mystery was what he did to make his cars—especially 55—go fast. Lund and Beauchamp were good drivers, but the car simply had more speed than the others. After one of the teardowns, the inspecting mechanic declared that the car was "on the level, one of the cleanest motors I've ever seen."[11] Sportswriters labeled Swanson "the leading stock car 'doctor'" and a "motor magician." He encouraged the belief that he had a secret to the speed. After one race he crowed, "Oh, we have a few tricks. And those other guys would like to know them, but so far they haven't learned."[12]

The formula for Swanson's magic was a combination of ingenuity and hard work. After servicing customers at his shop during the day, he worked until 4:00 a.m. on race cars, painstakingly assembling the engines. Not a speck of dust or dirt did Swanson allow anywhere near a motor. His engines had every connection tight, every aspect of the motor checked before he watched the car on the track to see how he would have to adjust the "springs." For consistent success, in addition to cleaning the carburetor after every race, he gave the engine a ring job and a thorough overhaul every eight-to-ten races or three-to-four weeks.[13]

During the weeks after Beauchamp's disqualification for spinning out Lilienthal, the track was inhospitable for the Harlan driver. He had car trouble, was spun out, and rolled 55 for the first time. In the midst of these setbacks, Beauchamp decided to try racing a midget, subbing for Jim Kirkpatrick, who had a bad ankle. Driving the number 5, Beauchamp finished fourth in his heat and ahead of five cars in the feature.[14] He later told his son, "I prefer stock cars."[15]

The midget experience had not recharged Beauchamp's racing success, and he searched for a solution to break his slump at the track. Struggling to win, he simply disappeared from the Friday, July 13, contest. Chris Nelson, a journeyman driver whose experience was primarily local in Harlan, was behind the wheel of 55. Reporters asked Swanson where Beauchamp was, and he cryptically answered, "John has gone to Denver."[16] Beauchamp had planned to miss this race date, but he also missed a second because Playland officials, giving only a few days notice, canceled the Tuesday midget races and replaced them with stock car races.

By July 20, when Beauchamp returned from his "vacation," more had changed than the 100 loads of dirt added to the south curve that increased the banking one foot. Beauchamp's point lead was threatened. Harlan boy Hooky Christensen had won four straight races, two features and two heat races — a feat never before accomplished at the track. Christensen was fifty-six points behind Beauchamp, and he had won as many features, three.

On July 24, Beauchamp won his first feature since June 15. Several competitors, determined to slow Beauchamp down, immediately demanded his car be torn down and checked. Number 55 was taken to an Omaha garage for the inspection. Swanson, irritated by the extra bother, watched until late in the night on Tuesday, when the car was declared legal. On the next night of racing, Beauchamp wrecked, and Christensen again won the feature. Vernon "Hooky" Christensen was about to become the top driver at Playland.

Beauchamp struck back a few nights later with his own feature win, and he followed this success the next evening with a win in the fourth heat race, but again his driving sparked controversy. During the contest, Beauchamp spun out driver Pete Huffman. After the race, and back in the pits, several drivers jumped Beauchamp, and he was in a fight. Huffman accused Beauchamp of deliberately spinning him out.

There was so much banging and ramming on the track during the typical race that a driver would usually need to demonstrate intent to do considerable harm to another car before officials would intervene. In this case, officials eventually gained control of the situation and declared Beauchamp had done nothing wrong. The racing continued, and Beauchamp won his second straight feature.

Building on these two victories, he won the next three feature events — a record five consecutive feature wins, beginning on July 31 and running almost through the first half of August. This kind of dominance was unprecedented, even from Tiny Lund.

The frustrated competitors turned to unusual measures. An anonymous, "mystery" car owner announced plans to enter a special vehicle for the sole purpose of beating Beauchamp. The owner said he would enter a 1942 Ford, number 287, and that Zane Bryan, winner of one feature during the season, would be the driver.

But it turned out that desperate measures to stop Beauchamp were not required, because circumstances on the track changed. In the next batch of races, Beauchamp encountered a lot of blocking and banging, but also new competition aside from Bryan. Glenn Robey, always capable,[17] began driving for the Williams brothers from Shenandoah, Iowa, home of the Everly Brothers. Robey had previously driven the number 8-ball, but his new car was number 117, and it was fast. Over the next few weeks, Robey won three out of four features, and he tied Christensen's record of winning four consecutive races.

Meanwhile, drivers continued using tactics to slow down Beauchamp, with Robey and Christensen the chief benefactors. On August 24, Beauchamp became more aggressive defending himself on the track. He, Tom Sloboth, and Vern Robey, Glenn's brother, tangled, and all three were suspended for two races.[18]

Johnny Beauchamp may have needed a break from the action at this point. His tumultuous life on the track mirrored his personal life. He had divorced Nettie Belle for the second time in 1950, but he was the father of three children: Robert, William, and Sanda. He remained friends with Nettie Belle's relatives, attending their family picnics. Her sister's husband continued to help Beauchamp with his stock car. As one of Nettie Belle's relatives remembered, "John was a happy-go-lucky guy."[19] He was too busy racing to stay home, and if he wasn't racing cars, he was visiting the horse races at the Omaha Ak-sar-ben track, betting on ponies with money he could not afford to lose and doing the same on cards elsewhere.

Now a local star, Beauchamp found that females sought his company. Girls came to the track to meet him, and Beauchamp was easily tempted. One of the young female admirers he met at Playland was Donna Richter from nearby Blair, Nebraska.[20] Donna, a recent high school graduate who was beauty contest pretty, became Beauchamp's main interest.

Although Beauchamp's personal life was unsettled, he was not a wild hell raiser. He was not involved in drunkenness, destruction, fighting, and trouble making. He was easygoing and enjoyed himself. Most of the drivers at Playland liked him, providing he did not win too many times. Leaving high school and marrying young had simply left him ill-prepared for money management and making good decisions. What he could do was drive a race car.

Despite the efforts of his rivals, by Labor Day weekend Beauchamp had clinched the 1951 season championship; he had too big a point lead for anyone to catch up. He was 500 points ahead of Robey and Christensen, having won eleven features, each worth 100 points in the standings, whereas Christensen and Robey had each won four. The remaining wins were spread out across sixteen other competitors.

Although the season point championship was not in doubt, the holiday races brought new excitement, because Tiny Lund returned on another weekend pass from the Air Force. This time, instead of kicking Beauchamp out of the 55, Swanson built a second car for Lund to drive. The new one was almost identical to number 55. They had similar black-and-white paint jobs. The main difference was the number on the side of the second vehicle—a five painted over a shadow double five. The new car was the phantom 55 or 5. The matchup between the two Swanson vehicles and their drivers—longtime rivals—added sizzle to the Labor Day weekend contests.

Although the cars were a formidable pair, their Sunday debut was not successful. Beauchamp failed to qualify for the feature and had to settle for a semi-feature win. Lund, racing with abandon in the feature, steered the number 5 into a pile of wrecked cars, mangling it. The Labor Day races were to be held the following night. After the shadow 55 car was hauled back to the pits, Swanson gazed at the torn up vehicle and said to the crowd gathered around, "Three of us have worked six straight nights on the car. One more night won't hurt us. It will be ready."[21]

Swanson, back at his Harlan garage with two cars to maintain, feverishly worked to repair the wreck damage on the Lund car. Lund and Beauchamp came by to discover their mechanic frustrated. Swanson complained, "Tiny, you have to be more careful and stop tearing up the car." Beauchamp chimed in, "Tiny, don't stand so close to my car. You might break something."[22]

On Labor Day the pair were once again unsuccessful, and Lund then returned to his Air Force base. Track promoters in 1950 and 1951 allowed the point season contest to continue on past Labor Day for as long as there were races. (In future years, promoters ended the season approximately on Labor Day and then held a post-season series of events.) Thus, with the

1951 season still in progress and Swanson possessing two race cars, Harlan driver Chris Nelson climbed behind the wheel of number 5 after Labor Day. Nelson, although not a great driver, started in front because he had few season points. He won a feature and did well in a few other races.

But the prospect of a race between Lund and Beauchamp was not lost. With an extra Swanson car available, Lund managed another weekend pass. Both he and Beauchamp qualified for the 6-lap trophy dash involving the top two finishers from each qualifying heat race. Fans eagerly speculated about how Lund, the old champion, would match up against Johnny Beauchamp, the new champion. Lund, with fewer season points, started in the front and jumped out to an early lead.

Beauchamp, starting from the back, held his foot down on the gas pedal deep into the corners. The spectators saw what appeared to be a smooth arc to the Beauchamp car as it turned the curves, but in fact, he feverishly spun the steering wheel back and forth as his car maintained near full power around the turns.[23] He caught Lund on the last lap, maneuvered him slightly wide on the last turn, cut inside, and edged ahead of him for the win. The press characterized the race as Beauchamp giving Lund "a driving lesson."[24]

After the race ceremonies, Nettie Belle proudly stood beside Johnny, both in front of 55 and both clinging to the trophy. The camera clicked, capturing the moment, but the image did not reflect the difficulties of their relationship. Nettie Belle was planning for her future without Johnny, learning to be a beautician to supplement her income as a waitress, and he continued to see Donna Richter.

During the limited fall schedule, Swanson, ever the entrepreneur, located another driver for his second car. Don Pash, "the Avoca Flash," as he was announced at the track, eagerly entered the Swanson orbit. One driver chortled, "Pash really was the Avoca Flash. He was passing cigars out on the streets after becoming the father of babies delivered by three different females."[25] On the track he was a driver of considerable ability.

With Pash and Beauchamp piloting Swanson cars, fans concluded that the motor magician was unstoppable. Not everyone was happy about it, though. One irate resident of Avoca sent Swanson an anonymous letter. The letter accused him of interfering with the livelihood of good Avoca mechanics that had worked on Pash's Avoca-based car earlier in the season.[26]

The anonymous writer did not realize that Swanson planned not to own a car for the next season. The man who built the vehicle that both Lund and Beauchamp drove to season championships was selling his cars. Don Pash bought number 55 and a Sioux City driver bought number 5. Swanson intended to build engines for all competitors who would pay his price.

Johnny Beauchamp began searching for a car for the 1952 season.

8 | Lilienthal's Revenge

T he nervous grind is too tough," Swanson said. The long hours working every night on the cars followed by more hours at the races left him exhausted. "Following my cars around the race circuit has kept me away from my business too long."[1]

Having sold his two successful cars,[2] Swanson took orders to build motors for whoever wanted them.[3] Like a military arms dealer, he did business with drivers in several states, selling motors for between $500 and $650, depending on "the size and finishing work."[4]

Swanson's withdrawal left Beauchamp scrambling, and he once again returned to his Avoca connections. The Leslies joined with another local farm implement dealer, Dutch Holtz, and the Avoca residents fielded a new Beauchamp 55 car. Although Swanson built the engine, the car did not have the daily and weekly massaging that it had when he owned the car.[5] The Leslie-Holtz car was fast, but it was not dominant; it suffered from more mechanical problems than a Swanson-owned car. Swanson was doing work for many cars, and making matters still more difficult, Beauchamp was competing against drivers who also had bought Swanson cars and motors.

Also, because he had won the previous season, Beauchamp was a marked man in 1952. The other drivers were determined to slow him down with the usual tactics: block, box in, spin out, and bang. One night in May, he had four separate tangles with other cars intending to do him harm.

Beauchamp continued to fight back as he had done a year earlier. The next night of racing, May 23, he was blocked by driver Chuck Terry in a heat race. On the corner, Terry made the mistake of not hugging the inside. Beauchamp held his foot on the gas pedal, cut inside of Terry, slamming broadside into him, using Terry's car for a bang board, and then speeding on to win. Although such metal scraping conflict was common, a contingent of drivers and mechanics protested, claiming Beauchamp had used rough tactics. Responding to the protesters, starter George Zenchuck changed the results of the race, dropping Beauchamp to fourth rather than first.

Robert Beauchamp, who went with the neighbors to many Playland races, was troubled by the attacks on his father. Johnny explained to Robert that when the other cars boxed him in, "Sometimes I have to move them out of the way."[6]

On Sunday, June 1, Beauchamp, battling for second place, became frustrated by Bud Drake's banging and spun his car out of the way. Beauchamp's tap was too hard, and Drake's car rolled over, initiating what became a firestorm of discontent from fans and pit crews. Officials stopped the race because of the wreck. Immediately, several spectators scaled the fence between the stands and the track and ran toward Beauchamp's car, which was still on the oval. Next, an enraged group of drivers and mechanics stormed out of the pits. Seventy-five angry people out for blood surrounded Beauchamp and his car. They wanted his head on a drive shaft.

Officials called the police and then disqualified Beauchamp. A number of drivers and mechanics did not believe the punishment was enough. The protest continued, and officials canceled the remaining schedule for the night.[7]

An inexperienced driver with modest promise and few top finishes, Drake believed he had raced Beauchamp fairly. There was some banging, but no more than normal in Drake's view. He said he had not left enough space to allow Beauchamp to slip between his car and the infield. Drake argued that "Beauchamp went down into the infield and off the track on the curve." Further, Drake believed, "Beauchamp didn't like anyone banging on his car, but on that little track a certain amount of banging went on all the time." He realized he was at a disadvantage racing against Beauchamp. "Those Harlan drivers had a hot rod club and had been practicing for years," he complained. "When I first started I didn't even know that I should turn my tires so the valves wouldn't get broken off during the race." Drake sensed the large, arrogant gap in the levels of professionalism between himself and Beauchamp: "Beauchamp would do anything to win. He was obsessed with winning."[8]

Officials had a difficult balancing act. On the one hand, Beauchamp was the biggest star. On the other hand, many competitors were needed for the show. To solve the dilemma, officials employed a double standard: when drivers banged on Beauchamp, they ignored it, but when he retaliated, he was disqualified and lost valuable points crucial to winning the championship. Officials were being pulled in two directions. They had to appease the majority of drivers in order to keep them competing, but they also needed stars like Beauchamp. Some rough driving was good for business, but too much was bad.

As Beauchamp struggled with other drivers' tactics to slow him down, Don Pash benefited. Pash won four of the first eight feature races, taking the season point lead. Beauchamp clung to second place but had won only a single feature.

Finally, Beauchamp began winning features, eventually nine in all. On June 29 he swept three races, and then on July 1 he moved into first place in the season point standings. During July and August, in one of the most intense and protracted battles of any Playland season, the two competitors rarely were separated by more than 100 points, the lead changing back and forth many times.

The seesaw duel between Pash and Beauchamp culminated in a showdown the Sunday night before Labor Day, during the last contests of the official season. Pash had accumulated 3,183 points; Beauchamp had 3,124 points. The Avoca Flash's narrow, fifty-nine-point margin meant that one Pash slip during this last night of racing and Beauchamp could repeat as track champion.

Spectators — 6,176 — jammed into the grandstand; the north and south bleachers overflowed. It was the biggest crowd in the history of the park. The pre-race music crackled on the sound system through the humid night air with a popular Guy Mitchell tune "Belle, Belle, My Liberty Belle." Ed Baron, a local entertainment personality, eventually welcomed the fans and made his usual observation, "Everything is ready for a good night of racing. The boys on the north turn are perched in their usual place." The boys who watched the race free from the huge tree that stood on the north turn outside the track's high, white wooden fence waved. Tiny Lund had returned on a pass from the Air Force and was now behind the wheel of Keith "Porky" Rachwitz's car, number 75. Lund's presence usually added excitement, but the electric atmosphere over the points battle overshadowed his presence. Nevertheless, he was a wild card whose involvement complicated the outcomes of this night.

And as it turned out, Lund won the first 10-lap heat race. Beauchamp won the second, with his Iowa buddy Mel Krueger running third. In the third heat, Pash had to contend with Bud Burdick, an Omaha champion and relative newcomer to Playland. Burdick, piloting a bright yellow car with a V-8 on the side, won and Pash finished second.

Next, there was a 6-lap speed dash involving the top two cars from each heat race. Lund jumped out into the lead, but at the beginning of the 6th lap, Beauchamp caught and passed him. On the last curve, Pash also managed to get around Lund for second place. Beauchamp had won two preliminary races and Pash had finished second in two races. The Harlan driver had shaved only ten points off Pash's lead going into the feature and still needed to make up forty-nine more. If he won the feature and Pash finished no higher than fourth, the season championship would go to Beauchamp.

In the 25-lap feature, Lund began near the front. He jumped into the lead while Beauchamp and Pash, starting in the last row of an eighteen-car field, struggled to work their way through the traffic. The roar of the engines circling was never louder. Fans, their eyes intent on the action, watched Pash and Beauchamp fighting their way toward the front, passing car after car. On the 14th lap, Beauchamp caught Lund and, after 3 laps, passed him, taking over first place.

Pash strained to accelerate through the clog of cars to catch the leaders. He first found himself in a bump and tangle with Ken Murdoch of Omaha. Once Pash cleared Murdoch, he found Hooky Christensen and Mel Krueger in front of him. Beauchamp, whose parents lived near Christensen in Harlan, had asked Hooky to help him if he could. He told Hooky, "I don't care about the prize money, I want the season championship." Christensen made it difficult for Pash to pass him. Krueger, too, was a friend of Beauchamp, and so once again Pash had trouble. The small, one-fifth of a mile track was like a footrace in a boxing ring.

On the 24th lap, Beauchamp was first, Lund was second, and Carl Lilienthal, one of Beauchamp's fiercest rivals, was third. During the 1951 season, Beauchamp had spun out Lilienthal, and the ill will between them lingered.

Pash was feverishly trying to move up, but coming out of the last turn, it was obvious Pash could not overtake Lilienthal. Beauchamp was going to win another season championship. Suddenly, in front of the stands but before the finish line, Lilienthal slowed his number 2 almost to a stop. Then "the Atlantic Arrow," with his arm out the window, motioned for Pash to come on by. A stunned, almost silent crowd watched Don Pash finish third and win the season championship by nine points.

Beauchamp said little and coolly accepted what had happened.

Beauchamp's finish-line loss of the 1952 season championship was a harbinger of tough times. In 1953 he was behind the wheel of the same car he had driven in 1952, and again it was not the fastest vehicle on the track. Once again Swanson did not own a race car. Beauchamp's competition was champion drivers from Nebraska, such as Bud Burdick, Lloyd Beckman, and Rex Jordan, and Playland regulars Bobby Parker and Keith "Porky" Rachwitz, who had upgraded their cars.

On Friday, May 21, Beauchamp clashed with the "roaring" Bud Aitkenhead. Frustrated and feeling that the other man was driving to make trouble, Beauchamp attempted to wreck him. Officials concluded both drivers were somewhat at fault and suspended Aitkenhead for one race, but because Beauchamp had made "several passes at Aitkenhead," he was banned for the night and suspended for the next three race days (or two weeks).[1]

Beauchamp argued that he did not initiate clashes on the track. He would, if provoked, defend himself and take action. But unlike some drivers, Beauchamp said, he settled his disputes on the track rather than fighting in the pits after the race. He believed he was justified in going after Aitkenhead. But Playland officials did not reverse their decision. Losing the right to earn points for two weeks scuttled Beauchamp's hopes of winning the season championship. He had conceded a potential 700 points.[2]

The harsh punishment was linked to the officials' new method of handling infractions. The previous season the track starter, in conjunction with a four-person dispute resolution committee composed of drivers and mechanics, had decided punishment. At the beginning of the 1953 season, officials created a new post—a referee to deal with conflicts. The new referee, perhaps ill-prepared to make decisions about racing disputes, meted out to Beauchamp the most severe punishment in the history of the track.[3]

It is possible that promoter Slusky believed this was excessively harsh punishment for Beauchamp, but in general Playland officials were proud of their management of the track. A feature article in the Playland Track News, an insert in the fifteen-cent program, said: "The Playland management has often been complimented by operators of other tracks throughout the country." Slusky had an extensive staff on the payroll to ensure that the races went smoothly. Those working full time in the office on the second level of the main stadium issued press releases; registered drivers and cars; monitored driver points; and performed other, similar tasks. When competitors arrived for a race, officials met them at the gate with an entry list of drivers, mechanics, and owners, with drivers ranked by their point total. Playland staff checked to make sure that drivers had health coverage and issued pit passes to the certified crew. Competitors also received at least two spectator passes. Finally, officials assigned drivers to a qualifying heat race and posted these heat race assignments on a blackboard in the pits.[4]

During the races, stewards monitored the track corners. In the middle of the infield, facing the grandstand, stood the officials' tower. A starter/flagman was stationed on the edge of the infield between the officials' tower and the track. Two separate, independent scorers, perched in the second story of the tower, monitored the number of laps each car completed. Because the races typically involved no more than twenty cars, no more than 25 laps, and no pit stops, counting laps was not excessively complicated.

When there were questions, though, Playland officials handled them fairly. In one case, there was no dispute that Karl Barkdoll, an Omahan and a seasoned competitor, had won the 25-lap feature, but some questioned whether Chris Nelson, driving a Swanson vehicle, had actually finished second. Nelson had spun out on the 2nd lap, and when the official lap scorers checked the records of laps completed, as they always did after a race, he only had 24 laps, putting him a lap behind the leaders. At promoter Abe Slusky's track, there was no question of any "funny business." Neither Swanson's car nor anyone's car received unfair benefits. Nelson was not awarded second place.[5]

The punishment inflicted on Beauchamp was disproportionate and, in addition, bad for business. He returned from his two-week suspension with a vengeance. He won the second heat and led in the feature until lap 22, when Bobby Parker passed him. Yet another Harlan native, "Rambling Robert Parker" as the announcer called him, was in first place for the season with 1,222 points, ahead of second-place Omaha champion Bud Burdick by 305 points. Beauchamp feverishly stayed on Parker's back bumper, hoping for a chance to pass on a corner.

On lap 24, Parker sped into the north turn but this time did not stay tight on the inside position. Beauchamp blasted his car into the opening and slammed inside Parker, forcing him even wider on the turn. Before Parker could recover, Beauchamp had won the race. He was back, and he was on top, at least for a Friday night in early June.[6] But although he had won a feature, Beauchamp was mired in tenth place in the point standings.

The Playland track usually featured excitement, even if Beauchamp was not winning. Promoter Slusky always welcomed Tiny Lund, who was still in the Air Force, back to the track. Lund returned July 24, 1953, on furlough; only on this visit he had more to do than just race. Tiny was to be married at the track. His bride was Irma Ruth Mears, "Ruthie," from Carlsbad, New Mexico, whom he had met while in the Air Force.

Lund was the first Playland champion, and now he would be the first person married there. In his Air Force uniform and Ruthie in a dark suit, they stood on the track in front of friends and drivers. Ruthie entered the union with a young son from her first marriage. The wedding ceremony was brief, and Ruthie then went to the stands to watch Tiny race in a borrowed car.

After the races, the wedding festivities began at an open air dance pavilion at Playland. Dale and Phyllis Swanson were among the light steppers on the dance floor. A subgroup of the wedding guests, particularly those without young children, eventually departed for a party financed by Delphine Kaufman and Joe Maloney, a couple representing an intersection in the lives of Swanson, Lund, and Beauchamp. Delphine, known as Gussie, spent her childhood on a farm near the Swansons' farm. Dale had known Gussie from the time he visited her parents' farm to help with the baling.

Eventually, Gussie married Joe, who owned the Chicken Hut restaurant, known to host gambling in its basement. They also maintained a bookmaking operation on their farm near Harlan and a tavern on the Harlan town square. In addition to their friendship with Swanson, Gussie and Joe were great friends with Tiny Lund,[7] years later even buying him a new race car. Beauchamp, also friends with them, ate plenty of chicken at their restaurant and did a little gambling with them as well.

Flamboyant, independent, and unwilling to take guff from anyone, Gussie had the look of a Hollywood B-movie actress. Into her eighties, she tended bar while wearing a cowboy hat and large, flashy jewelry. There was never any doubt who was in charge of the bar, except for the time when mobsters from Kansas City came to Harlan and demanded $50,000 of the take or else. "Those were some bad guys," Gussie said with a shudder.[8]

After Lund and his bride returned to the Air Force base, fans' attention returned to the racing season. At the diner in front of the roller coaster on Broadway, as the jukebox blared out Bill Haley's "Forty Cups of Coffee" and the Ames Brothers' "You, You, You," the regulars asked themselves what was going to happen to Beauchamp.

Beauchamp was so far behind the leaders in season points that he chose to compete elsewhere occasionally, missing several of the race dates at Playland. Attacked on the track and punished if he struck back, he was frustrated with the Playland situation and was forced to consider his options.

10 | The Invasion

B

eauchamp wanted to go up against national competition. His success had come by defeating local drivers of old model stock cars, and in the southwestern corner of Iowa he had achieved as much as possible. Racing additional seasons at Playland offered only repetition of past struggles and attainments. His challenges were to be found on more distant tracks with drivers gathered together from farther afield.

Several steps up was the Indianapolis 500. Indy racing, however, involved a type of vehicle and competition vastly different from the old model stock cars Beauchamp was used to. A stock car usually is a production automobile, manufactured for sale to the public to drive on the streets and roads. An Indy car is built to race. It is lighter in weight and without the top of a typical car. And one place it races is the Indianapolis 500. In the 1950s, an Indy car's typical speed was approximately 140 miles per hour in contrast to a speed of about 60 miles per hour on the one-fifth of a mile dirt track at Playland. In addition, Indy cars were open-wheel vehicles—they had no fenders, and the wheels were set beyond the body of the car. This design meant that contact between such vehicles could result in disastrous and deadly accidents, much like the hot rods and midgets driven at Playland. In contrast, however, Playland's old model racing was bang and bump; it was a contact sport, but the stock car's greater weight and its roof provided better protection for a driver than did the Indy car.

Typically, a driver interested in Indy racing might begin by piloting a midget. A midget had a smaller engine, and its wheel base was 72 inches, compared to an Indy car's approximately 96 inches. Playland's old model competitors Bobby Parker and Keith Rachwitz drove midgets regularly, and they had connections with Indy car owners that almost gave them a chance to race at the Indianapolis 500.[1]

Many drivers in the 1950s believed Indy racing was the ultimate in competitive motor racing. Young Playland driver Bob Kosiski told an *Omaha World-Herald* reporter he hoped to compete in the Indianapolis 500, and the reporter commented that Kosiski's "chief ambition is practically the same [as] all stock car chauffeurs."[2] Lund's mother in 1950 worried that her son would compete at Indianapolis: "I'm afraid his ambition now is to drive at Indianapolis."[3]

Hazel Lund did not worry for long about Tiny racing Indy cars. Beauchamp and Tiny Lund competed with midgets a few times, but neither continued with open-wheel contests. There was another path to move up in the racing world that appealed more to them: late model racing, also called new car racing. The adjustment to new cars was substantially easier than a transition to open-wheel, Indy-style cars. Although late models typically went faster and raced on larger tracks than the old models, how the driver handled the car with competitors nearby was similar. The spectators liked the idea that the cars on the track looked like the new cars in the showrooms, and many believed that new car races had better drivers than the old model events. As a result, late model events tended to draw larger crowds paying higher ticket prices resulting in more prize money, which lured competitors away from the old model events.

In 1953 Beauchamp heard about the biggest late model race in the nation, which was held in Darlington, South Carolina. It was billed as the "Southern 500," and in 1952 the prize money had totaled $25,500. Fonty Flock from Decatur, Georgia, had won the race and $9,500, second place won $3,500, and third place took home $1,500.[4] A first place at Darlington represented more money than Beauchamp could win in an entire season at the Playland track.

But it wasn't just about the money. Beauchamp wanted to compete in these high stakes events against the high-caliber drivers who raced in them. He believed he was the equal of or better than any stock car driver, regardless of region or racing association, and he was anxious to test the limits of his ability.

Beauchamp did not have long to wait for new competition. In 1953, two late model racing circuits sponsored events in the Midwest. One was the Circuit of Champions, formed by the Society for Autosports, Fellowship, and Education (SAFE), and the other was established by an organization based in the Southeast, the National Association for Stock Car Auto Racing (NASCAR).

Both SAFE and NASCAR portrayed their drivers as national champions. Although the many different tracks and racing organizations had no method of determining national champions, the exaggerated claims about these circuit drivers increased fan interest in seeing the show. Promoters urged local drivers to enter and compete against these hardened "national champions."

To take advantage of these new opportunities, Beauchamp began looking for a late model race car. For his search, he relied on his rural Iowa roots. Claus Behnken, an Anita Ford dealer who had carved a track out of land on his farm, came to the rescue. Lloyd Jorgensen of Audubon and Mel Krueger of Anita both drove old model Behnken race cars.[5] For the Midwest late model contests, Behnken provided Krueger a 1949 Ford two-door and Beauchamp a 1953 Hudson Hornet, the dominant late model at the time.[6] (Usually cars older than three or four years were not permitted in a late model event.)

SAFE's Circuit of Champions scheduled a visit to Playland on July 17, 1953, for what was to be the first late model events at the Iowa oval. SAFE promised to bring twenty-three cars, track owner Abe Slusky guaranteed a $2,000 purse, and ten local competitors indicated they would test their skill against the nonlocal SAFE pilots.

SAFE had been created in 1952 by Chuck Scharf, a Chicago promoter who in 1948 operated Chicago Land race track. In 1955 he also organized a convertible circuit that toured the United States. In December 1955 he sold the convertible circuit to NASCAR and from then on remained affiliated with that organization, promoting its races in the Chicago area.

The local papers reported Beauchamp naively saying, "I'll make monkeys out of those guys from Chicago and Detroit. Wait till I get them out on the track at Playland. See who's the champ after Friday night."[7] He confidently predicted, "I know the track. I'll get them on the corners at Playland. Nobody knows how to take the curves at Playland like I do."[8] Normally, good driving was a major ingredient of Beauchamp's success at his home track, but he did not realize what he was up against. He didn't grasp that he was competing against a group of rough individuals. Rumors circulated that SAFE cars were stolen, not uncommon in that era, and that SAFE drivers were an unsavory bunch.

Pat Kirkwood, featured as one of SAFE's top drivers, operated nightclubs and bars in Texas and was said to have connections with organized crime. Years later he was mentioned in the Warren Commission Report that investigated the John F. Kennedy assassination. Rumors about SAFE also extended to other drivers, among them Bob Pronger, who had connections with chop shops, car thieves, and other criminal types. Eventually, he was found murdered in his car, his face unrecognizable.[9] And the shady dealings of some of the drivers wasn't all of the story. The SAFE Circuit of Champions made certain its drivers had the advantage. Its cars were built with durable parts and special racing equipment.

By the night of the competition, only five local drivers had managed to locate late model cars to enter, Beauchamp among them. Defending the local drivers' reputation, Beauchamp placed third in his heat race, and his fellow Playland driver, Bud Burdick, won the fourth heat.

Burdick started in the front row for the feature and jumped out into the lead. After the 3rd lap Pat Kirkwood passed Burdick, who soon had to drop out of the 50-lap contest with tire problems. Beauchamp, meanwhile, struggled against the dirty tactics of SAFE drivers. At one point he was spun out, but he fought back and, though he didn't win, he managed to finish third. Hometown people thought he had held up well against the Circuit of Champions. The local paper reported that Beauchamp raced two of the better SAFE drivers "wheel to wheel" with the Iowa driver staying in front of them.[10]

During the next two weeks, the other circuit, NASCAR, which had been organized in 1947, held three races in the area. NASCAR promised to improve racing in the Southeast, but its major aspiration was to be a genuinely national organization. After World War II, racing in the South was perhaps less organized and more unpredictable than it was in other regions. Occasionally, promoters would hold a day of racing events, and while the cars were circling during the last event, they vamoosed with all the gate receipts. Drivers and mechanics also faced fly-by-night race schedules, never knowing far in advance where a race might be held, and often the racers received little money for their trouble at the end of the day.

NASCAR pieced together a circuit of tracks with definite race dates, made certain drivers got their gate receipt money, and scheduled separate event days for its old model modified division and its late model division. The late model NASCAR show drew the attention of a Nebraska promoter, Eddie O'Boyle of the North Platte Speedway. He was the catalyst for NASCAR's venture into the Midwest. After reading a report by Ken Purdy in *True Magazine* saying that NASCAR was a new race-sanctioning organization and was hoping to promote late model races, O'Boyle wrote to Purdy asking him how to contact NASCAR. Purdy forwarded O'Boyle's letter to Bill France, the owner of NASCAR. France and O'Boyle talked, and France agreed to a NASCAR tour in South Dakota, Nebraska, and Iowa.[11]

Beauchamp and Krueger drove to Rapid City, South Dakota, for the first NASCAR contest on July 22, 1953. The 200-lapper was a new challenge for the pair, because most of their experience was in races on smaller tracks with fewer laps. Late model race days at most venues throughout the nation tended to involve few contests, often just time trials and then one big event of perhaps 100 or more laps.

The governor of South Dakota was in the stands to watch a race that ads billed as "the biggest show ever presented to the people of South Dakota and adjoining states."[12] The big guns from the South were ready to show the fans and the race queen, Miss South Dakota, how good they were. Unfortunately, there were almost too few cars for the race. Usually, promoters aimed to have twenty cars in an event, although sometimes they had to paint a number on a tow car—the vehicle that pulled the race car on the highway—that would by prearrangement drop out of the event after a few laps. In this contest, however, there were only ten regional drivers competing against five NASCAR drivers so the field of cars was embarrassingly skimpy.

The race did not go well for the drivers from Iowa. Beauchamp exited the race early, after 34 laps, when on the north turn he slid into a slower car and damaged his radiator. Mel Krueger had only slightly better luck, breaking an axle later in the race on the same north turn.[13]

The trip to Rapid City netted Krueger and Beauchamp $25 each, while winner Herb Thomas collected $1,000 and second-place Dick Rathman won $550. They and the men in the next three spots were NASCAR drivers. Lee Petty, later to figure so largely in NASCAR history, finished fourth, earning $300. Mel Krueger said, "I didn't attempt to race the NASCAR drivers; I raced the other local drivers." Then he joked, "I pointed to which side of my car the NASCAR drivers could pass."[14] They had better equipment. Aside from their cars operating in peak condition, the vehicles of the NASCAR racers had heavy duty parts capable of withstanding the difficulties of a long contest. Reinforcing a car to withstand a grueling race usually would be considered a fair advantage. It was not dishonest for clever and well-informed mechanics to prepare a more durable race car.

It was at Rapid City that Beauchamp first met Lee Petty. The meeting was not memorable. Neither Beauchamp nor Petty realized that in slightly more than five years, they would be locked in a spectacular racing dispute, thrusting them both onto the national stage.

Four days after the Rapid City race, on July 26, NASCAR and local drivers competed again, this time at the North Platte Speedway, managed by Eddie O'Boyle. In the days prior to the race, he had indefatigably hyped the contest. Day after day stories appeared in the press announcing the entry of drivers for the event. Each of the five NASCAR competitors received considerable coverage.[15]

The $4,000 purse signaled a big race that, in turn, was expected to attract 10,000 fans. O'Boyle's problem was the shortage of seats for all the people he expected. He called France. France called General Curtis ("Boom Boom") LeMay, the commander of the Strategic Air Command (SAC) based in Omaha, Nebraska, and a well-known sports car race fan. LeMay, who used Air Force bleachers for his worldwide racing events, ordered the Corps of Engineers to bring them to North Platte, and military personnel assembled them for the contest.[16]

Behnken and Beauchamp delayed their entry to the North Platte event. After the drubbing in Rapid City and the observation that not enough cars were showing up for the NASCAR contests, they may have bargained for incentive money to enter—the promoter most likely was thought to be desperate for entrants. Incentive money was occasionally offered to attract more cars and ensure there would be a full field. In the end, the *North Platte-Telegraph Bulletin* reported that while twenty-two cars had entered, only seventeen had showed up, and one of those didn't race a full lap—most likely this was a tow car. O'Boyle needed every car he could find.

Despite the shortage of cars, more than 5,000 spectators watched locals challenge the NASCAR drivers. Beauchamp raced well, riding in fifth place until a right front spindle broke. One newspaper reported that the local drivers had a lot of "bad luck." The reality was the locals' cars were not as well equipped as the visitors' cars.[17] Beauchamp finished fourteenth and Krueger only finished ahead of the car that didn't last a full lap.

Although Beauchamp did poorly, the North Platte event offered unique excitement. The leader, Herb Thomas, who had won the Rapid City event, became bored with winning, so he and Dick Rathman decided to have some fun. Believing the Nebraska operation was small-time and easily tricked, they planned to tie, thereby arguing that both were entitled to first-place prize money. On the last lap of the race, Thomas slowed down and let Rathman's second-place car catch up so the two crossed the finish line in a tie.

But promoter O'Boyle was not so easily fooled. He refused to give both drivers first-place money. Instead, he called France, then awarded the race to Rathman. Thomas's fooling around cost him $350.[18]

The final stop of the NASCAR Midwest invasion occurred on August 2 in Davenport, Iowa. Beauchamp and Krueger traveled from the western end of Iowa to the Mississippi Valley Fairgrounds for this event. Only fourteen cars entered the contest, making it another slim field of competitors.

The Davenport press continued the tradition of garbling Beauchamp's name, reporting "Jerry" Beauchamp was entered.[19] Again the local newspapers hyped the NASCAR stars' great driving skill. Once again, Herb Thomas won and Buck Baker finished second, followed by Lee Petty, Dick Rathman, and Fonty Flock. Four of the local drivers lasted only about half of the 200-mile race.[20]

Making decent showings, Krueger finished seventh and Beauchamp eighth. The NASCAR racing machines remained superior to the local cars. By the Davenport contest, however, Krueger and Beauchamp had discovered how to keep their cars in the race, finishing close behind the NASCAR pilots. Beauchamp competed well against the locals, but this NASCAR thumping reinforced an important maxim he had first learned from Swanson: without a good race car, a top driver will have trouble winning.[21]

After the late model events and despite his mediocre performances against the visitors, Beauchamp was eager to compete on NASCAR tracks, particularly in high stakes contests. In the following months, he and Krueger entered several NASCAR events in the South. Beauchamp's brother, Gaylord, recalls discussions about visits to Darlington and Daytona Beach and remembers that John did not use his own name. Beauchamp believed there was a southern bias, so most likely the name he used could not be traced to any midwestern race driver but instead claimed a home state somewhere in the South. This was an era when credentials were not checked carefully, and promoters usually were happy to see extra cars and drivers. Johnny told his brother that during one southern race, he wore out twelve sets of tires. Darlington was a track likely to wear out many sets of tires, because the corners were sharp, requiring brake use.[22]

Mel Krueger, driving a Klaus Behnken–owned race car, visited the Daytona Beach race in 1954, and Beauchamp, as Krueger recalls, also raced a Behnken car. Krueger used his own name, but Beauchamp's relatives agreed with his brother Gaylord that John did not identify himself by his real name during visits to Darlington and Daytona Beach.

What is evident is that with Claus Behnken's support, Beauchamp and Krueger entered several NASCAR races in the South, probably in the last three or four months of 1953 and the first few months of 1954. Beauchamp still was unable to defeat NASCAR drivers, and he and his friend departed as they had arrived—quietly.

The 1953 Playland season championship was out of reach for Beauchamp. His bad beginning to the season and then his decision to split his driving time between late models and old models left the battle for champion of the home track to Bud Burdick and former Harlan resident Bobby Parker. It was not settled until the last race of the season, when Parker's car broke an axle, taking him out of the race and giving Bud Burdick the championship. Beauchamp, however, was on a new trajectory, edging away from old models and moving closer to late model racing.

t was 1954 and Beauchamp was behind the wheel of a Swanson-owned race car once again, lured back to old model racing by the opportunity to team up with the motor magician.[1] The Playland track had changed its rules, reverting to the 1950 standard: straight stock cars. The cars could not be souped up with expensive racing parts. Another important change had occurred in the middle of the 1953 season, when officials began allowing even older models, such as those from 1933 and 1934.[2]

With these rule changes, cars from neighboring tracks, such as those in Lincoln, Nebraska, and Sioux City, Iowa, that permitted the older-style autos, could visit Playland without major mechanical adjustments. Swanson saw a new type of challenge he liked. He believed he could a build a race car that, with Beauchamp behind the wheel, could win a championship. The new rules were likely to create a great show.

The competition at the Playland track was stronger than when Swanson last owned a car. Newcomer Bob Kosiski, if he wasn't the equal of Beauchamp, had the ability to win. In addition, Bud Burdick, winner of the 1953 season and multi-year champion on Nebraska ovals, was racing full time at Playland. Then there was Don Pash, the 1952 season champion, and Bobby Parker, powered with engines built by Ott Ramer, who fielded Indianapolis race cars.

Swanson rarely participated in an enterprise without a high probability of success. Taking advantage of the new rules, he built a sporty black-and-white 1934 Ford, lighter than the 1939 Fords, and Beauchamp eagerly joined the quest for another track title.

After the events of April 25 and May 9, the pattern was set. Bud Burdick and Johnny Beauchamp had each won a feature race. Beauchamp, by virtue of a slightly better performance in preliminary races, was twenty points ahead of Burdick. Burdick was a tough, clean-driving competitor who also flew airplanes, so he was accustomed to speed. A machine gunner in World War II, he had come under enemy fire and had a brave, battle-hardened spirit. If one glanced quickly at Burdick, one could believe one had seen the film star Vic Morrow, the tough guy in the *Combat* tele-vision series and a rough hoodlum kid in *Blackboard Jungle*. But despite his looks, Burdick was a happy, cheerful man, not looking to cause anyone extra trouble on or off the track. In third place was newcomer Bob Kosiski. These three would duel the entire season.

Beauchamp won the third feature of the season, extending his point lead over Burdick, who had car trouble. On June 11, Don Pash won a fea-ture in his first appearance of the season; then Burdick reeled off two more feature wins. He was now the track point leader, 89 points in front of Beauchamp.

Burdick's surge may have been the result of racing savvy. On May 21 the Playland oval was converted from dirt to smooth asphalt, which re-quired different tires than those used on a dirt track. Burdick bought tires, smooth without tread, from a California manufacturer and was ready to race. After a few asphalt races, Burdick said to one of the other drivers using the dirt track tires, "You will never do well with those tires."[3] Among those learning this lesson was Beauchamp. Beginning on June 13 his car, well fortified with the proper tires, won four of five features.

As Burdick and Beauchamp battled for the championship, officials struggled to keep order. One problem was cars with illegal parts. Burdick and Beauchamp, because they were winning races, were the prime tar-gets of teardown inspections. Their cars always passed. On one occasion, Swanson was away on a fishing trip when the Harlan driver won a feature. Competitors, seizing an opportunity while the motor magician was away, paid the money for the teardown of 55. Beauchamp fought back: "You are not tearing that car down until Dale can watch."[4] He wanted to make sure Swanson was there to explain anything officials might question. Officials impounded the car until Swanson returned to observe the inspection; the car passed.

Other drivers were not so lucky. Bob Kosiski won the Memorial Day Classic only to be disqualified because his car was not straight stock, and he was not the only one to get caught cheating. Jim Vana and Bill Peters also had cars that did not pass inspection. Others were torn down and passed, including that of the hard-driving Bud Aitkenhead.

Beauchamp led 1,524 to Burdick's 1,355 heading into the Fourth of July 50-lap Independence Day Classic. Officials doubled the points for the holiday event and guaranteed a $1,000 purse. Beauchamp relished such big purse events, but his car blew a tire in the heat race, leaving him out of the feature and humbling him with a spot in the consolation event, reserved for the biggest losers of the heat races.

Bud Burdick had better luck: he won his heat race and then captured the trophy dash. Tommy Leonetti, a rising singing star performing at the Omaha Seven Seas nightclub, presented the trophy to Burdick. Competing in the dangerous and raucous consolation event with inexperienced drivers, Beauchamp finished out of the money. His biggest competitor absent, Burdick cruised to an easy victory in the feature, piling up 350 points for the night and shooting back into first place in the point standings.

Beauchamp, Swanson, and Bud Burdick and his brother Roy competed against each other for almost a decade. Roy owned a garage in South Omaha, and he helped build the car Bud drove at the races. Through all these years of competition, the Swanson garage and the Burdick garage remained on good terms. One night near the time of Bud's heat race, he noticed a tire on his car was flat. Beauchamp, not in the event, pulled a tire off 55 and helped Bud put it on V-8.[5] After the races, Bud and Johnny would occasionally meet at the beer tent a few steps from the track on Playland's midway.[6]

Bud, a fun-loving fellow with five children, remained close to home to work his day job as a heavy construction equipment operator. In the early years, Bud had raced motorcycles with Tiny Lund, Bobby Parker, and the Harlan Handlebar Jockeys. Years later he laughed as he recalled, "John, Dale, and I all got along fine. The only time we had any problem was when old lady Swanson came over and told us we were cheating."[7]

Beauchamp had more problems than outrunning Burdick. Even though he had prominent rivals now, the banging and crashing by other drivers to slow him down continued. When he retaliated, competitors protested his "rough" driving, but Beauchamp kept winning. Importantly, Beauchamp had Swanson's backing in these track battles. Swanson said: "Drive clean, but if they start pushing you around purposely, hand it back even if it means disqualification."[8]

In several races, Beauchamp damaged his car defending himself on the track. In one event, while holding down fourth place, he rammed driver Bob Womochil's car, and Womochil's retaliation caused the 55 to lose a wheel, ending Beauchamp's efforts. During the Harlan driver's eighth feature victory on July 18, journeyman driver Chuck Riley attempted to give

Beauchamp unnecessary trouble, and finally Beauchamp bumped Riley into the fence. After the race, Riley and his friends complained to officials, but the officials allowed Beauchamp's win.

Beauchamp's star power had increased by the time the SAFE late model circuit returned to the Playland oval and inaugurated the official conversion of the track from dirt to asphalt. Beauchamp drove a Jaguar in the 100-lap feature. Starting from the last position, by lap 60 he was challenging the two leaders, Pat Kirkwood and Robert Pronger. In the end, the Harlan driver came in second to Kirkwood, and the following day the headline read: "Beauchamp is hero at Playland."[9]

But for local fans listening to Bill Haley's "Shake, Rattle, and Roll" at the diner near the Playland roller coaster, the rivalry between Beauchamp and Burdick remained the big show. Officials began to realize that Beauchamp (and through him, Swanson) should not be punished for protecting himself on the track. To damage Beauchamp's chances would undermine the hot competition with Burdick.

After the July 4 events, the Harlan driver won two features and Burdick had no wins. By the end of the month, Burdick's lead had vanished, and he was now 13 points behind. Complicating the Beauchamp-Burdick rivalry was the rise of Kosiski, who had won three features and was constantly in contention to win.

To settle the intense competition among the top three drivers, on Sunday night, August 1, track promoters held what they called a grudge race among Burdick, Beauchamp, and Kosiski. Burdick seized the lead, followed by Kosiski and Beauchamp in third. On lap 12 Beauchamp passed Kosiski and by lap 15 had his front tire at the door of Burdick's car. But Burdick won the race.

In the feature, Beauchamp pushed into the lead and Burdick left the race on lap 10 with a flat tire. Kosiski gained second place. Aitkenhead, who had not raced at the track in three weeks, finished third. With this victory, Beauchamp notched his ninth feature win.

Beauchamp, behind the wheel of the Swanson car, projected an aura of inevitability. He was the champion in the best car, and even if he didn't win, he was still the best driver and the champion. During his ninth win, as he circled the track in the lead, announcer Lee Barron told the fans, "Out of the north turn and into the backstretch, in the phantom 55, goes the ghost of Playland Park, Johnny Beauchamp."[10]

During much of August, Beauchamp clung to a narrow lead over Burdick. Kosiski won three features that month while Burdick and Beauchamp struggled to win. On August 22, the standings showed Beauchamp, 2,666; Burdick, 2,539; Kosiski, 2,375; and Aitkenhead, 1,434.

Although Beauchamp was locked in an intense battle for the Playland championship, he still managed to make time for some fun. Before the beginning of the racing season, Beauchamp, his ex-wife Nettie Belle, and the two small boys, Robert and William, took a vacation together. They traveled south to Lookout Mountain, the Great Smoky Mountains, and Florida.

In Florida, they stopped at a vast alligator and monkey farm that sold the creatures to tourists. John gravitated to the alligators, and he began talking about buying one. Nettie Belle said, "Absolutely not. I am not riding in any car with an alligator."[11]

John then turned his attention to the monkeys. Nettie Belle remained quiet while her ex-husband bought a monkey, and off they went again in the car. Then Nettie Belle chirped, "I think we should call the monkey John Junior."

John angrily replied, "I don't like that name, and I don't want him called John."

"Well I think John Junior is a perfectly fine name."

"No, he is not going to be called that."

Finally Nettie Belle said, "Then he can be Junior."[12]

The monkey, Junior, became great friends with John and often lived with his parents. Eventually, Beauchamp decided to show Junior stock car racing close-up. One night at the Playland races, Junior sat in the car with Beauchamp during a race. Unfortunately, the monkey was not cut out for stock car racing. Agitated, he climbed and jumped all over the car, making it difficult for Beauchamp to drive. As a final protest, Junior defecated all over the inside of the car. Once the car was back in the pits, Mel Krueger and some of the other drivers had a big laugh when they saw what Junior had done to the interior of 55.

On August 27, Lund finished his Air Force term of service and returned to Harlan. Lund, like some ancient Greek adventurer, returned with tales to tell, including being part of Operation Big Shot, an atomic bomb test at

Yucca Flats near Las Vegas, Nevada. Lund and other soldiers crouched in the shelter of trenches and climbed out about five seconds after the "awful white light" from the blast. Tiny explained: "The concussion hit a few seconds later and knocked us back into the trenches."[13]

Lund's frequent visits home during his service had not been without problems for Swanson. If the mechanic fielded only one car, then there always was the issue of whether Beauchamp would step aside to let Lund drive 55. On one occasion Beauchamp opposed Lund's getting to drive 55. Finally, after considerable dispute, Beauchamp said it was not worth all of the trouble, and he found another owner with an available race car.

Building a second car did not entirely solve the problem of Lund and Beauchamp. There remained the questions of which driver was allowed to drive 55 and whether one of Swanson's cars was faster than the other. In 1954, at the end of the season and knowing Lund would be coming home, Swanson built a second car for him. The second car was a 1939, slightly heavier than the 1934 car and perhaps slightly slower. Hazel Lund, Tiny's mother, who often intervened on her son's behalf, complained to Swanson about that possibility. Meanwhile, since Beauchamp had been driving the 1934 car all season, he expected to stay behind the wheel of that car.

Swanson, who attempted to make the cars equally fast, was not happy about the accusations, but it didn't amount to much in the end. Beauchamp and Lund, although always rivals, remained friends their entire lives. Lund rarely stayed unfriendly with anyone, and Beauchamp was usually easygoing and nonconfrontational. Swanson, somewhat more persnickety, also remained on good terms with both drivers. These were minor disputes in the heat of battle.

In his first night of competition, Lund, piloting the second Swanson car and with few points, started in front and easily won the first heat. Beauchamp, in his heat race, started last, behind twenty-one cars. Officials added 2 laps to the regular 10-lap heat event to give the drivers in the back more time to get to the front. On three different occasions, drivers attempted to spin out Beauchamp. He kept his cool and assumed the lead on the 9th lap. Track officials later observed that "Beauchamp drove one of his best races of the season."[14]

In the feature, Lund leapt out to an early lead and won easily. Meanwhile, Burdick and Beauchamp struggled. Burdick could not place in the feature event, and Beauchamp became locked with Tom Sloboth in a 14-

lap, bang-and-block mode of driving. The typically cautious Beauchamp bided his time, staying back to prevent Sloboth from spinning him out, and as a result settled for fourth.

On the next night of races, Sunday, August 29, during the third heat Lund tangled with struggling driver Ken Gooch. The cars crashed and came to rest in the infield. The 250-pound Lund sprang out of his car and began fighting with the overmatched Gooch. His assault caused officials to ban him for the remainder of the season, eliminating a wild card from the competition.

Burdick, meanwhile, had been plagued by engine trouble. To have a chance at the championship, he reasoned that he needed a better car than his 1939 coupe. He showed up Sunday, August 29, with a spiffy, bright yellow 1934 Ford with his V-8 number on the sides. His car appeared to be faster than Beauchamp's, and Burdick hoped it might turn the tide. In fact, with the wind whipping around the white scarf he wore to keep the track grime off his face, he won the feature, but Beauchamp won the third heat and finished second in the feature.

On September 3, Friday, Burdick still had a mathematical chance to win the championship, but he was unable to cut into Beauchamp's point lead. Beauchamp won the feature with Burdick second and Kosiski third. Burdick now was 152 points behind Beauchamp.

The final events of the official season were held on September 5. If he was to win, Burdick had to hope for a sweep of three races with Beauchamp earning no points.

Dale Swanson left nothing to chance. Not even a miracle was going to snatch the championship from him. Swanson calculated that if he put a good driver with no points in his second car, that driver, starting in front, could win the feature. Without a feature win, Burdick could not gain sufficient points for the championship, even if Beauchamp was wrecked and earned no points.

The problem was that Lund, the likely driver of the second car, had been banned from the race. Swanson thought of asking Chris Nelson, who had driven a Swanson car in the past, but Nelson was not capable of competing with Burdick one-on-one.

Swanson did know of another excellent driver who was capable of winning a feature. That driver was Harlan resident Hooky Christensen. He had demonstrated he could win races, finishing third for the season in 1951, but although everyone believed Christensen was good, he had never driven a Swanson car, so no one knew how good he could be. Swanson asked Christensen to drive the second car.

This September 1954 race would be the only time Christensen drove a Swanson car.[15] Although he was from Harlan, had done welding work for Swanson, was on cordial terms with him, and was widely recognized as an excellent driver, Dale Swanson had never asked him to get behind the wheel of one of his vehicles. Sonny Morgan, a driver who knew Swanson well, said when asked about this, "If Dale liked you, he liked you. If he didn't like you, he didn't like you. Sometimes it was unexplainable."[16] But in this instance, the season championship was on the line, and Swanson set aside any personal feelings. Hooky drove the second car.

Christensen, with few points, started in the front and won the heat race. Burdick and Beauchamp each placed third in their respective heat races, and this outcome ended the suspense. Even if Burdick won the speed dash and the feature, he could not make up the point difference in the two remaining races.

Christensen still had something to prove, though. He wanted to show how well he could drive a Swanson car. Starting near the front, he won the feature, lapping everyone but second-place Burdick and third-place Kosiski. Beauchamp, nursing a bad tire, finished fourth.[17]

Dale Swanson, with the 1954 season championship, had now owned or built the cars that won four of the five stock car titles: 1950, 1951, 1952, and 1954. He was the preeminent mechanical wizard of racing in the Iowa, South Dakota, and Nebraska area.

Beauchamp had won his second season championship at the Playland track and finished second in two other season point battles. He had won thirty-seven feature races in five years — more than any other driver. The accomplishment was made greater because of the competition. These Playland drivers were excellent, hardened, and skilled veterans. Other regions could imagine they had the best drivers, but it was only an assertion, difficult to prove, and not easily accepted with Playland drivers like Bud Burdick, Johnny Beauchamp, and the other Harlan boys on the track.

On opening day of Playland's 1955 season, Beauchamp only managed a fourth in the feature. He followed this inauspicious beginning in subsequent weeks with a second in the semi-feature, a first in the semi-feature, and a second in the feature. By July 4, Bud Burdick was the leader with 1,200 points, and Beauchamp not far behind with 1,121. However, Beauchamp's second-place standing was deceptive, because points were difficult to earn. The competition was stronger than ever. Winning was so difficult that Tiny Lund was not a threat; he was not even among the top ten point leaders.

Lund had no intention of building his race career around Playland. Although he shared a car with Hooky Christensen (when Lund drove, it was number 9; when Hooky was piloting, it was 99) and they planned to build a second car. The second car was never built. Lund's performance was so unsuccessful that the Playland track became more of a sideshow for him, and he redoubled his racing activities elsewhere. Tiny Lund, perpetually in motion, searching for races, cars to drive, and new challenges, operated as an informal clearinghouse for racing activity. The ubiquitous Lund was either at a track or had already been there and left.

Because he lived in Harlan, Lund sometimes intersected with Beauchamp and Swanson at the local races, while at other times he showed the way to new racing for them. A good example is how Lund's activities encouraged Beauchamp finally to make the move into late model racing. In the course of Lund's frenetic schedule, he crossed paths with Marvin Copple, a Lincoln, Nebraska, driver. Copple, the vice president of his family's savings and loan, the Commonwealth Company, had financial support. He began with old models in 1948 and in 1951 competed with a late model at the local track, finishing seventh. In 1955 he entered a new Oldsmobile in a NASCAR Daytona Beach event, finishing seventh.[1]

Planning to race late models in the Midwest, at the beginning of the 1955 season Copple purchased a 1955 Chevrolet from Ray Erickson Speed

Service in Chicago.[2] Erickson not only supplied the car, but sent along a bright, capable, mechanic named Robert McKee, who was fresh out of high school. Copple and McKee worked out of Bill Smith's Speed Shop in Lincoln, a nexus of activity for race enthusiasts. Beauchamp, Lund, and Swanson all knew Speedy Bill Smith from the hot rod days and from Playland. Lund bought the Copple Chevrolet, retaining McKee as his mechanic.[3]

Lund entered his new Chevrolet in July at the Des Moines, Iowa, Fairgrounds in what was billed as a 250-lap "American Grand Prix" with a purse of $3,500. Recognizing the opportunities, he had been urging Beauchamp and Swanson to leave the rough Playland scene for the more prestigious and lucrative late models. Beauchamp's decision came on June 22.

The trigger for the decision was a visit to Harlan by Junior Brunick, a successful driver from Vermillion, South Dakota. In 1950, at the Sioux City oval, Lund and Brunick's brother-in-law nearly came to blows after Lund spun Brunick out on the last lap of a feature race. In subsequent years, Brunick purchased motors from Swanson and by 1955 Tiny and Brunick had patched up their differences, and these fierce competitors had become friends. On this visit, Junior Brunick intended to buy an engine, so he stayed the night with the Swansons, much to the chagrin of Lund, who asked Junior, "Why didn't you stay with me?"[4] Brunick explained, "Dale and I are doing some business together, and I already accepted an invitation to stay with him."[5]

It was a race night, and they all went to Playland, where, as Brunick recalled, Beauchamp won the feature. They all stopped on the way out of Council Bluffs at a restaurant. Swanson said bluntly to Beauchamp, "You need to decide whether to race late model cars or the old stock cars." Beauchamp, never one to be the center of attention, thought for a moment and then said, "I believe I would rather race late model cars." Swanson, who lacked the energy to maintain an old model and a new model race car, at this point offered to sell Brunick his 1934 old model car rather than only a motor. Brunick bought Swanson's car, and the Swanson-Beauchamp team shifted to late model racing.[6]

Beauchamp had already worked out many of the plans for a transition to late models. He had brokered a deal with Merle Short, the owner of a garage in Omaha, and his brother George, who owned a drywall business in the same city. Merle had an old model car that frequently competed at

Playland, and it was here that Beauchamp and the Shorts talked. George agreed to put up the money for a new 1955 Chevrolet, and Swanson went on the payroll as the car's mechanic. Because often the old model race events at Playland did not conflict with date and time of the late model races, Beauchamp continued in old model races, driving Merle Short's old model Ford.[7]

An attraction of late model racing for Swanson was the prospect of working on Chevrolet's newly designed car, called the Hot One. The 1955 Chevrolet had been thoroughly redesigned. Departing from the earlier, six-cylinder "stovebolt six," the new engine had eight cylinders and was designed with lighter parts, so it had more horsepower. The Hot One was lighter in weight and smaller than the older model Chevy. In addition, it was loaded with many engineering improvements.[8]

The motor magician believed he could win races with this car. With owner Short's cash, Swanson purchased the vehicle from a Harlan dealer.[9] And Beauchamp, piloting the Short-owned Chevrolet, joined Tiny Lund in the late model races organized by the International Motor Contest Association (IMCA).

IMCA was founded in 1915, making it the oldest active racing association. It came into existence to sanction and manage state and county fair races, largely in the Midwest. Prior to 1915, these races had been sanctioned by the American Automobile Association (AAA). The fair organizers were unhappy with the AAA's handling of their contests but believed some entity was necessary to oversee and give credibility to their events.

Although one could hold a race at a track without a sanctioning body, most contests are sanctioned by a racing organization. The advantages include having standardized rules of competition, honesty in the conduct of the contests, and a legitimacy that an unsanctioned race might not have. For example, in 1953, when Eddie O'Boyle wanted to promote late model races in Nebraska, he located a sanctioning body, NASCAR, to help organize and give credibility to the events he sponsored.

In 1914, at the Chicago convention of the American Association of Fairs and Expositions, fair officials ended their connection with the AAA and set up a new sanctioning organization, the IMCA, largely consisting of fair members, to supervise races. Knowing that they lacked race experience, IMCA hired knowledgeable promoters to operate their events, but without a tradition, the new organization had difficulty attracting the best drivers. IMCA was considered by top competitors to be second class. Nevertheless, races held at fairs guaranteed a large crowd in the grandstand, a predictable race schedule, and good purse.

One problem with IMCA's image was the location of its races. Many activities at fairs, while enjoyable, had an air of hucksterism, and the fair races were accused of just that. They were suspected of being fixed, and fairground race operations were believed to be a "hippodrome" show, favoring entertainment over real competition. Indeed, one early IMCA promoter, Alex Sloan, may have conducted a few unserious races, such as one in which drivers, with the IMCA's approval, staged a race on a muddy track that became something like a professional wrestling match. The deceived fans were glued to their seats, watching what appeared to be hot competition and left the stands certain they had received their money's worth. In fact, the drivers took no chances on the muddy track.

Tom McGeehan, a college student working a summer job for Frank Winkley, recalled one instance when a track was in such bad shape that promoters paid the drivers $100 dollars each and told them to put on a good show.[10] This kind of thing was the exception, though, and Winkley, one of the two IMCA promoters in 1956, argued those days were in the past. He also pointed out that the same type of hippodrome activity had occurred in other association races.[11] Indeed, the NASCAR event of 1953 in Nebraska (see chapter 11) carried a whiff of the hippodrome mentality, a noncompetitive outcome.

In many respects, IMCA was a meager, shoestring operation, not unlike NASCAR and other racing circuits of the time. One insider account comes from young McGeehan, whose grandfather had been a mechanic in the 1920s for the famed Indy driver Ralph DePaulo. The IMCA organization traveled from track to track, and the sleeping arrangements for its staff were modest. At one stop in Mason City, Iowa, the Cerro Gordo Hotel issued young McGeehan a rope to lower himself out the window in case there was a fire.[12]

The vehicles on the IMCA tracks in the pre–World War II era were called speedway cars, sprint cars, or "big" cars, but these names all referred to the same type of vehicle. Essentially, they had the appearance of Indianapolis cars but were slightly smaller. For more than three decades, IMCA held speedway-style races throughout the middle section of the nation.

Lacking a list of strong drivers, IMCA nonetheless had several stars. One of the best was Gus Schrader, whom legendary driver Barney Oldfield argued was "the greatest driver ever to sit behind the wheel of a racing car."[13]

Most ovals of the era welcomed Indy-style cars and old models, while late model racing was less common, but not unprecedented. In fact, late models had been raced on occasion for many years. For example, in the first decade of the 1900s, Charles Howard, a Buick dealer eventually to become the owner of the great race horse Seabiscuit, entered his vehicles in San Francisco races because he realized such events could sell new cars.[14]

The first IMCA late model race may have been the one held on November 7, 1947, at Lubbock, Texas,[15] well before the beginning of NASCAR's late model racing circuit. By 1949, IMCA was regularly conducting late model races, but it did not have an official circuit, a well-defined schedule, or a system for recording race outcomes. It was only after the fact that IMCA declared driver Eddie Anderson the unofficial champion of the late model season in 1949. By contrast, in the same year NASCAR had an official circuit of late model races with a schedule and a record of the season points.[16] History is clear, however, that NASCAR did not hold the first late model races.

Despite lagging behind NASCAR in its organization of a late model circuit, IMCA officials quickly noticed the possibilities for late model competition. Archie Powell, a promoter with National Speedways, Inc., recalled that at the beginning of the 1949 season, car dealers in Milwaukee refused to sponsor late model race cars, but "when Kaiser won, it caused a lot of chagrin." Kaiser, a minor auto manufacturer, competed with the top brands, such as Ford and Chevrolet. Later in the summer, when Powell promoted a 150-mile race in Milwaukee, circumstances had changed. "There were a dozen dealer sponsored entries for the race," a newspaper reported.[17] Powell concluded that the dealer support for racing was powered by the axiom, "Win on Sunday, buy on Monday."[18] Fans wanted to purchase a car similar to the winner's.

In 1950 IMCA, recognizing the popularity of the late model contests, created two separate divisions: speedway and late model. Tiny Lund, driving Eddie Anderson's second car, participated in several late model events that year. Soon IMCA circulated newsletters about what was happening during each week of racing. The organization printed a yearbook beginning with the 1956 season.[19]

IMCA was an obvious choice for Beauchamp and Lund. It was the primary late model circuit in the region and offered more purse money than the old model events. The crowds could swell to more than 20,000 fans. The minimum number of spectators at an IMCA event was usually greater than the maximum crowd at Playland. Although it cost significantly more to race a late model machine than an old jalopy, and the travel time between contest locations was also substantially greater, a highly skilled driver could win more money and gain more glory.

Making the choice of IMCA easier for Beauchamp and Swanson was the fact that there was no recognized, superior late model racing association. The NASCAR circuit faced many of the same issues and problems as the IMCA circuit, but news coverage of IMCA and NASCAR was so limited that neither knew much about the other. Travel to distant tracks was arduous. Most racers competed in the region in which they lived, and in 1955 the Harlan racers could see little difference between the two circuits. Racing IMCA was a respectable option for midwestern drivers.

13 | The Flying Frenchman

On July 17, 1955, Dale and Phyllis Swanson, George Short and his wife, and several children, including twelve-year-old Dale Swanson Jr., piled into Short's Cadillac for the drive to watch Beauchamp compete in his first IMCA event at the Grand Forks, North Dakota, Fairgrounds, which had a one-half mile track.

In North Dakota, Don White, the IMCA point leader, gave Beauchamp a rude welcome, initiating some banging and bumping that slowed the Harlan driver and caused him to lose control of his car. Swanson didn't like what he saw on the track and was not going to be intimidated. He told White, "You better lay off because the Chevy may be lighter but it's faster down the straightaway and John can take care of you going into the corner."[1] Beauchamp finished fifth, slowed by a loose foot feed, or in mechanic's parlance, a throttle arm that came loose from the cross shaft in the firewall. The showdown with White was postponed for another day.

Beauchamp continued to perform unevenly the following week in Sioux Falls, South Dakota, finishing ninth in the time trials and second in his heat race. Then, in the feature, he had car trouble and once again had no chance to win. Tiny Lund, meanwhile, was also having mixed results in IMCA. In the same Sioux Falls event, Lund was seventh in the time trials and tenth in the feature race. Don White, from Keokuk, Iowa, and the eventual IMCA champion for the year, dominated the feature. Lund's luck improved later in the season. In Grand Forks, North Dakota, on July 31, about 3,500 spectators watched a 200 lapper on a half-mile dirt track. The hood of Lund's car came off on the 30th lap, seemingly taking him out of contention. Herschel Buchanan, a past season champion, kept his T-bird in front until lap 100, when Lund, amazingly, reclaimed the lead. Eventually, his topless car lapped the entire field. It was his first IMCA win of the season.

Still not successful in IMCA events, Beauchamp continued to race at Playland when there was no conflict with the late model events, but the Council Bluffs track had become his second option. Unfortunately, he had bad luck there as well as in the Dakotas. On July 4, the double flip of Beauchamp's car on the north turn added to his misery. Later in the month, after winning his heat race, Beauchamp, trying to avoid Aitkenhead's car during the second lap of the feature, crashed into the fence and flipped the car again.

Beauchamp and his late model car struggled until August 21 at the Wausau, Wisconsin, fairgrounds. Herschel Buchanan once again had the machine to beat, but Beauchamp eventually won the 100-lap, half-mile dirt oval race. The IMCA press release reported that "Beauchamp outgunned Herschel Buchanan before a capacity crowd."[2] After the event, the sportswriters gave Beauchamp the moniker, "The Flying Frenchman." Swanson declared that the "bugs are out of the car and it is performing beautifully."[3]

As Swanson's comment indicates, Beauchamp's first big win in late model IMCA racing was not entirely because of the driver's skill. The Swanson car was now mechanically more reliable, and the motor magician had managed to speed up number 55. Swanson had called Doane Chevrolet, in Dundee, Illinois. What prompted the call was his search for a heavy-duty axle housing assembly installed on one-half ton Chevrolet pickup trucks and police cars.[4] They operated with several different ratios of car wheel revolutions to revolutions of the drive shaft. For the half-mile track, the drive shaft could be set to rotate 6.33 times for every rotation of the wheel. Swanson believed that this half-ton truck axle housing offered maximum durability and power for the half-mile tracks.

The people at Doane Chevrolet, the headquarters for Corvette racing, told Swanson they had three of the half-ton pickup axle assemblies, but they refused to sell him one, preferring to keep such racing parts for their competition Corvettes. Swanson then called Chevrolet engineering in Michigan and, at first, they told him the part did not exist. He persisted, insisting the part was listed as a bona fide available GM part and that Doane Chevrolet had three of them, but the engineers wouldn't help. Swanson hung up the phone, frustrated. Then, to his surprise, shortly before the Wausau race, a half-ton pickup rear-end assembly arrived at the Harlan train depot. Chevrolet engineering and racing had changed its decision. Swanson installed it, and Beauchamp won his first big IMCA contest.[5]

Beauchamp, now occasionally missing events at Playland, saw Burdick extend his points lead. By August 16, Burdick had 2,130 points and Beauchamp had 1,850 points. The possibility of another season championship at his home track was slipping from Beauchamp's grasp. The Playland practice of reverse order starts—cars with the most season points must start the race at the rear—gave capable first-timers a big advantage. One such newcomer was Lloyd Beckman, a leading competitor from the Lincoln, Nebraska, area. Beckman was backed by mechanic Bill Smith. By the time the other veteran regulars had worked their way from the back through all of the slower cars, Beckman had built up a large lead. Even point leader Bud Burdick could not claim a victory. Starting in the front, Beckman eventually reeled off six feature wins in the second half of the Playland season. Winning races was the only way Beauchamp could have gained enough points for another season championship, and Beckman's arrival made winning almost impossible. The Playland season ended with Beauchamp finishing third in the point standings, two feature wins to Burdick's seven and Beckman's six.

At the same time, Beauchamp and Lund continued to improve their IMCA performance. At Lincoln, Nebraska, on September 9, Herschel Buchanan won the 200-lapper, but Beauchamp finished second, a mere two car lengths behind, and Lund was third. Beauchamp later won two more big races: in August at Sioux Falls and on September 16 at the Clay County Fair in Spencer, Iowa, where he broke the track record in a 100-lap feature.

On October 6, Lund snared a short, 10-lap race at the Tulsa Fairgrounds. By the end of the 1955 IMCA season, Beauchamp and Lund ranked sixth and seventh respectively, well behind the point totals of champion Don White and second-place Herschel Buchanan. In a half season of racing, however, they proved they could win, and they demonstrated that both could be threats to win a season championship.

Although Beauchamp and Lund finished near each other in the final season points, there was a reason Beauchamp finished ahead of Lund. Sonny Morgan recalls, "Johnny saved the car. Sometimes holes on the track could be deep. Tiny would go right at them—he never dodged the holes."[6] As a result, he had trouble finishing races because he was too rough on his car.

The Harlan boys had good reason to feel optimistic at the end of the 1955 season. Their transition into IMCA late model racing was going well, and 1956 promised to be better. But a series of events at the end of the season threw their plans into turmoil. Short and Swanson had a disagreement, probably over money. It is likely that Swanson had bought equipment for the car and expected to be reimbursed, but Short balked. The problem culminated at the Spencer, Iowa, race on September 16, that Beauchamp won. In the infield after the race, Swanson angrily pulled off the car's shock absorbers (probably the equipment Short didn't want to pay for) and severed his arrangement with Short.[7] Beauchamp was without a car to drive.

But the dispute did not end the possibility of Swanson and Beauchamp's late model competition. Swanson had discovered a path to being the owner-mechanic of a late model racing car should he choose to compete in the future. During the two months that Swanson worked on the Short vehicle, the motor magician had located other sources of support for a race car. Chevrolet began shipping free parts to Swanson, making it financially possible for him to own and maintain a late model car. Short's money had bought the car Beauchamp had been driving, but now Swanson, with free parts flooding in on the train every night from Chevrolet, could be the owner and mechanic of another car and run the show. Also, Swanson had discovered methods of speeding up the race car that made winning more certain. With lower costs and more prize money, Short was no longer necessary to his plans.

While Swanson and Beauchamp had stopped their racing activity for the season, Tiny Lund kept competing. His mechanic, Robert McKee, had enrolled at the University of Nebraska, and so Kenny "Red" Myler accompanied Lund to events. Myler, from the southwest Iowa community of Missouri Valley, had raced motorcycles and stock cars with Lund in the early days—1950 and before. Myler, however, was more of a mechanic than a driver, and eventually he worked for Richard Petty.

Always looking for a new challenge, Lund decided to take his car to a NASCAR race. The track at LeHi, Arkansas, the Memphis-Arkansas Speedway,[8] was one of the longest in NASCAR, a mile and a half around. The extraordinary size of the oval was not matched by its quality. It was rough, dangerous, and dusty—a driver's nightmare. Blinding dust caused races to be yellow flagged (a caution signal that slows the cars and freezes their order) while the track was watered down. The dust made it impossible for drivers and fans to see.[9] Unable to view the contest, spectators went home, and many drivers were anxious to do the same. In 1956 two drivers were killed in separate accidents at the track. Both were flung out of their cars.[10]

On October 9, 1955, Lund arrived at this treacherous track to launch his NASCAR career. The pre-race publicity touted the first place prize money of $2,900 and the large number of top drivers from all over the United States. The three Flock brothers, Tim, Bob, and Fonty, referred to as the "flying Flocks," were entered. Tim Flock was the point leader in NASCAR at that time and the eventual winner of the season championship. Fonty had been present at the founding meeting of NASCAR in 1947.[11]

In the early laps of the event, Lund competed well with the top drivers. Then, on lap 67, as he rounded a turn, his car's "A" frame broke. The vehicle began rolling over and over. On the third roll, Lund was thrown clear of the car. He landed motionless on the track. Cars sped by, dodging Lund on the left and the right. According to some accounts, he was run over by one car. Finally, the race was stopped and the unconscious Lund was rushed to the West Memphis Crittenden County Hospital.

Tiny was in shock. He had a broken arm, wrist, and toe, and he had injured his back. He spent two weeks in the hospital. The irony was that he had secured sponsorship for the race from Carl Rupert of Rupert Safety Belts. Unfortunately, the Rupert safety belt was not enough to hold him in the car. Lund's Chevrolet was destroyed. His reward for finishing twenty-fifth out of forty-one entries was $60.[12]

That winter, after the 1955 season, Beauchamp's plans for the next season were not settled. Because he lacked the skill to build a race car, he had to work with a good mechanic. Swanson, while a top mechanic, had not owned a race car every season and nothing was certain for 1956.

The weather turned cold and Beauchamp took his family to California. Robert and William missed some school, but they all went, including Nettie Belle. He remained on good terms with his ex-wife, primarily as a father for his kids. Beauchamp's female companion usually was Donna Richter, the girl he had met while racing at Playland.

During the winter, Lund recovered from his wreck, and at Bill Smith's Shop his mechanic, Robert McKee, built a new race vehicle financed with a commercial loan. At one point that winter, Beauchamp quietly asked McKee, "Why don't you come with me, and we will race NASCAR during the 1956 season."[13]

McKee, somewhat surprised by the proposal, said: "I have already told Tiny I would go race with him."[14]

Beauchamp changed the subject: "How is the preparation of Tiny's car coming along?"[15]

Eventually, the uncertainty at the end of the 1955 season cleared: Dale Swanson became an owner-mechanic and was ready to field a late model race car for the 1956 season with Johnny Beauchamp the driver. The previous year, Swanson had established two important connections that enticed him to become a race car owner. First, he made friends with Chevrolet dealers in the communities that held the IMCA races, becoming especially good friends with one dealer, Art Raduenz, the owner of Stillwater Chevrolet. The Swanson and Raduenz families in later years vacationed at the Raduenz's fishing cabin. Eventually, Art organized seven Chevrolet dealerships in the St. Paul–Minneapolis area to sponsor the Swanson Chevrolet race car.

This kind of relationship was not uncommon. Race teams often formed a bond with the local dealerships. Swanson, upon arriving in a community to race, usually paid a visit to the local Chevrolet dealer, the dealer often providing him with space in the garage to work and $100 or $200 to have the dealer's name brushed on the side of the car with wash-off paint.

Stillwater Chevrolet was situated in a center of late model racing; in the mid-1950s, the St. Paul–Minneapolis Fair held three events over seven days, attracting more than 20,000 spectators for each contest and offering a large purse. Gus McDonald, a mechanic at Stillwater Chevrolet, recalled, "The garage jumped with excitement when the race car showed up with Dale Swanson and Johnny Beauchamp."[1]

Aside from the local dealers' help, a second advantage that lured Swanson back to racing was that the Michigan Chevrolet factory, beginning even in the 1955 season, was supplying him with an avalanche of free parts. The heavy duty Chevrolet pickup truck rear end that had resulted in Beauchamp's first win of 1955 at Wausau, Wisconsin, demonstrated the value of Chevrolet factory support.

Although Swanson entered the 1956 season with several assets to improve his chances of victory, there remained a large barrier: Don White.

One IMCA official recalls that "White was one of the best drivers in traffic I have ever seen."[2] The reigning champion was considered by many unbeatable. Plus, White had an intimidating presence on the track. He was a tough, hard driver, while Beauchamp was merely a promising, largely untested newcomer. The savvy track observers had their money on White.

The season began in the Deep South at the historic Shreveport, Louisiana, Fair Grounds. Several Iowans, settling in over dinner a day before the race, were stunned to see Beauchamp with a flashy, painted female old enough to be his mother. A driver involved with Harlan racing who was at the restaurant reflected that Beauchamp was just being Beauchamp: "John usually had a woman with him."[3]

Before 9,523 spectators on April 8, after early hot competition between White and Beauchamp, White pushed his Dodge D-500 to the front. Texan Sonny Morgan finished second, and Beauchamp faded to ninth. On April 22, IMCA held a 200-lap event at Shreveport. Unlike the first race, this one was furiously contested. Beauchamp, along with Sonny Morgan and Marvin Copple, battled Don White for the lead. White eventually won, his second victory of the season; Beauchamp straggled in eleventh. The *IMCA Newsletter* concluded that the first two events were business as usual: "White is well on his way toward a third straight championship."[4]

Swanson and Beauchamp's start to the season was dismal. They barely made expenses. Compounding their disappointment was the success of young Sonny Morgan, a newly minted Lamar College graduate from Beaumont, Texas, who had bested them with a second and a sixth place.

The third contest of the season, at Hutchinson, Kansas, brought a surprising turn of events. A cold snap drove temperatures down to 42 degrees, leaving 4,500 shivering fans to discover that Don White would not be racing because he had had car trouble on the highway. With White not entered, the other drivers' odds of victory increased. Bud Burdick, earlier Beauchamp's competitor at Playland, and Bud's nephew, Bob Burdick, both hoped to win.

Sonny Morgan, who had the fastest time trial, seized the lead, but on lap 59 his fuel line broke. Harlan's "Flying Frenchman," profiting from Morgan's bad luck, took over the lead. He won the 200-lap race—his first victory of the season.

On May 6, IMCA was back in Shreveport for a split-feature format of two 100-lap races. Starting positions for the first race were based on time trials. The race stopped after 100 laps. Cars could be serviced with oil, gas, water, and tires during a brief intermission.

For the second 100 lapper, drivers started in a reverse order of their finish at the end of the first event. The winner of the initial contest started last, making it more difficult for the winner to succeed again, and the last place car started in front. With this arrangement, a driver could win two 100-lap races. To determine an overall winner, the points a driver earned from each race were added together.

In the first 100 lapper, White led until he went out with a broken axle. Beauchamp then took the lead and won, but in the second race he suffered from a steering problem and fell far behind. His misfortune allowed White to win, but barely, because Sonny Morgan clung to White's back bumper for 75 laps. After the race, Morgan climbed out of his car and collapsed from heat exhaustion.

The warm May weather shifted the schedule farther north. For the young Sonny Morgan, racing in Minnesota and Canada made it impossible to return between events to his hometown of Beaumont, Texas. He needed a base of operation in the North. At the same time, Swanson saw something in Morgan he liked. The Texan was intelligent, responsible, easy to be around, and an excellent driver. As a college student, Morgan had raced old model cars, competing against future four-time Indianapolis winner and also future Daytona 500 winner A. J. Foyt. The Texan, while still young, had learned how to wheel a race car. He was the type of person with whom Swanson could and did build a friendship. Many people believed Morgan was as good as Beauchamp.

Whatever Swanson's motive, he extended an invitation, suggesting that Morgan come back to Harlan with him: "You can work out of my garage."[5] Morgan accepted the offer. Swanson enjoyed having another good driver close at hand. The situation resembled the earliest days with Lund and Beauchamp.

Morgan and his friends, Gaston Phipps and Gerald Bernhardt, moved in at the Harlan Hotel just off the square.[6] He, Swanson, and Beauchamp became a loosely joined team for the remainder of the IMCA season, usually traveling together to the tracks. Morgan gained an important benefit from his friendship with Swanson, and a part of it arrived on the evening train through Harlan—boxes and boxes of free parts from Chevrolet.

This bonanza was critical to the viability of Swanson's drivers. He constantly replaced equipment on his car, changing key parts after three races and making sure all the nuts and bolts were tight. This was one of Swanson's secrets to success. He knew that in a 200-lap or longer race, new parts held up better than old ones.

Morgan explained how he benefited from the parts windfall: "Many of the expensive parts Dale Swanson replaced were still perfectly good. These old parts would last another three races." He replaced the parts in his car with the nearly new parts from the Swanson car. In other instances, Swanson shared new parts with Morgan.

The IMCA circuit visited Cedar Rapids, Iowa, on May 20 for a 200-lap contest. On the first turn, White was forced into the fence, damaging his radiator. His car then overheated, and he dropped out of the race. The Burdicks had come for the event, and Bud Burdick won, followed by Sonny Morgan, Bob Burdick, hometown driver Darrel Dake, and in fifth place, Beauchamp. A week later in Spencer, Iowa, the same drivers met again. This time a rain-soaked, muddy track caused drivers to lose control of their cars, with a few of them smashing into the fence. White seized the victory, and Beauchamp finished far behind.

Six weeks into the season, Beauchamp and Swanson had won two races, but these wins came when White was not in contention. White had the most points of the young season, winning four events. Beauchamp's championship prospects were dim.

But Beauchamp's luck was about to change. Topeka, Kansas, hosted a 200-lap Memorial Day event that attracted 14,503 spectators. As the race began, Beauchamp realized that his car had an exceptional power that allowed him to pass competitors as though they were stopped. He won effortlessly, defeating his old nemesis, Bud Burdick. White clung to the season point lead, but Beauchamp now was a formidable opponent.

Next, the IMCA drivers traveled to Sioux Falls, South Dakota, where 5,000 spectators watched a split-feature format of two 100-lappers. On this day, White was powerless to challenge Beauchamp for the wins, and although both Burdicks were present, only Bud Burdick, joined by Darrell Dake, threatened him. Beauchamp swept two more 100-lap features.

At Owatonna, Minnesota, Darrell Dake's hopes of victory were boosted when he won the pole with the fastest time trial. Dake, confident he could defeat Beauchamp, held the lead the first 44 laps, but then Beauchamp stormed past him. On lap 88, a spinning car smashed into

Beauchamp, bending his fender to within an inch of the tire. He powered his car back to full speed. His slowdown allowed White and Morgan to close the gap, their hot pursuit threatening Beauchamp's lead. But in the end, neither Morgan nor White was able to pass him, and he won the first 100-lap race.

The field reversed for the second 100 laps, sending Beauchamp to the rear of the pack. Twenty laps into the second contest, he blasted into the lead. Beauchamp swept two more 100-lap features.

By mid-summer 1956, Beauchamp was unstoppable. The other drivers began to wonder how they could ever defeat him. He had won the last five feature races: two in Owatonna, two in Sioux Falls, and the May 30 feature in Topeka. These wins, combined with his two wins at the beginning of the season, made him the top driver. The press called him the "Flying Frenchman," but some of the drivers, fed up with his dominance, preferred to call him "Johnny Hoseclamp."

Darrell Dake, who had challenged Beauchamp during several of the recent races, did not believe Beauchamp's car could be so dominant unless Swanson was cheating. Dake filed a protest to have the car torn down to determine if it conformed to IMCA rules. Away from the ears of IMCA officials, he vociferously muttered to several drivers that "the Swanson car could not possibly be legal." He went on, "The car must have illegal parts, because I have three illegal parts in my car and Beauchamp still goes faster than I do."[7]

In response to Dake's protest, the Swanson car was hauled off to Linderkugel's garage in Owatonna. IMCA rules specified what modifications could be made to the cars as well as procedures for handling a car suspected of infractions. Once a protest was filed with the race supervisor or promoter, the engine was sealed and taken to a designated location for a teardown. Following IMCA rules, Dake and Swanson each put up $50 and both observed the inspection. The loser lost the $50 while the winner got his money back.[8]

IMCA rules required the engine to be stock: the engine parts had to be manufactured by the factory. Legal parts would have a factory number. Enhanced parts, designed, manufactured, and sold by special speed shops, were illegal.

During this inspection, mechanics discovered an unfamiliar part—a different cam that could explain the speed that had propelled Beauchamp to his many victories that summer. Swanson insisted it was a legal part manufactured and sold by Chevrolet. By this time, it was the middle of the night, and there was no way to prove the truth until the Chevrolet offices in Michigan opened in the morning. The IMCA inspection team suspended any decision until after checking with Michigan.

I n the morning, the IMCA inspectors called the Chevrolet factory in Michigan. They were told that the strange cam in Swanson's car had the part number 3736097 and that it was indeed valid.[1] Dale Swanson's car was within the rules of IMCA.

The inspectors were not aware of the part's origin and that it had the name "Duntov Cam" after its creator, Zora Arkus-Duntov. He had come to the United States after an adventurous life in Europe, with stops in Belgium and Leningrad and an escape from fascist Germany with his wife, a Follies Bergère dancer. Thanks to his engineering background and understanding of European-designed sports cars, Chevrolet hired him as director of high-performance vehicle design and development. His mission was to improve the performance of the Corvette, first produced in 1953, so that it could outperform the Ford Thunderbird. The cam advanced this goal by adding power to the Corvette engine.

A cam regulates the opening and closing of air and fuel in the cylinder chamber. The shape of the cam lobs attached on the turning shaft determines how long the valves remain open, and thus the amount of air and gasoline entering the cylinder—the more combustible material entering the cylinder, the larger the explosion that drives the pistons and powers the car. The Duntov cam by its shape added power.

In 1955, when Swanson searched for the half-ton pickup axle/rear end, he had talked to mechanics at Doane Chevrolet located in Dundee, Illinois.[2] This garage was a center of Corvette activity. Dick Doane's interest in racing engineering attracted him to the Official Corvette Racing Team,[3] and while most Chevrolet dealers received only a restricted allotment of Corvettes, Doane Motors had as many as it could sell. It claimed in a *Road and Track* ad to be the biggest Corvette dealer in the nation. Significantly, the Corvette was manufactured by Chevrolet, making its parts legal for a Chevrolet race car.

One of the 1955 shipments of Chevrolet parts delivered to Swanson included an experimental Duntov cam.[4] The cam, at this point, may not have been an authorized Chevrolet part, and Swanson did not install it.[5] He had little time to experiment because of his breakup with Short. But when Short left with the race car, Swanson kept the experimental cam. It is not clear whether he ever tested this version of the top-secret Duntov cam, but it was tested at Pike's Peak in September 1955 with a 1956 Chevrolet that sported dummy headlights and taillights and had its other new features covered, one month before the 1956 Chevrolet arrived in showrooms. The cam Swanson installed in 1956 was actually a new and improved version of the 1955 test part. This cam came standard in the new model Corvette engines, but it was also available in a power pack that could be installed in a Chevrolet; it added a sensational thirty horsepower.

Why did the Owatonna inspectors not recognize the cam as a legal part? The most plausible explanation is that the inspectors lacked up-to-date information. Learning the cam was available required investigation—the same type of checking that Swanson had done to locate his parts. Years later, several competitors believed that the Duntov cam had been available for anyone to purchase.[6] Nevertheless, the exact date of availability of the cam at every Chevrolet dealer in the nation might not have been the same, and the speed with which the news spread about its availability could have varied.

The variability in the spread of knowledge about the part was compounded by the way racing worked in the mid-1950s. While in theory perhaps the inspectors could have known about the cam, this was an era when drivers entered rental cars in races, and other drivers were known to buy a new family car and take it straight to the track. The inspectors faced a wide array of cars, and they weren't necessarily well-equipped to do their job. Mechanic Robert McKee recalled one inspector using a yardstick to check micro features of the engine.[7] IMCA officials did not always reflect the highest standard of mechanical sophistication.

In short, it's possible that IMCA mechanics did not have an opportunity to learn of the cam. Duntov not only believed "to establish the sports car, you have to race it"; he also believed that to reveal Chevrolet had a cam which would boost horsepower would dull the edge of his company's advantage.[8] Duntov did not want Ford and other competitors to realize how fast the new model cars were until they were in the races. As a result, according to Mike Mueller, Chevrolet "never posted an advertised number" for the Duntov cam.[9]

Chevrolet had possibly concealed news of the cam and, even when the part was available, dealers may have kept the information on a shelf behind the counter, well out of sight. One has only to recall the difficulty Swanson had when he attempted to buy parts made for the half-ton Chevrolet pickup in 1955: the company clearly was not eager to share its more innovative equipment. But regardless of whether the cam was available, the other IMCA drivers and mechanics believed that it was not.

Their sentiments were reflected in a decision at the 1956 IMCA Banquet in December. The business meeting approved a new rule for the 1957 season: "All component parts of stock engines not immediately available to all drivers will not be permitted for use by any driver." The rule was promoted by drivers who complained that factory manufacturers had special racing parts that were not standard equipment but that some privileged mechanics had access to.[10]

But Swanson's success was more complicated than his having recondite engine parts or mechanical tricks. He put more effort and thought into his work than most others did. For example, when he visited the Chevrolet parts warehouse in Omaha,[11] he sifted through large bins of the same part, selecting those he deemed perfectly formed. Whereas an average mechanic might simply go buy a new part, Swanson carefully chose the ones he considered the best.

Once he had the parts at his garage, Swanson conducted engine work under conditions that would make most restaurant kitchen health inspectors proud. He kept all dirt and contaminants away from his parts and engines. The only exception, a source of frequent humor, was the risk of ashes dropping off his cigarette. Finally, he applied considerable skill to his work.

Engines have many valves and cylinders; gasoline and air enter cylinders through valves into cylinders. Any leakage caused by an improper sealing will reduce the power of the engine. To ensure the valves and other parts closed and opened properly requires delicate and precise machine work. Sonny Morgan, one of the few people with access to the Swanson operation, said, "Swanson was very good with cylinder heads—valve grinding, valve seats, and creating a thin seat."[12]

The Chevy engines worked optimally with careful balancing and leveling. With eight-cylinder connecting rods driving pistons rapidly up and down, balance was important. Unintended forces, torques, and part wear could be the result of a poorly balanced engine. Not only did Swanson carefully check the parts of the engine once installed, he would also take parts to a supermarket and weigh them on the scales to make certain they were all of equal weight.[13] Nothing was going to weaken his engine.

In the end, the advantage that Swanson's car had stemmed from a combination of factors: hard work, ingenuity, meticulous dedication to detail, and a willingness to plow time and money into the race car. And if he missed a detail or failed to build the fastest car, he had one ace in the hole: Beauchamp's driving.

After the Swanson teardown at Owatonna, more than three months of racing remained, and everyone driving a Chevrolet was aware of the Duntov cam. If Beauchamp was to keep his lead, he would have to do it with superior driving.

Beauchamp continued winning races after the inspection. In the ten 100-lap features before July 4 he won eight, losing only in Springfield, Missouri, and in Hutchinson, Minnesota.[1] Bob Burdick, fresh out of high school, led the Hutchinson event in a new Ford. Beauchamp was in hot pursuit when on lap 31 his car broke a wheel and almost overturned, forcing him out of contention. Before this race, Bob Burdick had never finished higher than third, and now he had won his first IMCA contest. Supported by his mechanic father, Roy (Bud's brother), he was poised to be a major contender.

Racing the IMCA circuit put a heavy burden on Swanson and Beauchamp. They were constantly either racing or on the road going to a race. The motor magician had little time to maintain the engine for the next event, even though his high school age son, Dale Jr., eagerly helped in the garage and traveled to the races. Swanson, always tired during a long season, had difficulty serving the paying customers visiting his garage. Finally, he ran an advertisement in the Harlan newspaper that thanked people for patronizing his shop but requesting that they not bring their cars to him for a few months because he was too busy racing.

Because they competed on consecutive days in events separated by long miles of road, the team had little time to relax in the beer tent after a race. Mechanics had time only to load the car and drive, sometimes all night, to the next contest, and drivers, if they won, permitted a quick press interview before they departed.

The schedule produced a frantic rush on July 3 when, after Beauchamp's victory at Jamestown, North Dakota, Swanson immediately loaded up and left for the July 4 race at the Kansas Free Fair track at Topeka. Even with their rapid exit at 10:00 p.m., they did not have an extra minute to spare—the drive was 850 miles and they needed to be there for the 1:00 p.m. time trial.

The Swanson/Beauchamp/Morgan caravan set out on its all-night drive. On the road, Morgan had trouble: his race car ended up in a ditch, and he had to pull the car out with his tow vehicle. Swanson examined the situation and decided Morgan and his friends could manage without him. Since he and Beauchamp were locked in an intense battle for first place, every point was important, and they hurried with the 55 car on to Topeka.[2]

Beauchamp had only enough time to grab a hot dog for lunch before climbing into his car to turn in the second fastest lap of the time trial.[3] Nevertheless, the local paper headline said: "White Heads Classy Cast."[4] White was the favorite because he was last year's season champion. However, the press believed Beauchamp was White's strongest competition, and one article noted that Beauchamp had recently set a new world's record in a half-mile time trial.[5]

But there was no shortage of other serious contenders. Marvin Copple, who had set the track record, 31.14 seconds, the previous year in the Chevrolet he eventually sold to Tiny Lund, was driving a 1955 Ford Thunderbird; this vehicle was permitted because promoters were experimenting with what they called an "international" race, in which foreign and domestic sports cars competed. (Sports cars were designed differently and had more power than stock cars, so promoters usually excluded them. In this case, and later at the 1959 Daytona 500, however, they were allowed.[6]) Complicating Beauchamp's chances was the late entry of Nebraskan Lloyd Beckman behind the wheel of a Pontiac Catalina. Beckman was the driver who had reeled off six feature wins at Playland Park in the second half of the 1955 season. If White, Copple, and Beckman did not pose enough competition, rising star Bob Burdick also hoped for victory.

Lennie Funk from Otis, Kansas, piloting a 56 Dodge D-500, sat on the pole as the winner of the time trials, 33.37 seconds to Beauchamp's 33.70. Funk, a good, well-liked driver and a farmer, was often close to the leaders, but he rarely won. During the 1956 Memorial Day contest, Funk had been named the "sportsman of the day" because while running in second place, he stopped racing to push Don White's disabled car into the pits. He lost several positions doing the good deed, and as the event progressed, he realized he also had burned out his clutch.[7]

The grounds crew had worked diligently to clean rocks and debris off the track and then smooth it down with heavy equipment. Recent rain meant the track would not be dusty, but it could be muddy. Even the concession operation was prepared: the "pop" was iced down and the "goobers" were bagged and ready for the 9,200 fans. The time trials were advertised as the device to narrow the field to the fastest twenty cars, but ultimately officials allowed all twenty-four to start, the slowest in the rear. This was a big July 4 event in Topeka.

Beauchamp, starting on the outside in the front row, gunned his Chevrolet into the lead. The muddy oval eventually became rough, contributing to several accidents. Bob Burdick recalled, "If a driver did not position his hands carefully on the steering wheel, hitting a deep hole on the track could break his thumbs."[8] Beauchamp had a reputation for taking care of his car, but even so, he was effortlessly extending his lead, going faster than the other competitors. As the contest continued, he pushed farther and farther ahead, lapping the others multiple times. Finally, an official went to Swanson and pleaded, "Tell your driver to slow down. If he gets too far ahead all the fans will go home."[9]

The appeal of the official did little good. Beauchamp kept his foot on the accelerator and continued to increase his lead. Finally, on lap 159 Don White took matters into his own hands, and from behind he tapped Beauchamp's car, sending it into the fence. With the remaining competitors circling about every 30 seconds, a truck pushed his car out of the loose mud and back on the track. A few quick repairs and he accelerated into the race.[10]

As he sped toward the corner, Beauchamp applied the brake, but there was none. The hydraulic brake line had been destroyed in the wreck. Still, he navigated the car around the corner. His lead had been so great that the Harlan driver remained in front, but he now was pressed by local competitor Bill Harrison in a 1956 Ford convertible. Beauchamp managed to stay in front of Harrison until lap 178, and then Harrison's car frame crumpled.

Next to challenge was pole-sitter Funk, and as with Harrison, Beauchamp negotiated the corners without brakes while maintaining enough speed to prevent Funk from passing. Funk finished one car length behind Beauchamp. Don White was 3 laps behind.[11] Beauchamp pulled his car up in front of the grandstand. Gulping down a cold beer someone handed him, he accepted a big trophy. Fans surged onto the track to see the champion up close.

The Topeka race was a big victory for Swanson and Beauchamp. They netted $750: $600 for winning the event and $150 for all the laps Beauchamp had led. The contest underscored the superiority of Beauchamp and his car. Even with a crash and no brakes, he could win.

After the event he stopped at the business office for his prize money. Don White was in line. Beauchamp looked at White and said, "I don't appreciate your driving that caused me to wreck. The next time you do that, I'll back off and really tangle with you."[12]

White innocently claimed, "You know I didn't do that on purpose. I just got tangled up in traffic and there was no place to go."[13]

A reporter heard of the quarrel between Beauchamp and White and went to the Swanson car in the pit area. He asked about White, and Beauchamp explained, "That's the second time this year I've been in an accident with White. No, I won't say it wasn't an accident. Maybe it couldn't have been helped. But I am getting tired of it."[14] Swanson, his cigarette almost all ash, solemnly added that "White caused a Beauchamp wreck in Shreveport during the first part of the season."[15]

Sonny Morgan also had tense moments at the Topeka race. Morgan was not in his best humor because he had driven all night, had trouble on the road, and not slept in twenty-four hours. After the race, he was told he had finished lower than he believed he had. He was certain officials had tinkered with his place in the finish order and angrily shouted, "I am going to get my rifle."[16] Phyllis Swanson saw what was happening and talked Morgan into calming down.

This is one of the few instances in IMCA in which a driver's finish was disputed, and it seems likely that the outcome was changed deliberately. Fifty years later Morgan was still certain he knew what had happened at that race.

Most events did not result in disputes over the place a driver finished. In the races that Frank Winkley promoted, his wife, Verna, kept score, counting laps, in many races alone. From all accounts she was exceptionally skilled and accurate, but it was possible to make an honest mistake in tracking so many cars. In the biggest races, promoters pressed volunteers, such as Boy Scouts, into service to help the regular staff.[17]

Leaving the track, the Swanson contingent, hot, grimy, and exhausted from two days of racing, went to a local motel. The desk clerk disdainfully told them, "Pull the race car around in back because this is a respectable motel, and we don't want the guests to know stock car people are staying here."[18] An indignant Swanson wheeled around, walked out, and found another motel.

The thermometer registered 100 degrees on July 15 in Des Moines, Iowa, site of the next IMCA event. This was a huge venue with 23,000 people in the stands. The race was 125 miles and 250 laps. The Harlan driver set a track time trial record of 30.12 seconds for one lap, but he had to share the success with Don Pash, also driving a 1956 Chevrolet, the competitor who wrested the 1952 Playland season championship away from Beauchamp. Pash did not race as widely or as often as Beauchamp, but he was a first-rate driver. He, White, and Dake appeared to be Beauchamp's toughest competition.

In spite of these excellent drivers, Beauchamp dominated the race, as he had in Topeka. Dake finished second, two laps behind, while White and Pash were forced out of the race with mechanical problems. Beauchamp netted $1,000, including $200 for laps led and another $100 for setting a new track record: 2 hours, 18 minutes, and 51.59 seconds.[19]

From July 15 to August 27, Beauchamp won twelve more feature races.[20] Morgan, White, and Burdick each managed only a single win.[21] In one event, Beauchamp was leading by several laps, but each time around the track the flagman failed to acknowledge his lead. Finally, in the middle of the race, Beauchamp stopped his car in front of the flagman and asked, "Are you ever going wave the flag that signals I'm in the lead."[22]

This wasn't the only issue he encountered. Although Beauchamp was the undisputed star of the IMCA 1956 season, he still couldn't get his name pronounced the way the family pronounced it. Auto Racing, Inc. announcer, Nick "the gregarious Greek" Nachicas, continued to pronounce the name as "Bow Camp" rather than Byou camp. Beauchamp was unconcerned—he only cared about winning. Other drivers wondered how they could defeat the "Flying Frenchman."

The end of August and early September served up a flurry of events. One of the biggest was on the track at the Minnesota State Fair, which held four high-profile contests from August 25 to September 1. This was a wide, one-half-mile track—five cars could race side-by-side.[23] In Minnesota, Beauchamp met an increased number of determined competitors. Among them was Bob Burdick, who had improved with every race. With 19,000 fans in the stands for a 100-lap opener of the Fair events, it was not Beauchamp or Burdick, but Morgan who pushed into the lead for the first 77 laps. But when Morgan's steering malfunctioned and Beauchamp developed car trouble, Burdick seized the lead and won the race.

Two days later, Burdick was back at the same track, winning a 90-minute race and setting a record. Once again Beauchamp had had trouble—midway through the contest, while he was in the lead, one of his tires blew out. Burdick had swept two races, winning $600 and $750 respectively, and he had defeated champions Don White and Ernie Derr as well as Beauchamp. Although Burdick won, Sonny Morgan recalls, "Bob was not as aggressive or as good as Beauchamp. His Ford was a pretty strong car."[24]

The 100-mile, 200-lap Minnesota Fair stock car classic was held August 30. Around 27,000 fans paid to see if Burdick could win three in row and collect the $1,000 first-place prize money. At the race's midpoint, Beauchamp blasted into the lead and held it for the last 100 laps. On September 1, the Fair ended with a split feature of 15 laps and 25 laps. Beauchamp and Morgan finished first and second, respectively, in both features.

Beauchamp avenged his Minnesota losses to Burdick with a victory in an IMCA contest at Sioux Falls, South Dakota, a 200-lapper with Burdick in hot pursuit but unable to pass. Then, after the last Minnesota Fair event, the IMCA competition shifted to the Iowa State Fair. Beauchamp, with driver Darrell Dake and his wife, strolled the midway, and he made certain that his friends, Don and Norma Brix, had front-row seats in the infield for the race and the entertainment. Beauchamp won before 22,000 fans, knocking almost four minutes from the previous record held by Don White. Five days later, on September 7, he won a 100-mile, 200-lap event at the Nebraska State Fair. In a span of a few weeks, he had won major races in four states: South Dakota, Minnesota, Iowa, and Nebraska.

The 1956 season was almost over when promoter Frank Winkley of Auto Racing, Inc., created an additional IMCA race: "The Great Gopher 500." A special sponsor, Midwest Sport Promotions, Inc., comprising St. Paul, Minnesota, businessmen in partnership with Winkley, leased the Fairgrounds track. The contest was advertised to be the longest race ever held at that site and the first race in nine years not associated with the Fair. The Great Gopher was a split feature, with two 250-lap events and $10,000 in prize money and a $2,000 maximum cap on what a single driver could win.

The Great Gopher hoped to attract competitors from other regions of the nation and from other associations. Because Beauchamp and Swanson, fielding a Chevrolet, had dominated the 1956 season, the promoters also expected other factories would send vehicles to defeat the champions' car. To their satisfaction, several drivers with factory backing from outside IMCA entered. One of these outsiders, driving a 1956 Ford, was Frank Schneider, a modified stock car champion from the East who looked for races with a big purse.[25]

Another outsider was Marvin Panch, a West Coast driver who had shifted his activities to NASCAR and the East Coast. Like Schneider, he was prepared to go wherever there was a big race. Panch picked up a 1956 Ford at the factory in Michigan and brought it to Morrisville, Pennsylvania. In one week Panch and a mechanic welded the body to the chassis, braced the engine, worked on the pick-up points on the suspension, and in general tuned the car. Then they left for The Great Gopher.[26] In other words, the Ford factory, after losing many races to Beauchamp and Morgan, sent reinforcements: Schneider and Panch.

Beauchamp brought his own type of reinforcements. Although more than a few people thought he was a "bird-dog," he often traveled to races with his sons and Donna. His son Bill wondered how his father would do against the added competition, and John said, "I can drive into the corners harder and faster than anyone."[27]

On September 30, more than 28,000 fans packed the stands. Beauchamp scorched the field in the first 250-lap feature, breaking track records for 50, 100, 150, and 200 laps. Gus McDonald, the mechanic from Stillwater Chevrolet, recalls the hum of Beauchamp's engine circling the track. "He never let up on the gas. On the corners he used the brake while running the throttle wide open."[28] Panch, for all of his effort, suffered from the heat and was not a factor. Morgan finished second. White stayed in the running with a fifth place, followed by Schneider.

In the second feature, Beauchamp once again flashed to the front, but he developed engine trouble, eventually blowing a piston. Panch passed him on lap 62, pushing on to win, with White third. White was the day's overall winner, and Beauchamp was third, with a first and fifteenth finish.[29]

Many events of the 1956 season ended with Beauchamp first and Morgan second—a one-two finish for Chevrolet. On several occasions, Morgan deliberately remained in second place rather than passing Beauchamp and winning. With Morgan operating as a friendly buffer behind Beauchamp, the Beauchamp-Morgan tandem became formidable and dominant.

Beauchamp had an insurmountable lead for the point championship, but Morgan was fighting for second place. Unfortunately for Morgan, he had a wreck late in the season and could not get his car repaired in time for the next race. To help Morgan earn points so he could finish the season in second place, Swanson decided that at Hutchinson, Kansas, the Texan, rather than Beauchamp, would pilot the 55 race car. The bonds between Morgan, Swanson, and Beauchamp were strong.

Morgan, grateful for Swanson's help, discovered the 55 car was not as easy to handle as his regular car. Morgan also remembered the time in Winnipeg, Canada, when Beauchamp and he swapped cars during some practice driving, and Beauchamp commented on how well the Morgan vehicle handled. Morgan, years later, concluded that "Beauchamp could manhandle a car. He could make a car go that wasn't a particularly good handling car."[30]

The IMCA season typically ended where it began, in Shreveport, Louisiana. Swanson decided that since they had a little extra time, they would also travel to Birmingham, Alabama, for a USAC (United States Auto Club) event. USAC was another sanctioning association that sponsored late model races. The Iowans did not do well, but they would return to the track to compete again in 1960 for a NASCAR event.

Still not prepared to leave the South, the intrepid Iowans decided to go to Beaumont, Texas, and visit Sonny Morgan, who had painted a lavish description of his father's big ranch near Beaumont, Texas. Arriving in Beaumont, they found Sonny's father operating a one-pump gas station, with no sign of a ranch, or even a patch of land with a few steers. The visitors checked out Beaumont and had a good laugh about Sonny's tall tales. The Iowans returned to Harlan. They would join each other after the Thanksgiving holiday for the annual IMCA Banquet.[31]

As the year came to a close, many in the IMCA reflected on a successful season and on Beauchamp's extreme dominance and record-breaking performances. Many no doubt recalled the open letter that IMCA promoter Frank Winkley published in the magazine *Speed Age* in July 1956. He had argued that the New York–based magazine neglected the Midwest racing circuit, refusing to admit that IMCA had excellent competitors in the "big car" or Indy-style vehicles. But another significant point by Winkley was that *Speed Age* ignored all IMCA racing. He closed by urging, "And don't forget to visit one of our late model stock car events where some of the nation's finest battle it out."[32] Without question, at the top of Winkley's list of excellent competitors were the emerging national stars Johnny Beauchamp and Dale Swanson.

IMCA drivers, mechanics, and supporting cast gathered at the Hotel Continental in Kansas City, Missouri, for the Saturday night, December 2, 1956, banquet. The press characterized the event as awards time for the "top drivers in the country." Beauchamp was the major star of the late model awards. He had finished with 4,075 points, and his stablemate, Morgan, finished in second place with 2,375 points. Morgan was voted the most popular driver of the season.[33]

Morgan was on top of the world. "I was fresh out of college," he reflected. "I thought it was a very big deal." Morgan, who usually did not consume alcoholic drinks, had one too many in celebration.[34]

At the end of 1956, Morgan, Beauchamp, and Swanson were a few months away from entering one of the biggest races of their careers.

Dale Swanson was one of many racing mechanics drifting into Atlanta, Georgia, in 1957. He was pleased by Atlanta's balmy late January weather, which compared favorably to the freezing cold of Iowa. Swanson pulled up to the Alamo Plaza motel on Stewart Avenue SW and arranged for an extended stay.[1]

Swanson was involved in a hush-hush Chevrolet operation. After the dismal 1956 season in which Chevrolet cars won only three of thirty-nine NASCAR Grand National races,[2] the factory, embarrassed, opted for a new strategy, and Swanson—under whose care a Chevrolet had won most of the IMCA races in the same year—was part of the plan. Chevrolet Racing decided to gather a group of its mechanics and drivers into a single, large shop, hoping a concentration of talent would boost the quality of its race cars.

Swanson reported for work at Southern Engineering Development Company (SEDCO), a ten-port garage, on Central Avenue in south Atlanta, near the airport. The name SEDCO concealed the connection with Chevrolet Racing that paid for SEDCO by funneling money through the local dealer, Nalley Chevrolet. Even the physical visibility of SEDCO was hidden, tucked behind the street-level business, Lee's Body Shop. SEDCO, renting from Lee's Body Shop, could be found only by going down a ramp-like road along the west side of the body shop that dropped on to a lower, basement-like level, invisible from the main road.[3]

At SEDCO, Swanson was a stranger—he was the only mechanic with no previous connection to NASCAR. Harlan, approximately a thirty-hour drive from Daytona, was too far to permit much competition or contact with competitors in the South, or even contact with reporters down there. Swanson had delivered the goods in the Midwest with a phenomenal number of wins, and Chevrolet gambled that he could transfer some of his magic to its floundering NASCAR effort. The agreement was that he would help build the race cars and his champion driver, Beauchamp, would be behind the wheel of one of them. The Chevrolets built at SEDCO would enter the February 1957 annual Daytona NASCAR Speed Weeks, a high profile set of activities culminating with an important and famous beach race.

Chevrolet paid $650 a month to most of the mechanics it had brought together, a good salary in 1957. Among them was Hugh Babb, a racing veteran from Alabama who had a reputation as a brilliant mechanic.[4] Also brought in were the highly regarded Louie and Crawford Clements, the former an important wrench man for Rex White in 1960, when White won the NASCAR championship. Bradley Dennis, who worked on the new fuel-injection technology, was an Atlanta resident with an engineering background from Georgia Tech. Dennis worked with Paul McDuffie in 1958, when Fireball Roberts drove for them and won almost every major NASCAR race. He was an all-round utility man who had become interested in racing by assisting NASCAR, without compensation, cleaning track debris at races.[5]

Swanson quickly became oriented. He and his fellow mechanics took many of their meals at the nearby Dwarf House, an establishment eventually to become the first location of the fast food chain, Chick-fil-A. These capable mechanics expected to be given the resources to build high quality machines. But what Swanson discovered at SEDCO was a bunch of grumbling mechanics. "We can't get the best parts for the cars," one mechanic complained. "We have to go to the junkyard to find parts for the suspension system," another told Swanson.[6]

The source of the problem was the keeper of the purse strings, Frank Delroy, the manager of SEDCO, who refused to release funds to buy the best parts. Delroy was unknown to the stock car community. He had a modest background in Indianapolis racing, but his main connection to the sport was owning a speed shop in New Jersey. He had an advocate, however: Mauri Rose, a three-time Indy winner who was employed with Chevrolet as a facilitator/engineer without portfolio. Part of Rose's responsibility was to interface with racing mechanics, and he had recommended Delroy to run SEDCO.[7]

The way Delroy was handling SEDCO made no sense to any of the mechanics.[8] His approach was contrary to the goals of Vince Piggins, the Chevrolet executive in charge. Piggins had developed the Hudson Hornet that dominated racing in the early 1950s, and the hope was he could do the same as head of Chevrolet's Performance Division. As an initial effort,

Piggins had assisted a number of mechanics and drivers in 1956, including Swanson, primarily with parts, supplies, and cash. In 1957, the Chevrolet executive used his clout to set up a large, quality race shop, and thus SEDCO was established.

Rex White recollects an ominous beginning for SEDCO. The first employee to report for work, he found a freshly painted, cement block, long, rectangular building with space to work on cars but no space for the storage of parts and equipment. Eventually, Lee's Body Shop would put up a second building for storage of parts and equipment. More significantly, there were no tools. White brought tools into the shop from his car.[9]

Swanson instantly realized that the situation at SEDCO was impossible. The frustrated drivers and mechanics had little incentive to work to their maximum ability and, although normally fun loving in any case, they engaged in particularly rowdy behavior after hours. The location for much of the mischief was a house rented by several SEDCO employees on Cofield Avenue in Hapeville, near the Atlanta airport.[10]

If the image of stock car drivers and mechanics needed any besmirching, the Cofield house inhabitants provided it. The house was unkempt and filthy. Its residents indulged in heavy drinking, and as Rex White, the 1960 NASCAR champion, and a mechanic as well, remembers, "There was something wild going on every night." At one point, the neighbors tacked a note on the door that accused the inhabitants of operating "a house of ill repute."[11]

This was not the operation Piggins had promised, and Swanson would not tolerate the situation. If Delroy would not authorize the spending to support a first-class effort, SEDCO was heading for failure. Swanson joined the other mechanics, informing Piggins what was happening, and soon Delroy began releasing the money for quality equipment.

SEDCO is mysterious for reasons other than its name and out-of-sight location. First, it went through three phases of management, and second, the personnel associated with it kept changing. A mechanic or driver claiming to be associated with SEDCO might not be on site all the time or might arrive several months after its inception. Only the people actually there are likely to know the full truth.

An example of the confusion about SEDCO is uncertainty about the exact model of Chevrolet that was converted into a race car. Many commentaries claim the model was a 150 two-door utility sedan, sold for several purposes but intended for racing. The automobile came right off the assembly line with the same half-ton pickup rear-end gear assembly that Swanson had struggled to obtain at the end of the 1955 season.

Chevrolet produced 8,300 150-utility sedans in several variations, including one dubbed the "150 Business Coupe" or the "salesman's Chevy" because it had no back seat, only a flat utility floor and back windows that did not roll down, leaving plenty of room for products and samples. A slightly different version of the 150, with a back seat, was sold to the U.S. Army and police departments. Painted in black-and-white color schemes, it became known as "the Black Widow."[12]

The problem with the above account is that while the 150, without the back seat, was an excellent potential racing car, it was not the one converted at SEDCO. The frames were built in St. Louis and it was a 210 (shortened from the official 2100 number) model Chevrolet that had a back seat. Rex White, working at SEDCO during its first days, recalls removing the back seats and taking them to the Banner Upholstery Shop immediately west of the SEDCO shop.

The 1957 Chevrolet, loaded with improvements, was the pet project of top executive Ed Cole, the general manager and, until July 1956, the head of Chevrolet Engineering. One of the important innovations of the vehicle was a fuel-injection system. As with the Duntov cam, Chevrolet wanted to keep the fuel-injection technology a secret so it could surprise the competition at the Daytona Speed Weeks in February.

But the new Chevrolet couldn't just roll onto the track as it came off the assembly line. The fuel-injection system had to be adjusted for race conditions. Piggins tested the technology at two locations: SEDCO and Smokey Yunick's garage in Daytona. Yunick had been working with Chevrolet since 1955, and a year later he was on the payroll earning $1,000 a month plus expenses.[13] When the plans for SEDCO were aired, Yunick refused to work out of Atlanta, preferring to maintain his Daytona shop. In fact, Yunick didn't think much of this organizational approach to racing, saying, "This team shit is busting up the poor racers and the newcomers. They ain't got a prayer. It's really wrong."[14]

Piggins recognized Yunick's creative ability and allowed him to work independently, but with two adjustments. First, Piggins sent Frank Johnson, a top engineer, to Daytona to assist Yunick. Later, Piggins relocated Johnson to SEDCO.[15] Second, when Yunick began experimenting with the fuel-injection technology, Chevrolet decided to upgrade the security at his garage, called the Best Damn Garage in Town. A few years before, the only protection Yunick had was a young alligator who had settled in at the shop. Now the alligator was gone, so Chevrolet erected a twelve-foot fence and hired a twenty-four-hour guard service.[16]

Chevrolet's desire to keep the improvements of its automobile a secret partially explains why SEDCO is sometimes considered a clandestine operation, but it's also true that the corporate structure of General Motors facilitated secrecy. GM, as Bill Collins of Pontiac's Advanced Engineering Group observed, was organized so that divisions could "stretch the rules and try things."[17] And another General Motors official, Ralph Kramer, explained that Piggins had wide latitude: "Piggins supported a number of mechanics and drivers. These were phantom operations because almost no one was aware of the support."[18] Setting up SEDCO was merely one more ghostly experiment.

SEDCO, rather than being secret, was a "backdoor" operation, one that upper executives at GM barely understood was happening. Although SEDCO was not widely publicized, the racing community quickly discovered it, and there was nothing illegal about it. In fact, the other factories were doing about the same as Chevrolet. Pontiac and Ford also had begun sponsoring garages, and the new initiatives were mentioned in newspaper coverage.[19]

At SEDCO, aside from the seven Chevrolets prepared for the Daytona race, two production (stock factory) Corvettes were prepared in the first two ports. These Corvettes competed at Daytona, returned to SEDCO for several weeks, and then went to Sebring, Florida, for the annual high-profile sports car competition at its track.[20] The SEDCO mechanics, including Swanson, all did work on most of the cars, and once they were able to buy good parts, they completed the first 1957 Black Widow. On a visit to SEDCO, Vince Piggins looked over the car Swanson had built for Beauchamp and said, "This looks good. Build them all like this one."[21]

Swanson and the other SEDCO mechanics had no instruction manual to help them create a race car. They had a practical knowledge of what to do: the production cars required engine, body, chassis, tuning, and track set-up conversion work. However, Swanson, a meticulous record keeper, frequently sent Chevrolet suggestions and notes about how the factory could build cars more amenable to racing. Driver Sonny Morgan had the impression that Swanson's notes and written advice to Chevrolet became the first draft of an instruction manual for mechanics.[22] The manual, titled *1957 Chevrolet Stock Car Competition Guide*, explained how to modify the 150 Utility Sedan Model 1512 for racing.

The *Guide* is well-known and much reprinted, and to this day it has readers. Robert D. Lund, GM national sales promotion manager, writes that the guide was "the first publication of its type in the industry" to encourage mechanics all over the nation to convert a passenger car into a race car.[23] On the last page of the guide, a map displays the five major associations and their race sites, documenting that racing was happening everywhere in the United States by 1957.[24]

Swanson, who was not credited for his role in preparing the *Guide*, was certain his hand appeared in one of the many photographs illustrating how to do the work. The *Guide* became a classic.

As the time for Speed Weeks at Daytona approached, Frank Delroy left SEDCO. Hugh Babb, second in command, was the mechanic of record on all of the SEDCO cars entered in the Daytona Beach event.[25] Swanson, who had played such a critical role in building the Black Widow, remained invisible. The drivers, some of whom, such as Rex White, had doubled as mechanics at SEDCO, began preparing for the race.[26] Among them was Johnny Beauchamp, the only competitor not from NASCAR, who would be behind the wheel of a Swanson-built race car that year, as he had been in so many previous years.

Florida's wide, hard sand beaches beckoned landlocked midwestern drivers, who had never competed with an ocean spray blowing across their cars. No other race was like one at Daytona Beach. For the Harlan contingent—Beauchamp, Swanson, and their friends and followers—the racing, plus ocean breezes, palm trees, and freedom from snow was a welcomed winter vacation.

When Beauchamp arrived in Daytona, he did not see condominiums soaring into the sky as twenty-first century visitors will, but instead stretches of open beach and small, unpretentious, dilapidated dwellings. Daytona in the 1950s was a sleepy, impoverished, and scruffy town. But the weather was warm, the ocean was a novelty, and the event had attracted many top contributors.

Beauchamp discovered Swanson tinkering with the 1957 Black Widow, which he was eager to get on the race course for testing and practice. The problem was the beach was too busy. Daytona's beach was in constant use during Speed Weeks because of special events, such as Pete DePaulo, the 1925 Indianapolis 500 winner, running a 1930 SJ Dusenberg[1] along the water's edge and, in addition, a continual series of speed runs and speed trials. These latter events involved passenger and sports cars, classified according to power and various modifications and placed in competitive brackets and tested with running starts, standing starts, and two-way runs up and down the beach.[2] Amid all this, it was difficult for the race car drivers to squeeze in practice time.

Beauchamp and Swanson finally discovered how to gain access to the beach to test the Chevy. Anyone could bring the family car, or any car, to the beach during an event called "the measured mile." This was a moment for the average citizen to race on the beach. If the automobile managed a 100-mph speed for the distance, NASCAR awarded the driver a certificate of membership in the Century Club.[3] More than one young boy clandestinely tested his father's pleasure car to make certain it would run at 100 mph.

Beauchamp's measured-mile run was ominous. He was one of the twenty drivers out of the ninety-four entrants who did not win the coveted Century Club certificate. He managed 98 mph.[4] The fault was not in his driving; it was that the Black Widow did not accelerate well, particularly at higher speeds.

Swanson went to work to solve the problem, eventually concluding something was amiss with the fuel-injection system. He suspected that the problem was caused indirectly by the lack of a heater. Race cars usually came from the factory as stripped-down, basic models without amenities like heaters. A car with a heater has an opening between the engine and the passenger compartment, but the Black Widow instead had a solid panel. Swanson concluded the solid panel prevented the release of pressure from under the hood, and that the pressure increase affected the fuel-injection system. To solve this problem, he cut a hole in the panel where the heater would have been installed and late at night hauled the car out on a secluded road for a test. The engine worked better now, with the passenger compartment not sealed off from the engine.

Unraveling this mystery was not the province of a regular mechanic. It was such an accomplishment that famed NASCAR mechanic Smokey Yunick carefully described it in his book. Yunick's explanation could leave the impression he discovered and solved the pressure problem, but a careful reading of what he says reveals that he is merely describing the steps he took to confirm the problem and the solution.[5] In fact, he first learned of the solution from Dale Swanson.

Despite fixing one major problem, Swanson remained uneasy about the fuel-injection system's reliability. When Vince Piggins arrived in Daytona, the Iowa mechanic asked him if he could replace the fuel injectors with a regular carburetion system. Piggins approved the switch, and Beauchamp's car became the only SEDCO Chevrolet entered in the race without the new fuel-injection technology.[6]

Meanwhile, the vastly improved Corvette was about to be tested on beach runs against the Thunderbird. Corvette tapped Beauchamp, along with experienced drivers Paul Goldsmith and Betty Skelton, to get behind the wheel of a production model for the competition.

Unlike Beauchamp, who showed up in Daytona from Iowa steering a traditional passenger car, Betty Skelton sported a brand new gold Corvette, compliments of GM. A sophisticated, attractive woman who was a pioneer of female aerobatics and had qualified to be an Air Force pilot,

Skelton was the first woman to take the same battery of tests as the original Mercury Seven astronauts. She definitely liked speed. She did not race oval or circle tracks, preferring straight ahead, drag-type events in which she held some speed records. In 1956 Skelton became an advertising executive with Campbell-Ewald, the company that handled all of General Motors' advertising. She was so closely associated with Chevrolet and Corvette that she arranged for the Mercury astronauts, whom she knew well, to each have one. NASCAR also benefited from Skelton's GM contacts; she drove the Corvette pace car at the '57 Daytona Beach race.[7]

At this time, she was probably the woman most involved with practicing the art of speed. At Playland and other, smaller contests, women competed against each other in the powder-puff derby events, but these events did not rise above the novelty category. Women also occasionally found themselves at the big events, competing not in the race but in the contest for race queen, wearing a swimsuit or prom dress. Finally, wives and girlfriends watched the men compete, brought food to the events, and in the case of NASCAR often became unpaid members of the workforce for races.

Although Beauchamp only had to drive the Corvette in a straight line, steering a car on the beach was an arduous task. The packed sand surface was not in good condition. Because the weather had been calm and the ocean tranquil, the tides had not been strong enough to wash away the holes and ruts. Before the race could even begin, one Thunderbird driver, Bill Norkutt, hit some rough spots, and the car barrel-rolled, then went end over end, finally bursting into flames. Norkutt was seriously injured, and the other events of the day were canceled.[8]

When NASCAR finally reopened the beach, the Corvette vs. T-Bird competition started. Beauchamp finished second from the standing start and sixth from a flying start. Goldsmith won the standing start and finished fourth in the flying start. The T-Birds finished first and second in the flying start.[9]

Beauchamp and his Iowa friends combined racing with some pleasure. Claus Behnken, who owned a second home in the area, hosted several Iowans, including Beauchamp's good friends Don Brix and his wife Norma. Unable to work in the frozen cornfields, the Iowans saw this as a perfect time to visit Florida. They went to the beach, enjoyed the warm weather, saw the sights, and watched the races.

There was a reunion at Speed Weeks. Beauchamp and Swanson discovered that a friendly face—their racing buddy Sonny Morgan—was in Daytona with a brand new Plymouth race car. After Thanksgiving, Morgan had visited Detroit in search of a free factory car. He and his friend, Everett Bresher, bunked in with national motorcycle champion Paul Goldsmith, who was also associated with Corvette testing and whom Bresher had met while racing motorcycles.

Morgan first visited Sam Samson, the IMCA contact for Chevrolet, but discovered Chevrolet was placing its hopes on SEDCO rather than the individual drivers and mechanics. Just as Yunick said, the centralized system left a lot of drivers out in the cold. Goldsmith, hearing what happened, suggested Morgan visit Ronney Householder, who was with Chrysler-Plymouth. Householder, aware of Morgan's IMCA success, warmly greeted him.

In December, Morgan returned to Detroit. Plymouth stopped the regular assembly line and produced ten barebones cars for racing, inserting special engines from California. One of these went to Morgan. The stripped-down vehicle had no heater, so the December drive back to Texas was chilly. Morgan, a good mechanic, then transformed his new Plymouth into a race car. In Daytona, when Morgan brought the car to an armory so that NASCAR officials could inspect it, he observed Smokey Yunick enter the armory, not with an entire vehicle, but with merely an engine.

As race time neared, Morgan adjusted the rear-end gear ratio of his car, reasoning that a higher ratio would give his car more bite through the sand and wind on the beach. The problem with this reasoning was that a high gear ratio also could burn up the engine on the asphalt highway part of the course.[10]

But Plymouth was not the main competition. SEDCO drivers were on a collision course with Chevrolet's two major factory competitors: Pontiac and Ford. Pontiac posed a serious threat because its racing team was led by Ray Nichols, an experienced Indy 500 mechanic from Indiana. His Pontiac team included none other than Robert McKee, who had briefly worked with Tiny Lund back in Iowa.[11] NASCAR veterans Cotton Owens and Banjo Matthews drove for Nichols. Ford centered its hopes on the race shop of Peter DePaulo, the winner of the 1925 Indianapolis 500.[12]

The Daytona race would settle two big questions: Which factory had the fastest car? And had the SEDCO effort improved Chevrolet's standing against the competition? Beauchamp was looking for the answer to another question: could he defeat the NASCAR drivers?

There was a new gunslinger in town. In 1957 Johnny Beauchamp came to Daytona Beach for a shootout with NASCAR stock car drivers. The man from Harlan, with a record thirty-eight season wins in the Midwest, was eager to test the NASCAR competition.

NASCAR claimed it had the best drivers, many of whom, legend says, honed their skills hauling moonshine on winding mountain roads. The southern drivers believed they could get the best of anyone, and they were not going to welcome any hotshot outsider. Beauchamp was invading foreign territory. Nebraska mechanic Bill Smith recalls the welcome the midwesterners received in the old Confederacy: "There ain't going to be any of those Yankees coming down here and winning any races from us good old boys."[1] NASCAR drivers and the press offered maximum contempt: they ignored the outsiders.

The night before the race, at Robinson's bar, a hangout for competitors, the live entertainment praised in song the exploits of the NASCAR drivers. The hard-drinking, boisterous members of the crowd reveled in their skill, confident that the following day, one of their own would win.

After the bar closed, ace drivers Curtis Turner, Joe Weatherly, and Fireball Roberts strode from Robinson's Bar to the rented beach house across the street—the Party Pad, as they called it. The cases of alcohol, stocked by friendly motor oil and spark plug suppliers, kept these stars well lubricated and partying all through the night.[2] The Party Pad guys drive hard and party hard. If they ever thought of him, they were sure that Johnny Beauchamp would be no match for such hard chargers.

Beauchamp, relaxed and confident, was unconcerned by NASCAR drivers' superior attitude. He was a veteran driver with three season championships against difficult competition. He had won more races piloting a 1956 Swanson-built Chevy than all the NASCAR Chevrolet pilots combined had won on their circuit. To prepare for the race, Beauchamp and Swanson had a quiet dinner with family and friends, drank alcohol sparingly (unlike many NASCAR drivers), and got a good night's sleep.

Racing on Daytona Beach goes back to 1903, but only in the 1930s was an actual oval track improvised. In 1957, the makeshift course of 4.1 miles followed the beach north and then returned south on Highway 1, a narrow, paved two-lane road. The beach made the contest special. Turning a corner on the sand required the driver to throw the car in a sideways slide well before entering the turn. During the race, ruts and holes in the sand develop, and if a car in a power slide hit one of the holes, the car might flip over. Making matters worse, at the speed the cars traveled down the beach, it was difficult to spot a hole in advance.

The straight part of the beach was as risky as the corners. A car would run faster on the packed sand near the water, but the tide and the waves did not always leave the course smooth. If a car passed over an uneven patch of sand, the driver might lose control. More than one competitor has been killed speeding on the beach.

Although Beauchamp had limited experience on the sand, he had plenty of experience sliding a car around corners on dirt tracks. During the time trials that fixed the starting order for the main event, he placed his Black Widow thirteenth. He was six rows of cars from the front. Starting behind him were more than forty competitors. Beauchamp was well positioned to win.

Around 30,000 spectators were ready to see the race. NASCAR encouraged fans to buy a ticket and enter through the gate, but some spectators chose not to pay to watch the event and instead hiked through the palmettos and rough terrain, ignoring the signs NASCAR officials had posted to "beware of snakes."

The scene was festive: the United States Air Force precision flying unit, the Thunderbirds, performed over the water in F100C Super Sabres—the fans enjoyed speed both in the air and on the ground. Recently crowned race queen Mary Jane Mangier, 35-23-35, was in place, ready to greet the winner. Beauchamp hoped to kiss her at the end of the contest.

The 39-lap event began on the highway side of the course with major competitor Cotton Owens, from South Carolina, speeding into the lead. Owens had finished third in the time trials, propelled by a 317-horsepower Pontiac engine.

Paul Goldsmith, driving one of the factory-backed Chevrolets, seized the lead from Owens on lap 11. Beauchamp, typically careful in the early stages, moved up to seventh from his starting thirteenth spot. Owens grabbed the lead again on lap 12 and by lap 20, Beauchamp had reached fourth.

The race, as usual, was kicking up sand everywhere, and all the drivers' windshields were covered with it. Drivers, speeding down the beach at 100 miles an hour, had to lean out their windows to see in front of them. Owens pitted on lap 23 and Goldsmith went into the lead. Beauchamp, lingering near the front, believed he had a chance to win. By lap 30 he had moved to third behind Goldsmith and Owens. At this point, Goldsmith's engine broke down and Owens went to the front. He had planned to set a torrid pace, hoping a few competitors would burn out, as Goldsmith had just done. Owens said, "I tried to set a pace which would force somebody out of the race."[3] Beauchamp, however, had carefully conserved his car, figuring that Owens himself might burn out because of his tactic, or at least be forced to slow down. But then random fortune struck.

Speeding up the beach, a driver had to decide when to prepare for the corner, let up on the gas, and put the car into a power slide. At the point where Beauchamp wanted to prepare for the north turn, he had spotted a family of four on the dune watching the race; one member of the family wore a bright red outfit. The person in red was the cue for him to begin making the turn. Unfortunately for Beauchamp, late in the race the person wearing the red outfit disappeared off the dunes. He failed to slow down in time and overshot the curve, losing precious seconds. All he could do after that was finish in second place, 55 seconds behind Owens. Marvin Panch recalled, "Everyone was talking about Beauchamp missing the north turn."[4] But even though he didn't win, Beauchamp was the only competitor on the same lap with Owens.

The experienced NASCAR drivers who raced in factory Chevrolets, although not winning, had done well. Buck Baker finished fourth and Speedy Thompson and Rex White finished a respectable eighth and ninth. Beauchamp, an outsider to NASCAR, had taken second. Overall, the Chevrolet team had four of the top ten spots and the second-place car. The Ford factory, a main competitor of Chevrolet, and its sponsored De-Paolo garage managed a fifth and seventh.

The sports writers and commentators never mentioned that Dale Swanson, the mechanical wizard, had built the car Beauchamp drove. In fact, when the stock car journalists assembled their retrospective information, they wrote, "Johnny Beauchamp, driving a factory backed Chevrolet set up by Georgian Hugh Babb."[5] Even in later accounts, Swanson could not get credit for building the car. Beauchamp had his own problems with stock car journalists. A 1993 book by Peter Golenbock quotes, with no correction, Richard Petty placing Beauchamp not in the little racing mecca of Harlan but rather in Keokuk, Iowa.[6] Beauchamp and Swanson pocketed the $2,400 second-place money; attended a SEDCO banquet for the participants; and left Daytona, scarcely noticed. The champion of the Midwest had defeated all of the NASCAR drivers but one.[7]

But the second-place finish and the lack of recognition were not the only disappointments. After the race, in the midst of the celebration, Vince Piggins told Swanson, "All of the cars built at SEDCO stay in NASCAR."[8]

Swanson was astonished. "I worked so hard building that car. This makes me feel very bad."[9]

Piggins replied, "I will give you another car to build for the IMCA season."[10]

Beauchamp and Swanson rushed to Michigan to pick up the promised Chevy. Swanson would have to work fast to build a new race car for the upcoming season. The good news was that Chevrolet planned to pay its most winning 1956 team to compete in 1957.

At a meeting with Vince Piggins and Mauri Rose, Piggins asked Swanson what he would like as a monthly salary. Swanson hesitated, not certain how much money to ask for. Under the table, Rose signaled with his hand for Swanson to bid up his asking price. Swanson said $500 a month, plus expenses. Piggins agreed and the season was set. What remained was the task of converting the new Chevy into a race car.

Back in Harlan, Swanson went to work, his fourteen-year-old son, Dale Jr., eagerly helping his father and being rewarded with permission to skip high school classes and go to Shreveport for the opening race of the season.

Weeks later, Chevrolet made Swanson a tempting offer to move south. Frank Delroy had left SEDCO, and Jim Rathman, his replacement, was managing the Atlanta shop temporarily. Piggins asked Swanson to take it over. The Harlan mechanic told Piggins he needed time to discuss the matter with his family.

Swanson pondered the offer, and his family sat around the supper table evaluating the pros and cons. Managing SEDCO appeared to be a good opportunity. He could become a prominent racing mechanic with Chevrolet in the increasingly important NASCAR circuit. But it also had downsides. Phyllis did not want to leave Harlan. Her family lived in the area and her children, born in the community, attended school in town. Dale, meanwhile, had observed the racial turmoil in Atlanta. In January 1957, six of the one hundred local ministers belonging to the Law, Love, and Liberation organization were arrested for sitting in the white section of a bus.[1] Also, civil rights leader Martin Luther King's headquarters, within a few blocks of the center of Atlanta, was not far from SEDCO's race shop.

The public schools were under siege because of the recent U.S. Supreme Court decision ending the legal segregation of public schools. Atlanta, although largely without riots and other violence, was a tense powder keg and a stark contrast to the pristine Harlan community. Another consideration was that Dale would have to close the Swanson garage in Harlan. The move would risk the modest security he had built up with his auto shop.

Beauchamp, on the other hand, saw the move as a good idea. If Swanson relocated to the South, his top driver would accompany him. He eagerly embraced the possibility to race for more money and to defeat the NASCAR drivers. Leaving Harlan would also put many miles between him and Nettie Belle, his ex-wife.

After much thought and discussion, Swanson decided not to accept the SEDCO position. He valued his family and his wife's wishes and chose to remain in Harlan.

In the first week of June, Swanson, who sometimes needed rest from the schedule, went fishing in Minnesota. Upon his return, he discovered that the Automobile Manufacturers Association on June 6 had unanimously voted to recommend that the industry stop supporting racing. Ford, Chevrolet, and the other companies promised to stop the flow of money for the sport. The factories divested their involvement, giving the cars and equipment to the mechanics. SEDCO closed. Swanson hurried to Atlanta to recover a promised car and his share of the parts and equipment, but everything had vanished.

The sudden termination of support from the automotive industry is usually blamed on the number of injuries and deaths occurring on the track. The most frequently mentioned event is a June 1955 European Le Mans race, in which a car careened into spectators, killing seventy-seven people and injuring many more. Drivers, mechanics, and fans died somewhere every racing season. Indeed, on May 19, 1957, at a NASCAR race, Billy Meyers's car crashed over a wall, seriously injuring spectators, including an eight-year-old boy. This accident fueled people's suspicions that the factory pullout occurred because management did not want to be associated with the injuries.

But it was more complicated than simply deaths at the track. The automotive companies were already ambivalent about racing. A number of executives preferred to have no connection with racing because they believed that the deaths and injuries at races, when coupled with an image of low-class combat on the tracks, tarnished the manufacturers' reputation.

The costs were not worth the benefits. Yet other executives were enticed by the belief that "win on Sunday, buy on Monday" was a valid maxim. They believed that success on the track meant higher sales in the showroom. Also, a few supporters of the factories' involvement in racing believed that competition encouraged the development of improved automotive equipment; the race technology could transfer to the family passenger car. However, the amount of transfer was debatable.

Other reasons may also help explain the factory pullout. NASCAR had recently cracked down on the exaggerated and overhyped industry ads about the quality of the cars that won. The organization had established an honest advertising and publicity rule and eventually prohibited the use of race results and horsepower in ads. After a March 24, 1957, race in which SEDCO swept the first three spots, Chevrolet violated the NASCAR rules by hyping its cars' horsepower in a national advertisement. NASCAR retaliated by denying Chevrolet its manufacturer points for the Hillsboro race.

From the companies' point of view, if they could not run ads about racing exploits, there was no reason to bother with any of it. On the thirteenth anniversary of D-Day, the Allied invasion of Normandy, racing had its own D-Day. The Automobile Manufacturers Association ended its support of racing.[2]

The "gravy train" was over. Swanson no longer waited for the late-night factory shipments of free parts. His monthly stipend also was gone. Things were back to how they had been when he and Beauchamp got started in racing: the only cash came from winning races. Swanson, as the owner-mechanic, received 60 percent of the purse, but the maintenance of the car drained away much of this cash. Never one to lose money, the mechanic reduced his commitment, and Beauchamp became co-owner for the 1957 IMCA season. He was now paying part of the maintenance of the car.

Compounding the loss of Chevrolet's support was a challenge from the Burdicks—Roy, Bud, and Bob. The Burdicks versus Beauchamp-Swanson was one of the great rivalries of stock car racing in the 1950s.[3] The Burdicks had begun their careers in 1950, when a customer came by Roy Burdick's garage and asked him if he could tune up a car for races. He said yes, and then Roy and his brother Bud went to an Omaha track, Grandview, to see how their engine work performed. The brothers were instantly hooked. They built a race car and Bud drove. Roy, a no-nonsense, smart, and resourceful mechanic, became a worthy competitor for Swanson.

After showing promise during the 1956 IMCA season, now in 1957, Roy's son Bob had become a tough competitor. Eventually, he would visit the South and win an Atlanta NASCAR race, but in 1957 he was barely out of high school, and the press still called him "young" Bob Burdick. The son turned out to be a lot of trouble for Beauchamp.

Before July, Beauchamp won eight races and Bob Burdick seven. At one point they were tied for the season championship. During a May 19 event in Cedar Rapids, Iowa, the contest heated up. In the first 100-lap race, Beauchamp's car flipped. Pushed back on its tires, the car and its driver recovered but could not overtake the winner, Bob Burdick.[4]

In the second 100-lapper, Burdick managed to get one lap ahead of Beauchamp. Later, when Beauchamp attempted to pass Burdick to get back on the lead lap, Burdick blocked him. Beauchamp, already frustrated because he had rolled over, was out of patience. He began trying to spin out Burdick. Officials finally black-flagged Beauchamp, the signal for a driver to leave the race and get off the track. Young Burdick's reaction was, "I thought the leader, when ahead of lapped cars, could go anywhere on the track."[5] Beauchamp's temper had flared, and he once again proved he would defend himself on the track.

Even with the intense Beauchamp-Burdick rivalries, the two camps were generally friendly and respectful. Roy Burdick and Dale Swanson were intelligent, level-headed men. In fact, the two mechanics were almost a matched pair: Swanson with the cigarette hanging from his lips, Roy Burdick with a cigar hanging from his lips. Youthful Bob Burdick, less experienced, was more impetuous.

As the season progressed, Beauchamp slowly pulled away from Burdick. Beauchamp won 24 more contests for a total of 32. Burdick won 15 more races and finished with 22 wins. Almost no other driver won a race, and Burdick remained close in points by finishing second or third when Beauchamp won. By the end of the season, Beauchamp had 4,376 points and Burdick 3,454 points.[6]

The fallout from the AMA's decision to stop supporting racing continued into the 1958 season. Swanson remained as a mechanic, but Beauchamp now was driver and full owner of the car. These circumstances made it harder for Beauchamp to make a living, so he began considering his options outside of racing. One possibility for him grew out of his interest in objects from the past. When traveling to the IMCA tracks, he poked around in the communities looking for antiques. Often he would return from a race not only with a victory trophy, but a car loaded down with old treasures.

Sometimes, Beauchamp's quest for antiques resulted in more trouble than he bargained for. On his way to Shreveport once, he stopped in a sleepy southern town for a haircut and asked the barber where he could find antiques. Beauchamp was particularly interested in guns. The barber told him there was a man who had guns he might sell, but he cautioned Beauchamp that the place was difficult to find. It was outside of town, down a road that appeared to end, but one had to drive on through what was more like a field filled with brush and woods.

Beauchamp followed the directions and eventually came upon a house trailer. As he approached the trailer, a young boy stepped out with a rifle pointed right at Beauchamp's chest. "I'm going to shoot you. You're trespassing."[7]

Beauchamp calmly told the boy he was looking for antiques.

The boy's father appeared and said, "Don't shoot him just yet, son."

The boy screamed, "Let me shoot him, dad. He is a revenuer."[8]

Finally, the father convinced the son not to shoot. Beauchamp explained why he was there and then hastily departed without looking or buying anything.

Although this particular search for antiques was dangerous, in general Beauchamp had better luck, amassing a large collection. Eventually, Beauchamp hoped to convert his interest in objects from the past into a profit-making business.

Perhaps thinking of his own struggle as a young man, Beauchamp attempted to direct his sons to occupations that would permit them to earn a decent wage. Bob Beauchamp, still in high school, was a lifeguard at the Harlan municipal pool when John stopped by and told him he was going to college—barber college. Bob gave up his job, left Harlan for the summer, and learned how to cut hair. He lost his chance to play football because when he arrived back in Harlan, classes had been underway for two weeks. He was almost too late to enroll for the term.

Even as he thought about alternative ways to make a living, Beauchamp continued to race. In 1958 he owned and drove a 1957 Chevrolet, only it was not as fast as the Pontiacs and Fords. Don White, the season champion, and Bob Burdick, the third-place finisher, both drove Fords. Ernie

Derr in a Pontiac was second. Beauchamp came in fourth with four season wins.[9]

He supplemented his IMCA racing with events at other tracks. But even if IMCA had a "still" date, that is, a date with no IMCA race, it banned its drivers from entering certain contests anyway. For instance, IMCA had ruled Pioneer Raceway in Des Moines, Iowa, unsanctioned and off limits because of some differences with the track's promoters. Beauchamp, however, sought to make some money by the method he knew best: racing. In 1958, following a common practice of the era, Beauchamp won a big race at the Des Moines track under a false name. He was Jack Davis of Dallas, Texas.[10]

Beauchamp, not as successful in 1958 as in previous seasons, yearned to find a way back to the top. He did not realize how soon he would take center stage in the biggest stock car race in the nation.

21 | An Indy Track for Stock Cars

The falling snow became a blizzard in the cold winter of 1959, causing rock sensation Buddy Holly's plane to crash in a frozen Iowa cornfield.[1] About the same time that "the music died," Beauchamp had the biggest opportunity of his life. Rival Roy Burdick needed a late model stock car driver. His son and brother were not options because Bob had joined the military and Bud had a day job, a wife, and five children, plus he had limited experience with late model cars. So Roy Burdick called Beauchamp and asked him to drive in the first Daytona 500.[2]

Burdick had been supported by Ford much like Swanson had been by Chevrolet. The major Ford racing garage in the nation was Holman-Moody, which had been owned by Pete DePaulo, who'd raced the Dusenberg on the beach in 1957. Although the factories would not admit to being involved with racing, the reality was that there remained clandestine support, not advertised but nevertheless present in limited and less visible amounts.[3] A competitor driving a Ford could get the best help from a Ford race garage, and most mechanics believed Holman-Moody was one of the best.

In 1959, Ford supplied Holman-Moody with nine partially assembled Thunderbirds from the Ford factory in Atlanta. The plan was to sell the T-Birds for competition in NASCAR's new premier event.[4] The people at this garage were aware of Roy Burdick, owner of the most successful Ford race shop in the Midwest, and they offered him a T-Bird for $5,500 to enter in the big race.[5] The complication was that Burdick had to travel to the Holman-Moody garage in Charlotte, North Carolina, to complete the building of the car—a minor matter for these two full throttle racers. Burdick and Beauchamp seized the opportunity.

Entering the Thunderbird at Daytona was controversial because the car was powered by a big Lincoln engine. In 1958, NASCAR had classified the Thunderbird a sports car and banned it from competition against showroom passenger cars. But "Big" Bill France, the owner of NASCAR, wanted a large field to inaugurate the new event, so he allowed T-Birds and Jaguars into the race. Seven T-Birds managed to enter, adding an extra dimension of excitement.

The Daytona track, in many respects, was the show. France had dreamed of a big, new race venue for stock cars. He became all the more eager to build his track after Indy officials threw him off the premises of the Indianapolis Speedway.[6] Indy officials wanted no part of anyone pushing stock car races, from their viewpoint a second-class motor sport. After this episode, he was determined to build a track better than the Indianapolis Speedway.

Daytona would not be the first super-speedway (a large, high-banked track). Darlington had been operating for a decade by the time France's track opened, and Raleigh's one-mile, high-banked track was open from 1953 to 1958. The Memphis-Arkansas Speedway, a 1.5-mile high-banked dirt oval, the scene of Lund's first NASCAR race and his horrendous wreck, operated from 1954 to 1957.[7] In the late 1950s, there were few of these tracks, and it was unclear how successful they would be, but France was determined to own a big super-speedway, better than Darlington and better than Indianapolis. France also had a practical reason to build his track. Daytona's historic beach course was dangerous—too rough, too unpredictable, and the highway portion too narrow; in addition, developers were eager to build hotels and condominiums where the cars raced. He was getting squeezed out. He had planned a new speedway by 1955 but struggled to find financial backing. France had the dream, but not the cash.

The Daytona community helped France with loans and anything else it could muster, because the big races generated hundreds of thousands of dollars of extra spending in the area. France borrowed additional money from private sources. His task was made easier because Daytona had more than half a century of racing heritage. Luck, determination, and daring finally helped France pull together the funds. In the end, the monster of a track that France built in Daytona cost $2.9 million, resulting in a facility larger than any that drivers had seen. The distance around the Indianapolis track was two miles, while the new Daytona Speedway was two and a half miles.

Even now, people remember seeing the track for the first time. Johnny Bruner, the NASCAR flagman, decided to give his wife Ann a treat and show her the track close-up in the family car. Ann remembers: "We came from a tunnel, from below, and we entered this vast track with the high banked curves." As Bruner chauffeured his wife around the track, suddenly Ann became frightened. "Johnny slowed down on the curve, and the curve was so steep, we dropped to the bottom of the curve and almost wrecked."[8]

Indeed, the 31-degree banking on the curves dropped the jaw of even the most experienced pilots. They quickly discovered that it was important to maintain speed on the corners, or they too would slide to the bottom of the track. Engineers had dug out a deep cavity for a lake in the infield, and they had piled the excavated dirt into the turns. Although banked curves were common at tracks, these curves were steeper, permitting competitors to run their engines wide open as long as the equipment could take it.

In addition to the steep corners, the course was not a regular two-curve oval. Reporter Morton Paulson described the shape as "a wide oval with an outward bulge in the north straightaway."[9] France called it a "tri-oval."[10] The strange shape was partially determined by the nature of the site on which the track was built. The new facility boasted a feature that distinguished it from most race tracks: two galvanized steel tunnels costing $80,000 so that people could reach the infield without crossing the track.[11] At first he called his creation Daytona Beach Speedway but then named the track Daytona International Speedway.[12] Many years later, NASCAR champion Darrell Waltrip would observe: "I don't know if Daytona is so much a racetrack as it is a shrine. There's a reverence about the place."[13]

Fireball Roberts was one of the many competitors taking a few practice laps. Arguably the biggest star in NASCAR, he was known for his penchant to charge faster than any competitor. Although he earned his moniker as a baseball pitcher, as a race driver he preferred big, high stakes events where he could make a lot of money. According to his mistress, they would arrive at the race track and Fireball would go directly to the office and pick up an envelope bulging with hard cash. This was his "appearance money."[14] In 1964 he was on the cover of Sports Illustrated.[15]

Roberts, after a practice session, brought his car to a stop, and before he could exit, a reporter approached the car window and asked, "What do you think of the new track?" Roberts took his hands off the wheel and just shook them.[16] Most drivers felt like Roberts. The track was scary. Beauchamp had the sensation that when coming out of those high-banked curves "the track just opened up in front of me."[17]

Beauchamp had both advantages and disadvantages racing on the Daytona oval. The powerful T-Bird engine posed a formidable threat to opponents on the high-banked track; however, the car's boxy shape made it difficult to maneuver. But Roy Burdick was aware of what Sonny Morgan once said: "Beauchamp could manhandle a car better than almost anyone."[18] Indeed, he could turn a fast car that handled poorly into a winner. Beauchamp and Burdick were both hoping he could do it again in 1959.

Beauchamp had one big obstacle before he could pilot Burdick's T-Bird at Daytona. He was not a NASCAR-sanctioned driver because he raced in what France considered a rival association. Atlanta reporter Greg Favre called Beauchamp an "outlaw." But the 1959 event was France's big kick-off race for the new track. He wanted a large field of cars and drivers from all regions of the United States, and even from other nations. France pardoned about fifty drivers, including Beauchamp, to clear the way for outsiders to enter.

By race time, although millions had been spent, little had been built except for the surface of the new track. In all other respects, the complex was not a model of a great racing facility. It had chain-link fences instead of walls. The garage area was simply a "weedy patch" in the infield behind the pit road (the road that exited the track so the cars could be serviced during the race). Bill France had spent every cent he could locate to build the track,[19] but the exterior facilities were deficient.

Unfortunately, France had not only spent all his money; he had also focused all of his attention and energy on building the track in time for the event, neglecting details crucial for the management of the race. As would be revealed, his organizational supervision of the contest matched his lack of attention to the infield's garage area. The management problems for the event would haunt the first big race. Yet France did have the big tri-oval ready, and he sought to ramp up the hype about his new speedway. The way he did it was enough to give any hardened veteran, including Johnny Beauchamp, pause.

France invited Indy cars to come to Daytona and try to break the world record. He believed that if the world speed record on a closed course could be broken on his track, this would prove that it was faster than the Indy Speedway or any other facility. Tony Bettenhausen Sr. had set the existing record, 177.038 miles per hour, in June 1958 at Monza, Italy. Mechanic Smokey Yunick explained: "France had a deal where the first guy who ran 180 miles an hour on the Daytona track, which would make it the fastest track in the world, would get $10,000."[20]

Driver Marshall Teague was the first to accept the challenge to go for the world record. He had won two beach races, but since 1953 he had raced Indy rather than NASCAR because of trouble with France. On February 11, he brought an Indy-style car, this particular one called a Sumar Special, onto the track to attempt the record. Teague, like everyone else, knew nothing about how the aerodynamics on the high-banked tri-oval would affect a race car. On the fourth turn, air got under the car, lifting it, and his car took flight, barrel-rolling and turning over multiple times. Still strapped in the seat, Teague was ejected from the car 1,500 feet from the spot where it began rolling. He died on the track.

Teague's death sent an ominous message: this track is not like any other, and it is dangerous. Nevertheless, France proceeded with the full schedule as planned, including events in two divisions: modified, featuring older model cars with souped-up engines, and late model, consisting of new cars, cars only a few years old—including both convertibles and sports cars. Time trials and two qualifying events determined the starting positions in the 500.

On Friday, February 20, two 100-mile qualifying contests, one for sedans and the other for convertibles, set the order for the late model division. The first twenty finishers in each race earned a spot in the big Daytona 500 on Sunday. France lacked convertibles for the race so he stopped at Marvin Panch's car and said, "I'll tell you what, boys. If you want to cut that top off those cars, I'll give you an extra $1,000."[21] With this offer, France cajoled nineteen convertibles to enter.

On Saturday, February 21, NASCAR held two races: one a 200-mile final contest for the modified old models, and the other, a 10-lap consolation race for the late model cars that failed to finish in the top twenty in the Friday qualifiers. The consolation established the starting order of the remaining late model cars that would line up behind the first forty cars.

By the time the big events started, France's hype seemed to be paying off. He had predicted 15,000 spectators for the Friday qualifying contests, but 17,000 attended. He anticipated 50,000 fans for the big 500-mile late model finale.[22]

The *Daytona Beach Journal* could not settle on one driver as the most likely to win the first Daytona 500. Photos of three favorites splashed across more than half of the front page: Cotton Owens, Fireball Roberts, and Lee Petty. These three NASCAR stalwarts had the pedigree for a victory. Owens had won the 1957 Beach race; Roberts was a big star; and Lee Petty was the 1958 champion. Bernard Kahn, sports editor for the Daytona newspaper, reported that according to the pit chatter, a number of different cars had a chance of winning: Chevrolet, Thunderbird, Pontiac, and Oldsmobile.[1]

Reporter Greg Favre of the *Atlantic Journal* handicapped the field of cars in his Sunday morning article. "The betting guys—they're picking Welborn for the most part with the T-Bird drivers, Wilson and Pistone, close in the running and Weatherly not far behind."[2] A number of the NASCAR stars, many of whom usually might have been considered favorites, had bad finishes in the 100-mile qualifier and were starting far back in the pack.[3]

As the cars lined up for the race, the sedan hardtops stretched out in a single line on the inside (the lane closest to the infield). Up front on the pole was the qualifier winner, Bob Welborn, in a 1959 Chevrolet. Behind Welborn was Fred Wilson in a T-Bird, followed by "Tiger" Tom Pistone in another T-Bird. Then came hard-driving Joe Weatherly in a 1959 Chevrolet, followed by Eduardo Dibos of Peru in a T-Bird. After Dibos, Beauchamp had the next T-Bird, but in between Dibos and Beauchamp were Cotton Owens, Tiny Lund, Lee Petty, Charley Griffith, and Rex White.

Starting in the eleventh row, and having the eighth best time trial for a qualifier, Beauchamp was near the front, close enough to win. But he was overlooked, scarcely mentioned as a threat, and this even though he was driving a T-Bird, a car believed to have a chance. The journalists failed to recall his second-place finish at the 1957 February beach race, and they barely noticed his exploits in the Midwest. From the perspective of the journalists covering the race, he was a phantom.

Beauchamp lined up his NASCAR-assigned number 73, an all-white car rather than the familiar black-and-white color scheme of vehicles he often drove. He looked right at, and smiled at, Wilbur Rakestraw, who revved his convertible's engine. The cars circled the track, two by two, and as they approached the starting line, with the grandstands on their right, the starter dropped the green flag. A vast flash of roaring metal charged ahead—the first Daytona 500 was underway. Fearful of the unknown track, most drivers were careful. Welborn, Pistone, and Weatherly took turns leading. Drivers led a few laps and then dropped out of first.

One reason the lead kept changing was because of what was called the slipstream. Bob Welborn, after the 40-lap qualifier event (Lee Petty finished eighth and Beauchamp eleventh), described the difficulty he had getting away from Fred Wilson: "As long as he was behind me I was pulling him," Welborn said. "Shucks, he could rest his engine while I did the work."[4] Tucked in behind another car, the following car glided along with less effort because the lead car bore the brunt of the air resistance. The car following could build extra speed and slingshot around the front car.

This curious phenomenon, eventually known as the draft, was negligible on the smaller tracks, and thus unknown before competition at the new Daytona. A review of the press coverage at the time shows that many motor jockeys discovered the draft simultaneously.[5] Drivers also discovered that the convertibles Bill France had paid so much to enter had no chance to win because they lacked the proper aerodynamics. Marvin Panch, driving a convertible, struggled to keep up: "It seemed every 20 laps the lead cars passed me."[6]

By lap 20, the fifty-mile mark, Beauchamp had moved ahead of eleven convertibles and four sedans to ride in seventh place. Lee Petty was in eighth place somewhere behind Beauchamp. By lap 23, favorite Fireball Roberts had passed Beauchamp, as well as everyone else. Roberts, starting forty-sixth, drove a high line around the speedway, flying on the outside, passing car after car and setting a blistering pace, extending his lead far ahead of second place. He held the lead until lap 43, when another important element of the race became apparent: tire wear.

Certain vehicles wore their tires out faster than others, so their drivers had to stop to get new tires more often. Since the cars were circling slightly less than ninety seconds a lap, a driver who made a few extra pit stops could easily fall two laps behind. Curtis Turner, who eventually finished thirteenth, made twelve tire changes and never got close to the front. Several cars did well the first half of the event, but in the later stages, the wear and tear on their suspension systems in turn caused their tires to wear out faster. Jack Smith made seven tire changes, most of them in the last third of the race.[7] To win a race—especially on a fast track like the one at Daytona—a driver had to think strategically about how and when to push his vehicle's limits.

A Beauchamp trademark was taking it easy on his car in the early part of contest. He had carefully moved up as the competitors in front dropped back with worn out tires or engine problems. He had taken his time but eventually found himself where he wanted to be: in second place. When Roberts pitted after lap 43, Johnny Beauchamp seized the lead.

While drivers discovered how to navigate the course, fans and officials had their own problems monitoring the running order from first to last. On the huge track, cars spread out—a substantial distance apart—and this distance between cars was a more realistic pinpointing of how close the competitors were to each other than the running order.

A consideration of the actual track conditions illustrates the difficulties of focusing on running order. For example, during the first part of the race, Fireball Roberts built a large lead over the second- and third-place cars. Later, on lap 100, second-place Tom Pistone was one and a half miles behind the front-runner, Jack Smith, and at this instant, Beauchamp, behind Pistone, was third. A car running farther back could be one lap or more behind the leader. It is evident that the listing of cars as second, third, fourth, or fifth fails to reflect how near these vehicles are to each other.

Spectators could recognize first place, but the remainder of the order was simply a spectacle of cars circling in uncertain running order. When the leader left the race either for mechanical reasons or for a pit stop and onlookers turned their attention to those cars that were a substantial distance behind the leader, the issue of whether those vehicles were on the same lap as the new leader became important. But at this first Daytona 500, neither officials, nor fans, nor drivers could be certain; confusion was rampant.

Fans and officials had no problem observing that Pistone snatched the lead from Beauchamp on lap 50, and Smith roared in behind Pistone, leaving Beauchamp in third, and somewhere behind these three, running in fourth, was Tim Flock, with Petty in fifth.

Examining the running order, one can piece together a possible sequence of track activity and understand how confusing it was to determine the action behind the first few leaders, but the task of analyzing the running order here is complicated by the lack of a record of when cars made pit stops; however, it affords an eye-opening understanding of what could have occurred. On lap 55, Beauchamp was not among the top five front-runners, most likely because he pitted; Petty ran fifth.[8] Then on lap 58, Jack Smith grabbed the lead from Pistone, who had been leading. By lap 60, Beauchamp was back in third place while Petty remained in fifth place. Because Petty held his position, as did Pistone and Smith, during these lap intervals, and because Beauchamp quickly caught and passed Petty after the likely pit stop, one perhaps can conclude that Petty was about one full lap behind Beauchamp when the latter pitted. In other words, when Beauchamp pitted, Petty had a minute or so on the track to cover a full lap and move ahead of Beauchamp, but not by much. When Beauchamp returned to the track, he quickly regained a position in the running order behind Pistone and Smith.

Indeed, between laps 43 and 148, Pistone, Smith, and Beauchamp traded the lead to the exclusion of all the other drivers. These three front-runners each led several times, with Jack Smith in front more often than Pistone and Beauchamp. After lap 105, Pistone faded from contention because of engine problems, and by lap 110 Beauchamp was again the race leader, but behind Smith by lap 120. On lap 149, Jack Smith stopped for gas and tires, taking a 135-second pit stop that left him well behind the front-runners.[9] Beauchamp inherited the lead at this point.

While Pistone, Smith, and sometimes Beauchamp challenged for the lead, farther back the running order (and the number of laps that the cars had completed) was less clear. Behind Beauchamp was a second group of racers: Charley Griffith, Cotton Owens, Joe Weatherly, and Lee Petty. Their order was murky. For example, from lap 50 to lap 70 Lee Petty was running in fifth place, but then by lap 75 neither Petty nor Beauchamp were in the top five; now Charlie Griffith and Cotton Owens, both of whom eventually finished a lap behind the leaders, were ahead of both Petty and Beauchamp. The most likely explanation why Petty and Beauchamp fell farther back was because they pitted, while Pistone, before and after the 75th lap, continued as leader and Jack Smith, always aware of his track position, was third.[10]

Surprisingly, by lap 80, Petty had somehow rocketed into second place ahead of Smith, who was still running third as he was 5 laps earlier, and ahead of Griffith as well. Beauchamp was running fifth at this point, having predictably fallen back in the order because he pitted. But how Petty moved ahead of Smith, Griffith, and Beauchamp during a 5-lap interval is either perplexing or quite an accomplishment.

Another puzzling change in the running order began on lap 140. Smith was in the lead, Beauchamp was second, Griffith third, and Petty fourth. Griffith was the one to keep a close watch on: he held the key to understanding the implications of what happened subsequently.

In the end, Griffith finished the race one lap behind Beauchamp, and during the race he ran a substantial distance behind the leaders. According to the lap order, between laps 140 and 145, Lee Petty passed Griffith, and then by lap 150 he had made up the distance between the lagging Griffith and the front-runners and took the lead. The question is: how could Lee Petty, running behind third-place Griffith on lap 140, make up the distance to assume the lead on lap 150? He would have had to be moving like Fireball Roberts did during the early stages of the race, but no one who was watching remembered anything like that.

The scramble that occurred between lap 140 and lap 150 illustrates the problems monitoring track position, but it seemed clear in the last quarter of the race that the likely winner would be one of two drivers. From lap 150 through lap 200, spectators saw Beauchamp and Petty running together. No other driver led the race during those 50 laps. Meanwhile, Charley Griffith, who had been ahead of Petty on lap 140, continued in third place the remainder of the race, finishing one lap behind. (Griffith had no problems with tire wear and had few pit stops.)

In the last 18 laps, Petty led ten times and Beauchamp six.[11] Also, Joe Weatherly appeared out of nowhere in the last few laps of the race to challenge Petty and Beauchamp. Officials were certain Weatherly was not on the lead lap, but they did not know how many laps he was behind.

Perhaps unaware of the confusion among officials, Beauchamp, always careful, appeared in no hurry to pass Petty. After the race, the Harlan driver explained, "It was all intentional. Petty dropped back to second as part of the plan and I did the same. After all, you can't run at 140 mph, full blast all the time, without taking a chance on your engine and tires. I save everything for the stretch."[12]

In this Daytona race, though, Beauchamp's strategy was complicated by Weatherly's presence, because he blocked one of the paths to pass Petty. The three cars often were racing side by side. Occasionally, Beauchamp followed behind Weatherly and Petty. One might assume Beauchamp was confident his car was faster than Petty's and he could pass him on the last curve, allowing Petty no chance to spin him out. But on the last lap with Weatherly in the mix, what part of the track was open for Beauchamp to pass Petty?

On the final turn, Weatherly was high on the track, Petty in the middle of the track, and Beauchamp came from behind to cut on the inside of Petty. Speeding from the curve, taking advantage of the downward slope off the turn, the Harlan driver pushed the accelerator to the floor. He did not need to save the car for any more laps. Beauchamp explained, "I let it all out on the final straightaway."[13]

The three cars flashed across the finish line in a blur at approximately 140 miles an hour. Weatherly was on the outside, ahead of the other two cars. Beauchamp in his T-bird and Petty in his 1959 Oldsmobile were so close it was difficult to see which car crossed first.

Flagman Johnny Bruner and Bill France did not hesitate. They agreed Beauchamp had won the race. He had proved that he could beat NASCAR's best on NASCAR's newest track at one of its marquee events. With his mechanic, Roy Burdick, and his friends watching, Beauchamp kissed the race queen, Scottie McCormick, a full five seconds. He basked in the attention while photographers snapped pictures, and he eventually went to a press trailer for interviews.

Afterwards, Beauchamp left for dinner with Donna and friends, and in the evening he went to the local television studio for an appearance on the late news. With Lloyd Jorgensen, a driver from Audubon, Iowa, Don Brix, a good friend, and others looking on, Beauchamp was interviewed by the anchor of the local television station.

Suddenly, Bill France appeared at the studio. He told the reporter and the television audience: "All this talk about a winner is premature. The outcome of the race is under review, and fans with finish-line photos or film should contact NASCAR. Johnny Beauchamp may not be the winner."[14]

At the moment of the finish, France and his flagman had not hesitated—Beauchamp won. They waved Petty, who was claiming victory, out of the winner's circle. If there had been a photo finish, why had France and Bruner declared the winner with unusual assurance?[1] Lee Petty, shunted to the side, mounted a barrage of complaints to the press. "If they let that decision stand," he grumbled, "it will be the worst under-the-table blow ever delivered in stock car racing."[2]

The angry accusations and counter accusations continued after the ceremony.

Petty had some support. Fireball Roberts, who was standing at the finish line, agreed that Petty's car crossed first. Joe Weatherly inflamed the dispute by asserting that Beauchamp "was the only guy on the track today who wasn't a gentleman."[3] Weatherly believed Beauchamp should have admitted he lost to Petty. Petty, seizing on Weatherly's rhetoric said, "If he [Beauchamp] were a gentleman, he would call it like he saw it."[4]

Beauchamp maintained his cool. When the press asked him about Petty's accusations, he insisted he had crossed the finish line ahead of Petty. "I was there by two feet," he said. "Not Petty. Petty is a real gentleman and a fine driver, but I beat him."[5]

In response to these claims and counterclaims, Bill France said only that he would review the situation. Eventually, the press and the crowds melted away.

Significantly, it was reported that "fourth place Cotton Owens and fifth place Joe Weatherly were told to stand by. A lap check would be made."[6] France had to review the records to determine if Weatherly finished ahead of Cotton Owens. But no reporter questioned whether Petty was on the same lap as Beauchamp. In fact, the press scarcely noticed that the final order of other finishers in the top five was under review.

Once France had a moment from the ceremonies and the press, he asked his photographer, T. Taylor Warren, to develop quickly and bring back an image of the race's finish.[7] Next, France began verifying the completed laps of the cars. He gathered all the scorecards from the race, one for each car, with their lap records. Examining the lap count for each vehicle required a substantial amount of time. In fact, Rex White, the 1960 NASCAR champion, recalls that on the occasions when he inspected lap count cards they usually were messy, making it extremely difficult to conclude much of anything.[8]

In any event, after six hours, France had a preliminary photograph, not definitive but suggesting Petty may have been ahead at the finish; also, by then France probably had confirmed a lap count for the top finishers. After France's announcement of a review, three days passed while he waited for the mail to bring photographs and film from journalists and spectators. It is likely he continued silently to ponder the lap counting.[9]

Nevertheless, the press coverage concentrated on the finish of the race, speculating on whether Petty or Beauchamp went across the line first. Those who believed Beauchamp won argued that observer position was crucial and that someone watching or photographing from an angle had a distorted perception. The Greeks understood this aspect of perspective when they built the Parthenon.

Among the witnesses were Larry Torson and his father, who were in the infield during the race. They worked all over the United States as welders on large jobs and happened to be in Geneva, about sixty miles from Daytona, the week before the race. They were fans, and so they went to Daytona to see the big event. Because the stands were full, they ended up in the infield, approximately seventy feet beyond the finish line.

Torson saw Beauchamp cross the finish line first and claim the trophy. He went home certain the Harlan man had justly won. When he heard that the outcome was in question, he was flabbergasted and disgusted—he believed France and his NASCAR organization were trying to steal the race. And he realized that only someone at the finish line could speak with accurate authority on the outcome.

Torson was so upset he positioned cars to mimic the order in which he thought Beauchamp and Petty crossed the line. He put Beauchamp one foot ahead of Lee Petty; next, he moved slightly to the side to create different angles of perspective. Torson said, "One didn't have to be very far to the side before it looked like Petty won, even with Beauchamp one foot in the lead."[10] The outcome of the first Daytona 500 burned into Torson's memory. He was troubled by how such a big race could be stolen from the winner.

In contrast, twelve journalists—in an effort to get a perfect view of the finish—had left the press area and moved to the finish line, putting themselves in an ideal position to judge the outcome. They unanimously said they saw Lee Petty cross the line first. All twelve of the journalists who claimed Petty won were from the South, and more than a few non-southerners believed NASCAR had a southern bias. Ann Bruner, Johnny Bruner's wife, disliked announcer Chris Economaki and labeled him "a Yankee." Smokey Yunick was certain the reporters were biased: "Reporters should be neutral, but they weren't and aren't. They had their favorites. Many times reporters get 'snowed' by some person with a vested interest."[11] Most fans from Iowa and Nebraska believed the good old boy reporters were pulling for a southerner to win. The following year, Roy Burdick even painted on the side of his 1960 race car, "Built by Nebraska farmers." He hoped that southerners might view a rural farmer, even from Nebraska, as kin to the "good old boy" NASCAR drivers.[12]

Relying on journalists often meant that race news was shallow and un-informed. Many of them did not understand racing. For instance, Max Muhleman worked for the *Greenville Piedmont* newspaper while a Fur-man University freshman. The sports editor had told him, "'Max, I'm as-signing you to cover stock car racing.' Muhleman's jaw dropped. He knew nothing about the sport."[13] Some of these writers, according to Smokey Yu-nick, may not have been able to tell the difference between Lee Petty and Richard Petty. Yunick asserts, "The early newspaper and radio reporters didn't know a damn thing about auto racing, and didn't want to know."[14]

Then there was NASCAR's owner. Bill France did not want an outsider to defeat all of his stars.[15] Attracting drivers from all over the United States—and from outside the nation as well—demonstrated the world-class level of the Daytona event and the NASCAR circuit, but who won the race was another matter. In addition to the protection of the NASCAR brand, there lingered a feeling, at least on the part of some participants, that NASCAR was a southern show, consisting of primarily southern racers. Outsiders, particularly Yankees, were not welcome.[16]

Meanwhile, fans waited to learn who won the first Daytona 500. Finally, at 6:00 p.m. on Wednesday, sixty-one hours after the race, France declared Petty the winner. He claimed a Hearst Metromedia news film decisively showed Petty in front at the finish line. He also relied on a photograph by T. Taylor Warren, who was on the NASCAR payroll. Warren explained the merit of his photograph: "People could see what the discussion was about."[17] This photo became the iconic image of the race finish. After studying the Hearst film, Warren's image, and other photos taken the instant before the cars flashed across, France concluded it would have been impossible for Beauchamp to reach the line ahead of Petty. But he did not release the film nor did he make any arrangements to have it released. In fact, Bill France has never released a photo that showed the cars crossing the finish line in the 1959 race, and no photo snapped exactly at the finish has ever been located.

However, films now are available of the race finish. Although the camera position was not directly on the finish line, stopping the film at every frame indicates that Petty finished in front of Beauchamp.[18]

But the photo finish wasn't the real story. Hidden beneath the surface, undetected by the lackadaisical press, remained a matter far more explosive.

A month after the crushing events of Daytona, Johnny Beauchamp still smoldered. He contemplated what he might do to reverse Bill France's decision. In Atlanta he sought the advice of veteran driver Frank Mundy. Mundy listened as Beauchamp told him, "I was cheated out of the win. What should I do? Maybe I should see a lawyer?"[1]

A former NASCAR driver who had left the circuit to become the 1955 AAA champion, Mundy knew France well, and he knew where the bodies were buried. Years before, they had promoted a Charlotte race, and another time, during a visit to Red Vogt's Atlanta garage (Vogt serviced engines for racers, moonshiners, and the police, the latter so they had vehicles fast enough to catch the moonshiners), France and Mundy had dived under a car after moonshiners pulled out guns and started shooting. Mundy was present at meetings at the Streamline Hotel in 1947 when NASCAR was formed. He held the flash for the group photograph.

But the two men eventually had a major disagreement in 1952 at Daytona. In the beach time trials, Mundy had finished first and Tom McCahill second, but France disqualified Mundy for not keeping a spare tire in his trunk. He told Mundy the car was not stock because it was sold out of the showroom with a spare tire, and not having the tire lightened the car, giving it an advantage. Mundy replied that he thought if he wrecked the car, the tire could come flying out and hurt someone. France sternly replied, "You are disqualified. If you don't like it, you don't have to run."[2]

Mundy replied, "That's right, and before I kiss your ass, I quit."[3]

Because the infractions of many other entrants were ignored, Mundy believed France was playing stock car politics with him—that France had deliberately disqualified him so that McCahill would win. His suspicion was that France thought McCahill, who wrote articles about automobiles as well as competing, could help NASCAR gain assistance from automobile factories.[4]

But Mundy offered Beauchamp no plan of recourse, just predictable advice: France ran NASCAR, and there was no opposing him. Mundy said: "I had no success influencing Bill France; the only thing to do is simply not to race NASCAR."[5] And Mundy's experience with France was not an isolated example. The NASCAR owner's ruthless, arbitrary, and self-serving actions are well documented. Knowing how he operated is important to understanding how he handled the 1959 Daytona 500 controversy.

For example, on one occasion Bruton Smith, a race promoter in the Charlotte area, had selected an open date for a race. An open date meant there was no conflict with a NASCAR race, and so Smith could expect to attract some NASCAR drivers, who were barred from racing in other contests when a NASCAR event was scheduled. France, desiring to stomp out competition, then scheduled an event for the same day as Smith's race. Many drivers had already signed up for the Smith contest before France caused the conflict, and they were forced either to break their commitment to Smith or to be punished by France. Mundy explained, "France [was] trying to knock Smith out of business" and would "step on anyone to get ahead."[6]

Then there's Tim Flock, the 1952 NASCAR champion who had several setbacks under the rule of France. In one case, Flock, driving a 1954 Oldsmobile at the Beach race in the same year, had led the entire event. Afterward, the top finishers had their cars torn down to verify that they were within the rules. Forty-eight hours passed before Flock learned his car had been disqualified because the butterfly shaft on his carburetor had been soldered, preventing it from shaking loose. Flock could not believe he would be disqualified for such a trivial matter, one that would not boost the car's performance. He went to France's house and asked him, "Bill, did you really disqualify my car?" France confirmed that Flock was disqualified. The driver stormed out of France's house, slamming the door so hard the glass broke, and yelled: "I'm through. I'll never run for you again."[7]

Flock believed France had deliberately disqualified him because France wanted a Chrysler to win the race to encourage Chrysler to become more involved in NASCAR contests. Flock then said: "I'll go to my grave knowing that that car was disqualified on account of Chrysler had something to do with it."[8]

France's greatest hornswoggle took place when NASCAR was formed. He organized the famous 1947 meeting at the Streamline Hotel while plotting to gain sole control of the new association. He plied the attendees, mechanics, and drivers with booze and women, and at the end of the meeting, the group voted to give him the go-ahead to draw up the incorporation papers. Red Vogt, famed mechanic, recalls in private conversations that his ex-wife presciently said, "I don't trust that man."[9]

As it turned out, France had tricked the people at the Streamline Hotel into believing they had a democratically created organization that was theirs. But he quietly had the legal documents prepared in a manner that made him owner of NASCAR. None of the drivers and mechanics at the hotel realized at the time that France planned to seize legal ownership of the association. At first no one paid much attention. They went on racing, but Ray Parks, another NASCAR legend, recalled: "The next thing we know, NASCAR belongs to Bill France."[10] In 1948 Red Vogt said that he was "pissed off" because "France had created an association using [Vogt's] ideas, his acronym" and then left Vogt out of any leadership role.[11]

This bold ruse clearly demonstrates the lengths Bill France would go to take him and his vision to the top.

France's reanalysis of the 1959 Daytona 500 photo finish had given a southern driver the victory, but the real sticking point was who that southern driver was. Within NASCAR there was a rough competitor who would do anything to win, and he was not afraid to take some liberties with Bill France's organization. It would be an understatement to say Lee Petty was not well liked in the NASCAR pits. Smokey Yunick, always prepared to "tell it like it is," recalled: "There wasn't too many people who liked Lee Petty. . . . Lee Petty was a two-faced dirty driver, and I would find it real hard for him to scrape up too many friends in racing today."[12]

Rather than welding his doors shut like other drivers, Petty bolted plates onto the car to hold the doors secure, leaving the huge bolts sticking out from the sides. The plates worked to keep the doors closed, but they also had an interesting side effect. If he hit another car broadside, the bolts worked "just like a can opener."[13]

Petty raced to make money, and for Lee Petty it was a business. He watched every penny and competed tenaciously. When Elizabeth Petty, Lee's wife, sat in the scorer's stand, she cheered when the car in front of her husband wrecked, never mind that the wrecked driver's wife was sitting right next to her. For her, the wreck meant that her husband moved up a spot and brought home a few more dollars.

During the Depression of the 1930s, the Pettys were as impoverished as most rural people in the South or anywhere in the nation. Lee Petty, however, claimed he never dealt in moonshine. Bob Welborn, one of the early NASCAR drivers who first practiced racing by hauling moonshine, disagreed: "All I know is I used to take fifty gallons a week to Lee's house."[14]

Lee Petty's wily, competitive nature showed up in his youth during foot and bicycle races. "He was not always the fastest or the strongest, but he almost always found a way to win."[15] As an adult, his competitive intensity gave off a whiff of dishonesty. Given a chance to get in front of another car, Lee Petty would do what it took: wrecking that car, driving rough, or any other method possible. He lacked the camaraderie of competition present among many drivers. Instead, according to some, "He was a churlish despot who would do anything to win."[16]

Whatever Lee Petty's limitations, Bill France considered him a reliable soldier who entered all the NASCAR races, regardless of how insignificant the contest or its distance away. In an era when France needed competitors to fill out his field of cars so the crowd would at least believe it was a viable event, Petty was valuable. While Petty was important to NASCAR, NASCAR was important to Petty. Petty was the kind of man who would scratch for every penny, nickel, and dime he could obtain. By doing his own mechanical work and driving the car, he received 100 percent of whatever prize money was won. Even $50 in the 1950s could be sufficient money upon which to live.

Unlike Petty, most NASCAR competitors did not enter all the races. It was too much effort. At a small venue with little prize money, it was not worth the drive to the track to risk wrecking a good car. Fireball Roberts, probably the biggest NASCAR star, had a reputation for only entering the big races with the big prize money, and in 1958 Roberts, piloting his Paul McDuffie–built vehicle, entered ten and won six of the bigger races in NASCAR.[17]

So at the February 1959 NASCAR Victory Dinner banquet, where the awards were passed out for the 1958 season, most observers believed Paul McDuffie, with almost unprecedented success, was likely to win the Mechanic of the Year award. But it was Lee Petty, winner of seven of fifty races, who won the award. On top of the surprising mechanic of the year award, Petty had won the season point championship. An *Atlanta Journal-Constitution* article explained how Petty managed to finish on top for season points: "Petty won only a few minor championships [races] but compiled enough seconds, thirds, and fourths to claim the national title."[18]

Lee Petty, a good friend of NASCAR, consistently showed up, but he was not considered one the best drivers; however, if competitors had mechanical problems or if he could knock out an opponent with a stiff bump or bang, or figure out another angle, then success could be within his clutches.

Beauchamp was up against two of the most ruthless and cunning people he had ever come across. The 1959 race, such as it was, had ended, and Beauchamp was now about to realize that when Lee Petty and Bill France were involved, a race won on the track could be lost off the track.

France was likely troubled by the controversy over the 1959 race. Questions lingered about who had really won. His organization was gaining importance, and it was not good to have his first big event tainted. Still, he had done everything he could do immediately after the race. That included checking the laps, even though the press focused almost exclusively on the photo finish. In fact, his behavior at the race's end and his flagman's judgment, contrary to the majority opinion on the finish line, suggested they had thought Petty was a lap behind Beauchamp. But the records he reviewed later showed Petty had as many laps as Beauchamp. France probably was puzzled. An old race man like him was not likely to make such a mistake about who was ahead on the track, particularly when Johnny Bruner, his flagman, saw the race the same way he did. But there it was in the records: Petty had as many laps as Beauchamp.

France had to know that it was possible for someone to add a lap to Petty's scorecard, but he had no way to prove that something like that happened. If France made the charge that the event had been decided improperly because of an error in the lap totals, he might discredit his big race by revealing poor management or, worse, malfeasance within the organization.

But none of this discrediting was necessary. The records showed Petty with the proper number of laps, the southern reporters were adamant that Petty had won, and Beauchamp was an unknown in the South anyway. France owed Beauchamp nothing. Whatever doubts France may have had, naming Petty as the winner validated that NASCAR had the best drivers, and that would benefit the organization. To have an outsider, even a champion from another association, come in and win would be an embarrassment. At least Petty was his faithful soldier, showing up at almost every race. Under these circumstances, the NASCAR owner trotted out the best photograph he had that showed Petty in front near the finish line.

The nagging worry for France was that someone would come along and figure out that there might have been a problem with the lap counting. He needed a description of the event that made Petty a plausible winner. In 1965 France wrote a book with the writer Bloys Britt that put considerable polish on the early days of NASCAR, including the big race in 1959.[1] By placing the Britt and France account of the race next to the more accepted accounts by newspaper reporters, one can see how France attempted to revise reality.[2]

Britt and France describe Fireball Roberts working his way to the front and taking the lead, and then they write: "Other drivers, never staying far behind, began to push a little harder and close the gap. Lee Petty was one of them. Johnny Beauchamp was another." A few sentences later, they write that Beauchamp "saw Lee Petty overtake Roberts." A few paragraphs later, Britt and France write: "Beauchamp watched the rear of Petty's car for almost 150 laps."[3]

The France account fails to match the contemporary reports of what actually happened on the track regarding Petty and Beauchamp. First, the cars were spread out on the track; about midway in the race the leader, Jack Smith, led by one and a half miles over the second-place car. Second, during the first thirty lap reports (one every 5 laps of racing reported by the press), Petty ran ahead of Beauchamp four times. In contrast, Beauchamp appears to have run ahead of Petty in a minimum of sixteen 5-lap intervals. In two of the intervals in which Petty was ahead of Beauchamp, he accomplished that by surprisingly jumping from too far back even to be recorded in one interval to second place in the next interval!

The France account is also at variance with newspaper narrative accounts. The race reported in the newspapers said Beauchamp took the lead on lap 44 and led until lap 49. He then dropped back out of first place, staying near the front but not pushing his car at full speed. He again led from lap 107 to lap 116, and once again he led on lap 149. The on-scene reporters did not mention Petty being near the front (see chapter 23) or even mention Petty at all during these stages of the race. From the spot of Petty's running order during much of the race, he could easily have been one or more laps behind the front-runners.

Then, three-quarters of the way through the race, with 50 laps to go, Petty took the lead on lap 150. This is the first mention in the press coverage that Petty was near the front. France and Britt, as they recount the first 150 laps, never say exactly whether Petty was running second or third or where he was. All they say is that Beauchamp was behind Petty for 150 laps! In fact, Petty was behind Beauchamp and other cars most of the first

150 laps. France's account is a substantial departure from the established facts. Why would he permit something so obviously contrary to the facts go into print?

One might suspect that France was hoping to make Petty look more like a contender for the lead, all the while downgrading Beauchamp's chances of success. But the newspaper accounts at the time make it clear that Beauchamp's presence at the front the last 50 laps was no surprise. He ran in the front all along. Yet we are expected to believe that Petty, on the other hand, suddenly appeared out of nowhere around lap 150 to join the leaders. This is the mystery that needs to be explained. Not the photo finish.

The photo finish was similar to "the juicy piece of meat carried by the burglar to distract the watchdog."[4] Had there been no photo finish and Petty then claimed he had won, all attention would have focused on the laps, and any problems with lap-counting might have been considered. As it was, the photo finish became the entire story. Beauchamp believed he had lapped Petty and that Petty had never made up the lap. Petty went down a lap and never passed Beauchamp again to gain the lap back. What of the possibility that Petty was a lap behind?

n fact, the people closest to the race—the drivers and the pit crews—focused on the lap count from the moment the race ended. The Petty and Beauchamp pit crews stood eyeball to eyeball, and both crews claimed victory. Beauchamp's mechanics, a few spaces from Petty's pit, had counted the other driver's stops, and they were positive Petty had made more than four stops, while Johnny had made only four.[1] They had witnessed Petty make his stops and observed the consequence: Petty was lapped by the leaders, including Beauchamp.[2] They were so sure that in the last 50 laps of the race, they signaled their driver to take it easy on the car. He drafted behind Petty, saving his car and not going as fast as possible.

After the event, the competitors hashed over the race in the pits. Jack Smith was running third on lap 75 when Petty was not in the top five. Then, while maintaining his third place on lap 80, he observed Petty listed as running second (see chapter 23) and ahead of him. He told Paul Hudson, the owner of the third-place car, "You might want to file a protest. Petty was a lap behind." Smith believed that somehow, an extra Petty lap had been added, and he thought possibly it had happened when Petty made one of his pit stops.[3]

The fact that France and his flagman had not hesitated to call Beauchamp the winner, even when people on the finish line believed Petty was slightly ahead of Beauchamp, supports the view that the southern driver had been a lap behind. The argument made by several observers that France's vision was blocked, causing him to choose the Harlan driver rather than Petty, implies this veteran of the sport and a veteran flagman would be so dumb that they would choose a winner without clearly seeing the finish line. The argument strains credibility. The more obvious explanation is that although the three cars flashing across the line together made for a good show, France and Bruner believed Weatherly and Petty were at least one lap behind Beauchamp.

Adding substance to this understanding of the race is that when Petty complained immediately afterward, France ignored him and all the other comments about the finish. Only hours later, after France had a chance to review the scorecards and found Petty had the same number of laps as Beauchamp, did the photo finish become crucial. Once the laps were checked, all France could do was announce that he was studying film and photos and giving himself time to ponder how he mistakenly believed Beauchamp had one more lap than Petty.

Perhaps that's how it was. But in the past, a dangerous precedent had been set by giving the impression that occasionally a race outcome was manipulated. Drivers and mechanics grumbled and complained, but they also loved to race and refused to be discouraged by France. Some, such as Mundy, left NASCAR to compete in other associations. Others visited NASCAR, saw what was going on, and did not stay for many races.

To give another example, Ray Chaike, driving a Gus Holzmueller Chevrolet out of Ohio, visited NASCAR for the 1956 beach race. A capable and seasoned veteran, he finished ninth. After the race, when he walked into the office to pick up his winnings, he was told he had finished in fourteenth place. Chaike demanded the money and recognition for his ninth-place finish. Unwilling to accept anything less than what he had earned, he stood there, his voice growing louder and louder. Other drivers in line for their money heard him accuse NASCAR officials of dishonesty. It was not so much the $150 difference in prize money as it was his better finish in the race that Chaike wanted to defend. The NASCAR staff threatened to call the police.

At this point, a Chevy representative pulled Chaike aside and told him, "We will take care of you and also your owner/mechanic." Then he added, "We are pushing Herb Thomas for the championship and moving him to ninth will help in the season point standing."[4]

Chaike's experience wasn't isolated. NASCAR's early years of operation are littered with stories that the association played favorites.[5] (IMCA had similar problems with race finish order, but these were isolated and rare.) If NASCAR revised the outcomes of races, it is a small step from there for a driver to decide, and find a way, to move ahead in a race by a paper and pencil adjustment in the results. In fact, to cheat on the results could be easier than to cheat with an illegal engine part to make the car go faster, since a winning car might well be torn down afterward and disqualified. But did drivers cheat this way?

Suddenly, an arcane, rarely mentioned aspect of racing—scoring— becomes important. "Scoring" is the word people in auto racing use to describe lap counting. Today, the scoring process is handled almost entirely by electronic communication devices on each car, backed up by professional lap counters. But during the early years of NASCAR, novices and volunteers were the scorers. At best, honest scorers can make mistakes; for example, a bad wreck on the track could distract a scorer from counting a lap.

NASCAR scoring was particularly vulnerable to dishonesty because the wives and girlfriends of the drivers and mechanics counted the laps, along with fans who were given free tickets in exchange for their labor. The association exercised minimal control over the people selected—no check to determine whether the volunteers were fans of a particular driver or friends with the other scorers. There was simply no credential check.

Once in the scorers' box, a scorer was given a card that listed the number of laps and left a space beside each one. The scorers sat together facing a special clock. Each scorer watched a particular car and, after that car completed a lap, recorded the time showing on the clock.

The main way that scorers could cheat was by shaving seconds from a small number of laps. For example, in the Daytona 500, the cars circled the track about every ninety seconds or less. If a scorer reduced the actual time it took a car to go a lap by ten seconds, then after 9 laps, the car would have gained ninety seconds. The scorer would then mark the time for the lap gained and so show 10 laps even though the car would actually have completed only 9 laps. A second method of adding a lap would be marking credit for a lap when the car was actually in the pits getting serviced. Drivers were aware that scorers could play games like these, and eventually a volunteer second scorer, usually for the big races, was added for each car. At the 1959 Darlington race (a NASCAR event) and after the Daytona race, two scorers followed each car.[6] At this time, Darlington and Daytona were the two biggest stock car tracks in the nation. Eventually, NASCAR adopted other reforms, such as having an official check of scorers' cards every 10 laps. At the smaller tracks with fewer cars, fewer laps, and less importance, the scoring process was not systematically reformed.

However, the 1959 Daytona race occurred before Darlington and, apparently, before the reforms were in place. One of the scorers at the 1959 Daytona 500, Helen Hudson, the wife of the owner of the third-place car, remembered it vividly: all scorers were grouped on a bleacher near what was the pit area. The higher up on the bleachers a person sat, the easier it was to view the cars as they passed, but everyone seated in the bleachers could see the track. She was given a card with 200 laps and a space to write the clock time each lap her husband's car passed by.

She was on her own: no one checked her scorecard during the race and no one asked her if she needed anything. If she had a question, needed a drink of water, or required a bathroom break, for example, no one was around to take up the slack. The extent of the supervision, at least in her case, was receiving a scorecard before the race and handing in a scorecard after the race. She did not notice a second scorer for each car, and the difference between 60 people (one for each car) and 120 (two for each car) would have been easily discernable. What Hudson remembers about the scoring was that after sitting near the track for more than three hours without leaving, her face was covered with black tire dust.[7]

But even if the scoring reforms had been in effect at the 1959 Daytona 500, the possibility of fraud remained because of the race's circumstances. The longer races, such as the 500, lasted more than three hours. Even if there had been two scorers for each car, it is possible one scorer would need a break and the second scorer, who remained, would have had ample opportunity to manipulate the laps.

Of course, the opportunity for cheating doesn't mean that cheating actually took place. However, during the 1958 season, there were rumors that Elizabeth Petty was adding laps to her husband's scorecard. Since cheating on scorecards appears possible, specifically how easy would it have been for Elizabeth Petty to tamper with a scorecard?

NASCAR, from its earliest days, had an official, Joe Epton, responsible for scoring. The association added another official to help with scoring when, in 1952, Morris Metcalf attended a NASCAR race, entering free in return for scoring work. He soon became Epton's assistant, handling most of the supervision of scoring. After 1957 he supervised the counting of laps at most races. At the Daytona 500 in 1959, Epton was listed as the head scorer.

On the surface, Metcalf was an excellent man to be working in a matter involving numbers. He held a master's degree in engineering and worked for Western Electric. Compared to many of the uneducated NASCAR employees, Metcalf stood out as a star of mathematics and calculation. One might believe that with Metcalf at the controls, cheating would be difficult, if not impossible, but one fact casts doubt on such reasoning. In 1955 Morris Metcalf had created the first NASCAR driver fan club. And that fan club was for Lee Petty.

Although there's no evidence that Metcalf cheated or knowingly permitted anything dishonest,[8] he might have contributed to circumstances in which other people could do so. Did he watch Elizabeth Petty closely as she counted her husband's laps? Or did he simply trust her as an experienced scorer and friend? Having the Petty Fan Club president oversee the scoring of a race in which Petty was competing simply does not pass the smell test. In fact, when asked about the possibility of Elizabeth Petty adding laps to her husband's cards, Metcalf said: "You're talking to the wrong person; I started the first Lee Petty fan club."[9]

The pattern of suspected cheating occurred over several years until the uncontrolled, wild days of NASCAR came to an end in the 1960s. The compromised scoring system provided opportunity to cheat, and the evidence that people took advantage of that opportunity makes the official outcome of the first Daytona 500 look dubious.

After that race, Bill France must have wondered if Lee Petty had ended up with an extra lap on his scorecard, because France and his flagman had already heard the rumors about Elizabeth Petty's scoring and dealt with a barrage of complaints after a race the previous year. On March 2, 1958, 12,000 fans and NASCAR officials watched Curtis Turner lead every lap at an event in Concord, North Carolina. There was a caution two laps before the end of the race, slowing the cars down. When the race resumed, Petty sped around Turner. Turner was certain Petty was a full lap behind and so was everyone else, including the officials who flagged Turner the winner, Speedy Thompson second, and Petty third.

Then Petty protested, and France reviewed the scorecards. Four days later he announced Petty was the winner. Turner angrily responded: "The entire audience of 12,000 and other competitors know the real outcome."[1] And he said he knew how the race was stolen and who did it: "That Mama Elizabeth has the fastest pencil in NASCAR."[2]

If Turner was upset, Speedy Thompson was furious. Thompson had finished second but was bumped down to third by France's decision, losing $175 in prize money. It was not the loss of the money that Thompson objected to so much as the fact that the race outcomes could be sabotaged and stolen by behind the scenes manipulation. Threatening to quit racing, he pointed out, "If they can whip you once like this and get away with it, they'll do it again."[3]

Less than one year later, at the 1959 Daytona 500, the Beauchamp pit crew believed they were the victims of an almost identical injustice.

And it didn't stop there. Four months later, on June 14, 1959, in Atlanta, there was yet another bizarre scoring occurrence. The contest was loaded with top competitors: Lee Petty, Richard Petty, Buck Baker, Curtis Turner, Jack Smith, and Fireball Roberts. In addition, Bob Burdick, who had completed his military duty, piloted his father's 1959 T-bird, the same car that Beauchamp had driven at Daytona. Tiny Lund was there, too, behind the wheel of a 1957 Chevrolet convertible.

The race was chaotic, and officials stopped it twice because of dust. This was precisely the kind of event—with limited visibility and interrupted racing—that encouraged dishonesty and errors with scoring. After other drivers suffered wrecks and mechanical failures, Richard Petty grabbed first place, followed by his father, Lee Petty.

Young Richard was jubilant because the victory came on his twenty-first birthday, and it was his first win. Fans, particularly young fans, crowded around their new hero. He signed autographs and basked in his triumph and newfound popularity. But his success was short lived.

Richard's own father, Lee, protested the outcome, claiming he had one more lap than his son and demanding that the scorecards be checked. Flagman Johnny Bruner examined the scorecards and found that, indeed, Lee Petty had one more lap than officials believed. Though usually not involved in the details of the competition, Donna Richter, Beauchamp's longtime companion, was still angry over the Daytona race and chastised Lee Petty: "You are so bad; you even take races away from your son."[4]

Lee Petty defended himself by arguing that his son should "earn" his victory. "This wouldn't be the right way for him to get his first victory."[5] The reality was that Lee's winning earned $100 more than Richard's victory. NASCAR paid this extra amount if the winner was driving a current model, and Lee Petty was driving a 1959 Plymouth while his son was driving a 1957 Oldsmobile. Lee Petty's protest earned an extra $100.

His son seemed not to mind. One hour after being acclaimed the victor, Richard was told he had not won after all. Admiring teenagers then asked Richard who won. "Either Pop or me," he answered with a smile.[6]

"Where's Lee?" asked a bystander.

"Over there wherever the money is," laughed Richard. "Don't get me wrong, I'd like to win this one . . . but Pop said he won and he's been in this game about fifteen more years than I have. I'll have to take his word for it."[7]

NASCAR officials must have noted that Lee Petty's scorecard kept showing up with one more lap than people thought it should have; sometimes it happened under the radar, with Petty protesting to get a slightly improved finish, such as from fourth to third.

The following season, the circumstances appeared to be a rerun of previous lap-counting problems. In this case, on April 24, 1960, at Weaverville, North Carolina, in a 200-lap race, Petty had been declared the winner, but veteran driver Joe Johnson was certain Petty did not have as many laps as he claimed. As in early similar situations, officials examined the scorecards and declared Petty the winner.[8]

By June 1960, anyone paying attention to auto racing was aware that during the previous two years, Petty in four races had protested his loss and succeeded in being named the official winner. In one of these, the Daytona 500, his strange surge to the front sent rumors of cheating swirling through the pit crews. The reaction in each instance suggested that something was amiss, that Petty had not won, even though the lap count said otherwise.

In part because of the four high profile races in which Elizabeth Petty's scoring apparently worked to her husband's advantage, there was a steady undercurrent of rumor. Jim Reed, a New York driver who raced NASCAR with considerable success, said he told his girlfriend that when she scored she should watch his car with one eye, counting every lap, and with her other eye, "she should watch Elizabeth Petty at all times."[9]

At one point around the time of the 1959 Daytona, Holman-Moody—the well-known Ford racing organization—became so disgusted that it took action, setting up a second lap-counting operation. The company hired the accounting firm of Price Waterhouse to count laps to dramatize the problem. Price Waterhouse only watched NASCAR scoring for a few races, and it found no counting errors.[10]

Nevertheless, everyone remained reluctant to confront the problem. Even many years later, when one of the highly regarded old drivers was asked about the rumor of Elizabeth Petty adding laps, there was a pause but no answer to the question.[11]

One son of an old driver was asked, without mentioning any aspect of the Petty lap-counting issue, if there was ever a race his father believed he had won, but—after the scorers counted the laps—he hadn't won. The son innocently replied, "There was one race when my father was positive he had won, but the other driver, when the laps were counted, won. That other driver was Lee Petty."[12] Others familiar with the racing of the era agreed with what Wanda Lund said: "I believe at some point the rumor was that Elizabeth Petty was caught adding laps to Lee's total."[13]

Petty's suspected activities posed a problem for Bill France. He was not going to allow scorers to manipulate an event. And as racing became more important and visible to the press, France had to clean things up. He could not permit race fixing. By the time of the April 1960 Weaverville contest, the evidence and rumors associated with lap counting were probably becoming too apparent for France to ignore. France had to stop the trouble to protect his organization's reputation.

France's opportunity came on June 19, 1960, and he hammered Lee Petty with a hornswoggler's stealth. The event was the first World 600 on Charlotte's new 1.5-mile oval.

After the exhausting drive from Iowa, Beauchamp, accompanied by Donna and his son William, arrived in Charlotte, and as William Beauchamp recalls, attempted to check in at the Miracle Hotel. The clerk refused to give them towels to use for showering. Beauchamp argued back. The clerk pulled a gun, calling them white trash, and then with a knife partially concealed, stepped out from behind the counter and gave them the towels. It was a rude welcoming to Charlotte, North Carolina.[14]

In the race, Johnny Beauchamp finished second, winning $9,110, and Tiny Lund secured $1,350 for eighth. But of greater significance was what happened to the Pettys.

Prior to the contest, competition director Norris Friel called a meeting of the drivers, warning them that cars must enter the pits only on the special pit chute (pit road) and drivers who did not enter on the pit road chute would be penalized.[15] The reason for the rule was that driving on the dirt infield would cause blinding dust.

On about lap 100, Richard and Lee Petty both had problems and cut across the infield to their pits. Four other drivers also violated the rule: Bob Welborn, Junior Johnson, Paul Lewis, and Al White. Officials permitted all six violators to continue, only telling them about the penalty for their infraction after the race: no points and no money for the race.

Lee Petty and NASCAR officials disagreed about what happened next. NASCAR officials Johnny Bruner and Norris Friel said they decided on the penalty soon after the race and informed Petty. Later, Lee Petty denied that he was told about the infraction and the penalty.

A closer inspection reveals the Pettys were the only drivers for whom the penalty constituted a substantial punishment. Of the other four violators, Welborn managed the highest finish, sixteenth, and so he lost $400. The other three finished far out of the money and points and consequently had little to lose.

The situation was entirely different for the Pettys. Richard and Lee had finished fourth and fifth, respectively, according to their lap cards. Together, they would have received prize money of over $6,000, and they would have earned substantial points toward the season championship. In fact, the loss of the points doomed father and son's chance for the season title, valued by some observers at $100,000.[16]

The evidence that this penalty represents France's move to punish the Pettys for their rumored cheating lies in its severity. France could have punished the Pettys less harshly by penalizing the violators only one or two laps. They would have lost some money and points, but not everything.[17] Furman Bisher, an Atlanta sportswriter, observed that one Charlotte newspaper launched a massive defense on behalf of the Pettys because of the harsh punishment.[18]

Why take this subtle approach to asserting his power? A plausible explanation is that France could not openly discredit the Pettys for adding laps because that would have cast all the previous race outcomes into doubt. Plus, the entire NASCAR operation would have been disgraced. Severely punishing the Pettys for an infraction that all drivers were told would get them penalized was a cunning move.

Indeed, after the Charlotte race, the problem of Petty's laps not agreeing with the officials' count did not occur again. For Johnny Beauchamp, Curtis Turner, Speedy Thompson, Joe Johnson, and others, though, putting a stop to the lap-counting problems came too late.

There were no eyewitness claiming to have seen laps added to a scorecard at any of these races, and no one is likely to step forward to tell what happened. Few people were privy to the scoring protests, so it would have been easy to keep the scandal quiet. On the other hand, examining the entire stream of evidence suggests where the truth lies, and the evidence in its totality is powerful. Often in historical research, there is no eyewitness or document that offers proof beyond the shadow of doubt. Professor Annette Gordon-Reed[19] writes, "There are not many things in the world where you can look at one thing to totally prove the case. It's [instead] the totality of the circumstances."[20]

Months after the Daytona 500, Beauchamp told Petty, "You just as well admit you didn't win. You know you didn't win."

Petty replied, "Yeah, but I got the money."[21]

Beauchamp had something to prove after the 1959 Daytona race. He announced, "I've been thinking about shooting for NASCAR's grand national championship. I expect Lee Petty is the man to beat."[1] Beauchamp's problem was that he didn't have a race car. Bob Burdick, who had completed his military service, was back driving his father's Thunderbird.[2] So Beauchamp bought from Delta Airlines pilot Beau Morgan the Thunderbird that Tim Flock drove at Daytona,[3] and he had Holman-Moody tune the car. Promoters, eager to capitalize on the Harlan driver's fame, promised him appearance money, cash sometimes given to a star driver to boost the sizzle of a contest, to renew his rivalry with Petty at the March 22 race at the Atlanta Lakewood track, a major southern venue that had hosted such stars as Barney Oldfield. Beauchamp led the entire race, was never challenged for the lead, and by the end had lapped every NASCAR driver. It was a big win, but the Thunderbird required repairs, and he sold it. He was back to looking for a car to drive.

Beauchamp also continued to explore methods of earning money outside of racing. In 1959 he had finally turned his love of antiques into a business, opening on North Broadway in Council Bluffs a co-owned antique store, the Frontier Trading Post. The store had guns, old windup record players, coins, and a large range of other items. Donna Richter, his longtime girl friend, worked in the store.

Amidst the antiques, the store became a gathering place for the Beauchamp children. Sanda played among the old clocks, record players, and furniture, while Bob, who worked at a barber shop a few doors away from Frontier Trading Post, visited during his lunch hour and after work. In some respects, the store underscored and increased Beauchamp's dilemma: on the one hand his roots, family, and racing support were in the Midwest, but on the other hand, his opportunities to win money in NASCAR races were at tracks 1,000 miles away.

Promoter Ed Otto gave Beauchamp his next opportunity: a race at the famed Polo Grounds in New York, the former home of the New York Giants baseball team, now relocated to California. Otto promised Beauchamp $500 for an appearance,[4] even locating a car for him to drive—Jim Reed's backup Ford. Otto paid Reed bonus money for his help, and Beauchamp in a separate agreement with Reed promised not to challenge him for the win.[5] For Beauchamp it was about the excitement of racing at the Polo Grounds and the money. While the stock car drivers were dealing in hundreds of dollars, Willie Shoemaker won $5,000 on a horse named Sword Dancer in a preliminary race leading up to the Kentucky Derby.[6]

Around 15,000 fans and twenty NASCAR drivers were at the Polo Grounds for the April 25, 200-lap, 50-mile event. Reed suggested that Beauchamp scuff up his right front tire before the race to help make the car corner better. On the first lap Beauchamp darted into the lead. After 6 laps, as planned, he yielded to Reed, who proceeded to lap the entire field. At the finish, Beauchamp and Speedy Thompson, in second and third place respectively, were far behind.[7] Lee Petty and Rex White battled it out for fourth and fifth with Cotton Owens in sixth. The following day, Beauchamp brought Reed's car to Reading, Pennsylvania, for another race, but the brakes failed midway through the contest, ending his hope for a good finish.[8]

Beauchamp persisted in his efforts to gain a foothold in NASCAR. On May 3, 1958, he drove a Beau Morgan–owned 1957 Chevy at the Virginia 500. The Martinsville Speedway, on the NASCAR schedule since the opening 1948 season, was two drag strips with difficult turnarounds. The modest, 12-degree banking on the sharp corners forced the drivers to slow down on the curves and promoted a fender-banging show. It was a difficult contest that replicated February's Daytona 500 finish: Lee Petty first, Beauchamp second, the latter winning $1,625.

Although Beauchamp entered several other NASCAR events in 1959, he spent most of the remainder of his time in Iowa. He had neglected several matters in his quest to win in the South. He was concerned about his sons' future ability to earn money. He believed a barber would always have an income, and so he pulled his eldest son, Robert, away from his summer job as a community lifeguard before his senior year to go to barber school. Because barber school extended a few weeks after Harlan High School began, Robert almost was not admitted to begin his final year and did miss a chance to play football. But because Beauchamp was racing farther away from Harlan the summer before William's senior year; he escaped his father's close supervision and became the starting quarterback, attending barber school the following year.

Beauchamp's 1959 foray into NASCAR competition told an interesting story. Although he had a big second-place finish at the Daytona 500, another second at the important Virginia 500, and a convincing win in the historic Lakewood race in Atlanta—these successes alone enough to rank him high in the final season standings—NASCAR did not mention him. He was an outsider, considered an outlaw for not driving exclusively in NASCAR, so the association deprived him of the points he had earned. As far as Bill France's organization was concerned, Beauchamp scarcely had been there.

The Flying Frenchman began the 1960 season behind the wheel of a Holman-Moody Ford, a good circumstance because this garage maintained a fleet of race cars.[9] Unfortunately, at Daytona during a preliminary event, he became involved in a pileup. His car wrecked, and he was eliminated from the big race. But Beauchamp did have an exceptional moment during the NASCAR Speed Weeks.

Autolite, a spark plug manufacturer, sponsored a 4-lap contest, taped and shown later by NBC,[10] for the six fastest cars in time trials that used its plugs.[11] Such factory events were part of the hoopla. At stake in the Autolite demonstration event was a $1,000 purse, with the winner to be interviewed by Dave Garroway on the *Today* show. Ned Jarrett recalls that "all I wanted to do was win so I could get on television."[12]

Jarrett almost won, but Beauchamp edged him out. In the Daytona track infield, *Today* set up a display of standard engine parts and racing parts. With the camera running, the winner of the race explained to Garroway the comparison between standard production car parts and race car parts and the importance of various parts for the speed of a race car.[13] Not being a mechanic, Beauchamp faked his way through the interview. He looked good on the small screen. Dale Swanson Jr. recalled that as a teenager, "I thought he was Elvis Presley."[14] *Today* aired the Beauchamp interview on Monday, February 15, 1960.

The Burdicks were all involved in the 1960 Daytona 500. Bud, driving the 1959 T-Bird, finished eleventh out of sixty-eight drivers in the race, but Bob had mechanical issues and completed only 31 laps. Roy, while at Daytona, attended a banquet and to his surprise, Lee Petty arrived and sat down across from him. Roy said to Lee: "Lee, did you really win that Daytona 500 last year?" Lee replied: "I got the money."[15]

At the end of that month, Beauchamp drove the Holman-Moody 1960 Ford one last time at the Charlotte Fairgrounds. He had the third-fastest time trial, but as in Daytona, was caught in a wreck and became one of fourteen cars not to finish. After this bad luck, his fortunes turned even worse. Although the automobile factories claimed to be not supporting stock car racing, help was still flowing profusely through many secondary product manufacturers and suppliers of products such as motor oil, tires, seat belts, spark plugs, and every imaginable auto part. Beauchamp had support from Champion spark plugs, and since Holman-Moody was using Autolite spark plugs, the latter company did not want a driver who had endorsed a competitor's product. The Harlan driver had, in the parlance of race-talk, "lost his ride."[16]

Beauchamp left for Iowa. Upon his arrival, he had time to focus on his business venture and what he found was unsettling. He believed his partner in the Frontier Trading Post had made bad bargains buying merchandise, so he closed the business. His first major effort to earn money outside of racing had met with a setback. But he planned another campaign into NASCAR territory, and when he returned to the South, he would be driving a Swanson 1960 Chevrolet.

Swanson smelled the cash, and so he prepared a car for the inaugural race on June 19 at Curtis Turner's big new Charlotte Superspeedway. The first World 600, held on this 1.5 mile paved track, had attracted sixty cars competing for a $27,150 first place prize, more money than Bill France offered at his Daytona 500. The 600-mile race was a constant turmoil of dust, crashes, and car trouble, but Beauchamp finished second, earning a purse of over $9,000. Swanson and Beauchamp left the South with plans to return for a second assault.

The Harlan pair arrived in the South on July 31 for eight NASCAR races. The car had mechanical problems in three; Beauchamp won in Nashville; and he finished fifth, eighth, ninth, and twelfth in other races. Entering only eleven events during the season, Beauchamp finished eleventh in the NASCAR point standings.

After their strong 1960 showing despite racing only a limited NASCAR schedule, Beauchamp and Swanson believed they had an opportunity in 1961 to surge to the top. Even NASCAR appeared to embrace the idea that Beauchamp was a threat by putting his photo in the program as a star for the 1961 Daytona Speed Weeks. Swanson prepared a new Chevrolet, sporting the familiar 73 that was Beauchamp's number in NASCAR.

In the 40-lap qualifier, Beauchamp found himself directly behind Lee Petty's car, both vehicles rocketing at 150 miles an hour around the Daytona speedway's steeply banked curve. The Harlan driver was still angry about their 1959 contest and had told his racing buddy, Bud Burdick, "I'm going to get that sonofabitch."[17] Suddenly, Petty slowed. Beauchamp, with a split second to react, jammed his foot on the brake before slamming into the rear of Petty's car, sending Petty toward a flimsy guardrail and a forty-foot drop off the track. Beauchamp, smooth and patient, may have been waiting for an opportunity to settle the score with Lee Petty. On the other hand, the Petty-Beauchamp wreck could have been an accident. Petty had been directly in front of Beauchamp in other races since the disputed 1959 event, and Beauchamp had done nothing. Moreover, at these speeds, any wreck was much more than mere jolt.

A microsecond later, Beauchamp realized his front bumper had latched onto Petty's back bumper and that his rival was pulling him toward the precipice. The steep bank of the curve served as a ramp to launch both cars into the air. Turning upside down as he soared off the track, Beauchamp braced for the hard landing. At this speed and plunging from this height, death was likely. The two cars almost landed on the small building where Bill France's wife, Annie, worked.[18] Few people believed either driver would live. Petty's car was said to look like a pretzel.

The first medical news reported both men were seriously injured: Petty with a punctured lung, fractures, and broken bones, and Beauchamp with head injuries. After one day, the story changed. Both were badly banged up, but their situation was not as critical as first believed. In the hospital, Beauchamp rested comfortably one floor above Petty. After the first reports, the press updates focused on Petty and said little about Beauchamp.

Even though the accident wasn't as bad as it might have been, when Beauchamp was released from the hospital, he was not in good condition. Donna and eleven-year-old Sanda Beauchamp had remained in Daytona after the wreck, and they all made the long return trip to Iowa. The wounded warrior stopped at motels every night to rest. Beauchamp suffered from cracked ribs, an injured eye, an aching back, and a pinched nerve. His recovery was not immediate. Several months after the crash, at his home, he passed out while walking to the mailbox. Still recovering, he married Donna on May 5 while they were visiting Cañon City, Colorado.

In the months and years after the wreck, according to the much-repeated story, Petty raced a few more times and Beauchamp never raced again. If these accounts consider only NASCAR events as racing, then it is true.

Back in Harlan, not long after the disastrous wreck, Beauchamp walked into the Swanson garage. Swanson pulled his head out from under a car hood and asked Beauchamp, "Before you say anything else, I want to know if you deliberately plowed into the back of Petty."[19]

Beauchamp replied, "No, it all happened too fast. I had no time to do anything."[20]

Later, sipping a beer with Fred Miller, who had raced the first Playland season in 1950, Beauchamp said, "It is too fast on those super-speedways." Then he told Miller he was not going back to NASCAR because "a few of those NASCAR drivers might go after me on the track."[21]

But "Beauchamp," as Bill Smith reflected, "raced to live." Beauchamp, his income largely from racing, was back behind the wheel on July 1, finishing sixth at a Knoxville, Illinois, IMCA event. He entered at least twelve races that year.

In 1962 Beauchamp was back competing in IMCA, driving a Swanson car. The Harlan duo had one big win on July 8 at the Des Moines, Iowa, Fairgrounds. But Swanson, as in several other race seasons, opted for a part-time schedule. Beauchamp needed to race all the time to earn a living, so he began searching for another race car and mechanic. Peoria, Illinois–based mechanic Wally Satterfield saw his opportunity. His car had had only modest results while competing in IMCA, but with Beauchamp as his driver, the prospects appeared much better. Beauchamp, dividing his driving almost evenly between Swanson and Satterfield, entered twenty-five IMCA contests in 1962 and finished eleventh in the season standings.

Swanson, meanwhile, pared back his racing activity even more; the grueling weekly diet of races at distant tracks ended. However, in 1962 he won the Minneapolis Gopher 350 with Sonny Morgan the driver. In later years, his garage entered a car at the nearby Denison, Iowa, track; his sons, Dale Jr., Richard, and Kim, helped with the mechanical work; and in 1968 the Swanson magic once again won a track championship, this time for his new local driver, Bill Wrich, dubbed "king-of-the-highbanks."[22] Dale Sr.

then sold the race car, remaining even further behind the scenes. In the early 1970s his son Richard, born in 1947, raced a Camero stock car in the Harlan area and became a winner.

Eventually, Dale Swanson would say that he dabbled in racing, calling it "hobby racing."[23] Instead of racing, he concentrated on his expanding business ventures. The 1962 opening of a man-made lake, Prairie Rose, near Harlan suggested many more local people would need a boat, a motor for the boat, and repair work on the boat motor. Swanson was ready: he had applied for a contract to represent Johnson Outboard Marine products, which he secured in 1956. Then, in 1964 he moved his automotive and marine business from the little garage on Fifth Street South to a larger facility on a main highway on the outskirts of Harlan, agreeing to the bank's requirement that he tend to business and not have an extensive racing schedule.[24]

In 1965 Beauchamp shifted his racing activities eastward, still driving for Satterfield. Usually, they raced in Peoria, Illinois, and Davenport, Iowa. At Davenport, his friend Mel Krueger recalled that the track promoters gave Beauchamp appearance money, and all he had to do was "just show up at the Davenport track and drive." In 1965 Peoria Speedway had moved to Farmington Road from its Pioneer Park location. There, Beauchamp finished fifth in the season standings, high enough to be labeled the "outstanding driver of the year." Satterfield's assistant summed it up: "He was quiet, but he loved to race."[25]

In 1966 Beauchamp won the season championship at the Peoria Speedway. Living, at this time, in Atlantic, Iowa, he made many trips to eastern Iowa and Illinois during the racing season. John and Donna would arrive at the Satterfields' house with steaks and spend the night in warm hospitality. They all became good friends.

Peoria race historians reported that it was said of Beauchamp that he was a driver of great natural ability and a deserving champion.

T he story of the great racers from Harlan must include what happened to Tiny Lund. After almost being killed in his first NASCAR race in 1955, he borrowed the money to buy a 1956 Pontiac that was built into a new race car with the help of Robert McKee.[1] In 1956 McKee, Lund, and Ruthie, Lund's wife, left for NASCAR and South Carolina. In twenty-one races, the Harlan driver managed one top five finish and eight top ten finishes, earning only small amounts of money.

With so little success, Lund's first effort to conquer NASCAR was a sad debacle: the car was repossessed because he failed to make his payments. Since Lund could not support his mechanic, McKee left and eventually went to work for Ray Nichols, whose garage built Cotton Owens's winning 1957 Daytona Beach car. McKee went on to have a distinguished career as an automotive designer.

Despite the massive setback, Lund would not be stopped. He loved to race, and he pulled together his grit for a second southern invasion. Later during 1956, he and one of his many friends, Kenny "Red" Myler of Missouri Valley, Iowa, again left for NASCAR. Lund, with Myler's assistance, finished the season driving for owner Gus Holzmueller, based in Cincinnati, Ohio. But Lund had no better fortune with Holzmueller's car than with his own.[2]

Between 1957 and 1962, Lund had fifteen more top five finishes and thirty-six top ten finishes, but again they earned him little money. By 1960 he appeared to be withdrawing from NASCAR's top division, Grand National, entering only eight events.

The years on the road were difficult. He would sleep in the car near a motel, and when a guest left early in the morning, he would sneak into the room, shower, and sleep in the bed. When he could, he would bunk in with other people. Part of Lund's problem was that, although he was thirty years old, he behaved like a teenager. Rex White, who had pulled together a serious racing team in hopes of winning a 1960 championship, finally had to encourage Tiny to spend less time in his garage because "Tiny was always cutting up and fooling around. He distracted everyone from the work."[3]

Lund had another problem, too, the same old one that had frustrated Swanson—Tiny was a "hard charger." He seemed deliberately to aim for the deep holes on the tracks. He needlessly banged and battled with the other cars. Many people over the years told Lund, "Tiny, you could break an anvil."[4] A car owner and a mechanic did not appreciate a driver ruining the equipment. Owners preferred pilots who were careful with the car out on the track and therefore were reluctant to let Lund get behind the wheel.

In the midst of this adversity, Lund signed a long-term lease for a fish camp in South Carolina.[5] The camp was primitive. Larry Frank, one of Lund's closest pals, rigged up a bucket system so Ruthie could take a shower. Eventually, Lund had six house trailers and one small cabin on the property. At a minimum, this camp ended the precarious road life for Ruthie and gave her a place to live while Lund disappeared for weeks of racing.[6]

Frank "bottle" fished with Lund and "stood back-to-back with Tiny in bar room fights."[7] Marvin Panch remarked, "Frank, although not a big man, was about the only person Lund could not beat in a fight."[8] Once, Lund and Frank were arrested on a moonshine run, and Tiny became upset because he had never spent a night in jail. Frank graciously said he would take the jail night if Lund would call to make the bail arrangements.

By January 1963, Ruthie Lund was weary of the hardship of the fish camp and her husband's neglect. Ruthie now had another option, because her first husband had been released from prison and was available. Lund, with a few dollars in his pocket, departed for the 1963 Daytona 500. He had no car to drive in the big race and was suffering from trench mouth, a painful infection of the gums.[9]

On February 10, ten days before the race, Lund's luck changed. Marvin Panch, scheduled to drive for the Wood brothers, was test driving on the big track. The Ford factory had installed one of its stock car engines in a Maserati, hoping that with this car Panch would break records. Instead, the car went airborne, sliding and bouncing down the track, coming to a stop upside down. Panch undid his seat belt, but he was trapped inside because the doors opened upward and the car was upside down. And he saw flames.

Five men—Bill Wimble, Ernie Gahan, Jerry Rayburn, Steve Petrasek, and Lund—rushed to the car. As they struggled to free Panch, the car exploded and the force pushed the men back. One of the men, Steve Petrasek said, "He's still kicking boys—let's go get him."[10] Petrasek temporarily lost his eyesight and burned both his hands lifting the blazing car. Lund pulled Panch out of the car. Panch was forever grateful to the five men who risked their lives. Lund happened to be the most well-known of the rescuers, but all five received Carnegie medals for their heroism.[11]

Panch's misfortune meant that the Wood brothers needed to find a new driver for the Daytona race. They decided to ask Tiny, and they emphasized that his role in the rescue had little to do with the selection, but that Lund was the best available driver. Tiny Lund, although without a win in 134 NASCAR races, was recognized as always a threat. The Wood brothers visited Panch in the hospital and told him that Tiny Lund was going to drive the car, and Panch approved.

Lund finished sixth in the 100-mile qualifier, and he started twelfth in the Daytona 500. The Wood brothers had set the gears of the car so it had less speed but would have better gas mileage. Their plan was for Lund to make fewer pit stops for gas than the faster competitors, who would burn up more gas and wear out their tires.

A strategy to win based on going slow frustrated a hard charger like Tiny Lund, but he had no choice—his car lacked speed. Driving out of character, Lund took care of the car and behaved himself on the track. Larry Frank remembers "drafting" with Tiny, but Lund was not fast, and "I finally drove on."[12] He lingered near the front, even leading for 5 laps. Nevertheless, he did not appear fast enough to win.

With only 10 laps remaining, Lund was in third place, unable to outrun first and second. But the Wood brothers suspected Fred Lorenzen and Ned Jarrett, both ahead of Lund, did not have enough gas to make it to the end of the race without a pit stop. Running in third, Lund could win the Daytona 500. As Jarrett and Lorenzen dropped out, Lund on lap 193 moved into first. He cruised in first place for 7 laps and then coasted across the finish line, out of gas, first. The hard charger had won the biggest race of his life with a slow, gas mileage strategy.[13]

Tiny Lund, although his marriage had ended, found his racing career soaring. After winning the big race, mechanics offered him better cars to drive, and he finished races closer to the front. In the midst of the revival of his good fortune, a Michigan factory was prepared to back Lund with support and a new car. He boarded a plane for Detroit to seal the deal. On the flight he celebrated his good fortune with drink—too much drink, and too much flirting with a female flight attendant. The two left together when the plane landed and continued the party. Tiny missed his appointment and lost his opportunity for factory backing. His irresponsible behavior had again cost him one of his best opportunities.[14]

Lund, nevertheless, was a success in the NASCAR division immediately below Grand National. In the Grand American division, a "pony" division in which the cars had less power, he was a three time champion between 1968 and 1972,[15] winning 41 of 109 races.[16] He was selected the most popular driver four years in a row in the pony Grand Touring/American circuit.[17]

As his NASCAR career began to decline in the 1970s, Lund remained a big hit at the short tracks. He was a favorite at a Jacksonville, Florida, oval. After the competition, Tiny would give the kids rides around the track for as long as they wanted. He drank deeply of life and had improbable experiences. In 1963, fishing in Lake Moultrie, he caught a 55-pound striped bass. This catch broke the record for South Carolina, and there were those who could not believe such a catch was possible. Yet he seemed always to manage the impossible. A few years later, in 1967, the film *Hard Charger*, with Tiny Lund the focus of the documentary, was shown briefly in movie houses across the nation. He appeared on the network television program *What's My Line* and in the Elvis Presley film, *Speedway* (1968). Lund was a celebrity.

EPILOGUE

The Playland track is gone. The asphalt oval became a grassy park; for many years the faint outline of the track remained visible.[1] Looking over the grounds, those who remember the track may imagine they hear the roar of engines and cars banging and rolling. They may even imagine Johnny Beauchamp battling Bud Burdick.

The track fell to the winds of progress. In 1964 a new bridge stretching across the Missouri River, part of the interstate highway system, replaced the Ak-sar-ben Bridge. To make room for the highway changes, the roller coaster was torn down. The amusement park property was condemned. All that remained were twenty acres, enough for the track, the stadium complex, and twelve amusement rides. In 1966 the track, like its drivers, fought back with a full schedule of racing.

In 1970 Abe Slusky, the operator and owner of the facility since 1948, died at the age of 59 of a heart attack. What was left of the amusement park closed, but still the competition continued. The racing finally ended in 1977, a victim of progress and the loss of leadership. The scene of Beauchamp, Swanson, and Lund's great beginning disappeared.

Tiny Lund, Playland's first champion, died on August 17, 1975. He had raced twenty-five more years after his first championship at the Playland track. Lund won his last race August 13, 1975, at Summerville, South Carolina. He was competing in Savannah, Georgia, two days later, when his car blew an engine. On Saturday night, August 16, he finished fifth at Hickory, North Carolina. The winner of that race, Butch Lindley, recalls that Tiny "was physically wore out, just really run down so bad that you wouldn't believe it was Tiny."[2]

Lund then went to Talladega, Alabama—the 2.6 mile super-speedway tri-oval. Lindley believed "Tiny needed the money. He was down there at Talladega trying to make money."[3] Lund told his mechanic, Roger Byers, "I do not want to go to Talladega." But Tiny had promised the owner, A. J. King, he would drive the car, even though he believed the 1974 Dodge was not good enough to perform well.[4]

Forty-five-year-old Tiny Lund, his racing career in a downward spiral, was going to race the biggest and most dangerous track in NASCAR. He departed in driver Bobby Allison's plane for Alabama after the Saturday night Hickory race.

Lund started thirty-first out of fifty competitors, and on lap 7 he saw an opening to squeeze in between J. D. McDuffie's vehicle and the wall. But his car went into a spin and stalled sideways in the middle of the track. Terry Link, a rookie, came out of the dust and dirt, spinning out of control and into the driver's side of Lund's car—a broadside or a "T-bone." Lund died instantly of severe internal injuries. He won $620.[5]

Tiny Lund's funeral at Saint Michael's Lutheran Church at Monck's Corner in South Carolina overflowed with mourners. Loudspeakers brought the service inside the church to the throng outside. They ran out of room to put the flowers and so the family finally told the florist to stop bringing them. Lund had touched many people, usually with fun, good times, and generosity. They remembered him on this day.[6]

Dale Swanson, always exhausted during the long racing seasons, finally found relief when doctors discovered he had a heart problem that was fixed with an operation. But there was no return to the glory days. As the motor magician's later years swept by, he was increasingly ignored and forgotten. Swanson dropped in more frequently to see his old friend Gussie, who owned the Chicken Hut restaurant and operated a tavern on the Harlan square. He had helped her father baling hay sixty years earlier.

The new generation of race competitors rarely thought to consult Swanson about how to make their cars go faster. He had many tricks, but no one asked. Swanson would visit Randy Rath's auto supply store in nearby Denison and reminisce about the old days and lament the minimum clout he now had. Rath recognized that Swanson had exceptional native intelligence and "the common sense to figure how to make a car faster."[7] Once, Swanson advised a young mechanic that the weight on his race car was distributed wrong. The mechanic ignored Swanson's advice, and the car rolled over during the race. Swanson was left to make his boat go faster, which he did.[8]

In 1989, at age seventy-one, Swanson, not ready to sit back and rest on any laurels, still strived for more success. He purchased the defunct drive-in movie property near his business. No one, including members of his family, was certain this was a wise move. Still a man of vision, he believed condominiums could be built on the property. Ultimately, he put the land to use to store his inventory of boats.

Meanwhile, Swanson delighted in his grandson's accomplishments. Ken Swanson, Dale Jr.'s son, had grown up in the family business. He raced modified cars and learned mechanics. Ken left for the South in 1994, building engines that raced in NASCAR, and in 2002 he built the motor that won the Daytona 500.

In January 1996, Dale Swanson was dying. Dale Jr. and his brother Kim were running the business. Dale Jr. asked his father one more time whether he had figured out the reason for the problem with the fuel injection of the 1957 Chevrolet. The father assured his son that what he had said before was all true and exactly as he had told it.[9] The next day, January 28, Dale Swanson died.

Some years later, at a racing convention, Dale Jr. saw Smokey Yunick, who had been on good terms with Dale Swanson. Yunick had claimed he was the one who discovered the pressure problem with the fuel injection system. When Dale Jr. asked Yunick about his claim, Yunick replied, "I can't remember—it's so long ago."[10]

The years were sweeping away the truth. All that remained was an imperfect memory of what had occurred. The problem was what to do with the truth, and often, under the guidance of NASCAR, writers, if they even knew the truth, applied the questionable axiom, "When the legend becomes fact, print the legend."[11]

Legend was slowly pushing Swanson and Beauchamp out of their just place in history.

Swanson did live long enough to see the completion of a dominant late model racing association. In the first two decades after the Second World War, there was near parity among racing associations that slowly gave way to NASCAR dominance.[12]

Several factors helped Bill France ramrod his way to the top. First, although not caused by anything France did, NASCAR became identified as the stock car association with what eventually was called a super-speedway. The idea for a big, high-banked track was that of Harold Brasington, and he built one in 1950 at Darlington, South Carolina. Brasington's 1.3 mile track and dream of a 500-mile race was not instantly accepted by France. France was not certain he even wanted to associate with the Darlington track. In fact, for a time it appeared France was going to be outmaneuvered by Brasington and perhaps other attractive venues that the founder of NASCAR did not control.[13] The tail was wagging the dog. Eventually, NASCAR held races at Darlington, and ultimately Darlington, then Daytona almost ten years later, followed by other, bigger speedway tracks, gave NASCAR unique racing venues. The one-half mile, unbanked dirt tracks of the IMCA summer fair could not match the velocity and thrills of the super-speedways.

A second factor that gave NASCAR an edge was that it was based in the South, where warmer weather than in the Midwest allowed it to stay in business about nine months of the year. A third factor that propelled NASCAR to dominance was the changing technology of mass media. CBS Sports Spectacular aired a part of the 1960 Daytona 500, and then, in 1961 and 1962, ABC covered several races, but it was cable television and its need for programming that yielded lucrative deals beginning in 1981 with ESPN.

The winners of wars write the historical record of right and wrong; similarly here, the story gradually became that all great racing and great drivers were associated with NASCAR. The early NASCAR racers became transformed into legend that often defied reality.

The wild, hard-drinking, hell-raising, impoverished NASCAR competitors became fed up, died, or too old for racing. NASCAR's pioneers, almost to the man, had worked for little money and had come away at the end with scarcely anything. These people raced for the love of the sport and because they didn't know any other way to make money; only a small proportion became prosperous by racing. The ruthless, arbitrary, and sometimes unfair actions of NASCAR lingered like ghosts in the wind. Bill France became extremely wealthy.

Johnny Beauchamp remained in the Midwest. After the 1966 Peoria season championship, he was forty-two years old.[14] Men raced in their forties,[15] but Beauchamp's back was racked with pain, much of it from the banging up when going over the wall with Petty.[16] He may have raced occasionally after 1966, but his glory days were gone. Over the years, he had attempted several other ventures to make money. His wife Donna reminisced, "John always had some money-making business going on."[17] None of his efforts to make money were especially successful. Beauchamp was exceptionally good at only one thing: auto racing. One evening, John and Donna went with friends to the Chicken Hut. The parking lot was full of cars. The only open space was between the iron poles that held the store sign high in the air. John, driving, said, "I can park here." He wheeled his car between the signs, barely an inch to spare, and he didn't have to maneuver the car. Norma Brix said, "It was amazing."[18]

While racing, he was known as Johnny Beauchamp. His friends said that was his "stage" name, and they mostly called him John, though occasionally he was called J.D. (from John David). By 1967 the racing was almost over, and Johnny Beauchamp transitioned to John Beauchamp. Instead of driving a race car, he drove a school bus. He lived in a mobile home on a small acreage near Atlantic, Iowa. Donna recalls that John always liked animals and that he maintained goats and other barnyard creatures.[19] When races were on television, John turned his entire attention to the screen. Nothing disturbed his watching the races.

During racing season, he found a way to be at the track. He managed the Audubon, Iowa, facility and was also the flagman at the Des Moines track. His friend, Don Brix, who often accompanied him to the races during the glory years, still went with him, but now Brix assisted with the management of races.[20]

Beauchamp's son, Robert Beauchamp, told his father he felt like he might be able to drive a race car. John advised his son, "I believe I would try something else."[21] In later years, both of his sons lived in Reno, Nevada. John and his son William bought a duplex in Reno, yet another of his investment ventures.

John and Donna visited Reno annually, saw his sons, and did maintenance work on the property. On one of these visits, he and his son William were repairing the roof. William was on the roof, and John was below bringing shingles from a nearby garage. John felt pain in his chest. He fell to the ground and was near death when the rescue unit arrived.[22] The Ghost of Playland Park, as announcer Lee Barron called Beauchamp, died April 17, 1981.[23] He was fifty-eight. The heart condition that made him ineligible to serve in the military finally ended his life.

Johnny Beauchamp died certain he had won the first Daytona 500.

SOURCES

The endnotes, combined with the list of individuals interviewed, represent, with perhaps a few exceptions, all the sources for the book. I drew information from scrapbooks owned by four people: Dale Swanson Jr., Norma Brix, Russell Leslie, and me. My scrapbooks consist of newspaper coverage of most of the Playland races from 1951 to 1954.

I supplemented scrapbook articles by personally spending many hours in library microfilm rooms copying articles, mostly dealing with Playland racing. For these photocopied articles I have precise dates and page numbers. Not all articles in the scrapbooks have dates and page numbers. I was able to put together a full record of the Playland schedule by carefully reading the articles and employing the dates I did have. I also enlisted the help of many libraries in the Midwest and the NASCAR region, and in almost every instance, the newspaper articles that I accessed there have dates and page numbers.

Although the interviews were extremely important, the printed information was invaluable. Another important aspect of preparing the information for the book was determining which people were involved in certain events and activities and then locating these people. Even after the interviews and the print information were assembled, there were puzzles that required sifting through the facts to determine the most likely explanation of an action. In general, the work of gathering the information required a massive amount of research and investigation, and this perhaps explains why so little has been written about the story told here.

INTERVIEWEES

Ackerman, Lee
Anderson, Jack
Archibald, Dick
Baker, Al
Ballard, Rex
Bean, Roger
Beauchamp, Donna
Beauchamp, Gaylord

Beauchamp, Robert
Beauchamp, William
Bertsch, Opal
Blackledger, Keith
Boehlander, Don
Bowman, Mary
Boyles, Ray
Brix, Norma

Bruner, Ann
Brunick, Junior
Burdick, Bob
Burdick, Bud
Burger, Linda
Buwalda, James
Byers, Roger
Cartmill, Leonard
Chaike, Ray
Christensen, Vernon "Hooky"
Chubbuck, Bill
Cisar, Stan
Clements, Mike
Cole, David
Cooper, James
Dake, Darrell
Daub, Joe
DeHart, Howard
Dennis, Bradley
Dolan, Dick
Dorsey, Ronald
Drake, Bud
Economaki, Chris
Epton, Juanita
Erickson, Lesley
Favre, Gregory
Flock, Francis
Fox, Ray
Frank, Larry
Funk, Lenny
Gans, Arlene
Gazaway, Gwen
Givens, Jerome
Goldsmith, Paul
Havick, Dallas
Hellerich, Dave
Holenbeck, Sandra
Holland, Lou
Holman, Lee
Holzmueller, Gus
Hudson, Helen

Hudson, Paul G.
Hufstader, Gib
Jacobsen, Faye
Jacobsen, Ron
Jarrett, Ned
Jensen, Ron
Johnson, Charles
Johnson, Ralph
Jones, Judy
Jorgensen, Lloyd
Judge, Judy
Kaufman, Keith
Killion, Ray
Kosiski, Dan
Kramer, Ralph
Krueger, Mel
Latham, Beverly
Leslie, Russell
Lewis, Randy
Liebe, Jule
Lund, Tom
Lund, Wanda
Mair, Alex
Malcom, Paul
Maloney, Gussy
Massey, James
Mays, Bob
McCuen, Milton
McDonald, Gus
McGeehan, Tom
McKee, Robert
McKim, Buzz
McQuagg, Sam
Metcalfe, Morris
Miles, Cliff
Miller, Fred
Miller, R. L.
Morgan, Sonny
Mundy, Frank
Nelson, Chris
Ostendorf, Don

Owens, Cotton
Palumbo, Charlie
Panch, Marvin
Parker, Bobby
Parks, John
Pash, Ollie
Peers, Richard
Pistone, Tom
Prout, Warren
Rachwitz, Elaine
Rath, Leslie
Rath, Randy
Rathman, Jim
Reed, Jim
Renfield, Marlene
Roby, Glen
Rogers, Paul
Samples, Eddie
Sappenfield, Earl
Satterfield, Kathy
Satterfield, Larry
Shannon, Herb
Short, Dan
Schroeder, Juerelle

Sindt, Sanda
Smith, Bette
Smith, Bill
Sorensen, Roger
Summers, Charles
Swanson, Dale Jr.
Sisson, Frank
Slusky, Jerry
Squier, Ken
Sykes, Mike
Thomy, Al
Torson, Larry
Trybulec, Joe
Ulmer, Steve
Valasek, Ray
Warren, Taylor
Weis, Joan
Weiss, Violet
Wheeler, Humpy
White, Don
White, Rex
Whitman, James
Wickersham, Reb
Williams, Susan

NOTES

Notes that do not contain complete source information are from scrapbooks in the possession of the author.

Preface
1. Donna Beauchamp interview.

Chapter 1. The Natural
1. Sanda Beauchamp Sindt interview.
2. Robert Beauchamp interview.
3. Gaylord Beauchamp interview.
4. "Pottawattamie Shows Gain," *Omaha World-Herald*, June 30, 1950; Shelby County Historical Society, A Look at Shelby County (Harlan, Iowa: Shelby County Historical Society, 1974).
5. "Stock Car Races," *Harlan Tribute*, August 15, 1947.

6. "Swanson Family Has Long Business History in Harlan," *Harlan News Advertiser*, February 1, 2008, p. 1. At first his business was on the corner of 6th and Durant in an old Phillips gas station. Later he moved to 5th St. south in a small building behind a farm implement business two blocks from the courthouse square. In the 1960s, he moved the business farther from the town center.

7. Dale Swanson Jr. interview.

8. "Stock Car Races," *Harlan Tribune*, August 15, 1947.

9. Dale Swanson Jr. interview.

10. Dale Swanson Jr. interview.

Chapter 2. Racing among the Cornfields

1. Ron Jensen interview.

2. Junior Brunick interview.

3. Beauchamp was born on March 23, 1923.

4. Arthur Rix, ed., *Manning Centennial Book, 1881 to 1981* (Odebolt, Iowa: Odelbolt Chronicle Print, 1981), pp. 431–432.

5. Speedy Bill Smith interview.

Chapter 3. The Mafia Race Track

1. Wally Provost, "Dogs Across the River," *Omaha World-Herald*, June 6, 1974.

2. The criminal elements remained after the dog races stopped. By 1950 the Stork Club profit had soared to $200,000 a year. The Kansas City–based Binaggio gang decided to come to Omaha and seize the business. Thugs from the gang held a gun to the head of Stork Club owner Cy Silver and told him to sell his club for no money or he would be shot. He sold. In 1953, the owner of the Riviera, Edward McDermott, was found shot dead in his garage.

3. Dave Smedley, "Playland: From Dogs to Stockers, Barron Remembers," *Nonpareil*, June 9, 1974; Wally Provost, "Dogs Across the River," *World-Herald*, June 6, 1974; *Nonpareil*, February 16, 1958; *Omaha World-Herald*, June 21, 1990, p. 11, p. 16; *World-Herald*, June 21, 1990; *Nonpareil*, March 27, 1977; Richard Warner, "Playland Speedway Brought Racers and Fans to Council Bluffs Local Landmark," *Midland Business Journal*, September 24, 2004, p. 26.

4. Richard Warner, "Playland Park Drew Midwesterners to Council Bluffs," *Member Journal, Historical Society of Pottawattamie*, 2008.

5. Jerome Givens interview.

6. See http://www.calebarmstrong.com/cars.aspx; http://www.ehow.com /facts_7331042_history-midget-race-cars.html; Gene Crucean, "The History of Sprint Car Racing—Mission Impossible," July 5, 2012, at http://polypopculture .blogspot.com/2012/07/sprint-car-history.html; Tom McGeehan (an IMCA official in the 1950s and 1960s) interview; Joe Scallop, "The Shreveport Inci-

dent: Gus Schrader and the IMCA," *Automobile Quarterly*, First Quarter, 18, no. 1 (1980); V. Ray Valasek and Bob Mays, *Valley County Thunder* (Lincoln, Nebraska: Fasttrack Publishing, 2004); and Don Radbruch, *Roaring Roadsters*, vol. 2 (Driggs, Idaho: Tex Smith Publishing, 2000).

7. At the precise time when Beauchamp raced a hot rod, the writer Henry Felsen, residing in Des Moines, Iowa, witnessed the thrills and excitement that he captured in his cult novel *Hot Rod*. Felsen described the hot rod as follows: "Bud's car, variously called . . . strip-down roadster, heap, hot rod, jalopy or set of wheels, was . . . oddly-assorted parts." Henry Greg Felsen, *Hot Rod* (New York: E. P. Dutton, 1950), p. 17.

8. Felsen, *Hot Rod*, p. 11; Beauchamp had to locate and build a hot rod. Lawrence Holtz in nearby Avoca had one, but after test-driving the hot rod, Beauchamp parked it and told Holtz, "It is fast, but difficult to turn." Richard Holtz interview.

9. Dan Francisco, "Ford 4-Barrell Speed Secrets, Part II," *Hot Rod*, November 1950, pp. 16–17.

10. When John's brother, Gaylord, who was younger by six years, entered the military, he sold Johnny his 1932 Ford. At the end of Gaylord's service, Johnny sold the car back to Gaylord. But when the brothers decided to convert the car into a hot rod, Johnny again bought the car from Gaylord.

11. Gaylord Beauchamp interview.

12. Dale Swanson Jr. interview.

13. "Hot Rods Make Playland Debut," *Nonpareil*, July 7, 1949, p. 18; "Big Crowd Sees Hot Rod Crackups," *Nonpareil*, July 10, 1949, p. 23.

14. Don Hill of St. Joe, Missouri, won; Bill Flickhein of Kansas City was second; and Roger Young of Los Angeles was third.

15. "Encore for Hot Rods at Playland Track," *Nonpareil*, July 16, 1949, p. 5; "Hot Rod Feature to St. Joe Man," *Nonpareil*, July 17, 1949, p. 24.

16. http://www.findagrave.com/cgi-bin/fg.cgi?page=gr&GRid=50062536.

17. "Curtis Ross," *Racers at Rest*, vol. 1 no. 4 (July 2011), pp. 1–2; online at http://www.racersatrest.com/uploads/Racers_at_Rest_Newsletter_Issue_July_2011 .pdf.

18. Bill Smith interview. Mechanic Bill "Speedy" Smith explained that from his vantage point in the pits it was difficult to see the injured drivers out on the track, but he heard that Pettit and Ross were both decapitated. Although policy could vary from track to track, most promoters needed more cars to make their races look good, so they did not discriminate against black drivers wanting to race. Fellow drivers could be a different story, however. They could purposely wreck the car of a black competitor. In reality, there were few black racecar drivers.

19. "No More Hot Rod Races, Playland," *Nonpareil*, August 2, 1949, p. 12.

Chapter 4. Winning with a Hot Rod

1. John Beauchamp, "My Topper," *Nonpareil*, August 1, 1951.

2. Beauchamp, "My Topper."

3. Dan Radbruch, *Roaring Roadsters* (Driggs, Idaho: Tex Smith Publishing, 1994), pp. 128–129; Radbruch, *Roaring Roadsters*, vol. 2 (Driggs, Idaho: Hot Rod Library, 2000), p. 74. The 1994 volume of *Roarding Roadsters* was not identified as volume 1. The Iowa hot rod activity developed at the same time, much of it in central and eastern Iowa, producing two organizations that sanctioned races: the Central Iowa Racing Association (CIRA) and the Hawkeye Hot Rod Association (HHRA).

4. Robert Beauchamp interview.

5. "Big Crowd Views 'Hot Rod' Races," *Beatrice Daily Sun*, August 29, 1949.

6. Radbruch, *Roaring Roadsters*, p. 133; Bill Smith interview. The *Harlan Tribune* reported that Swanson and Beauchamp won over two hundred dollars at Beatrice, Nebraska, hot rod races. "Harlan Hot-Rods Win Frequently," *Harlan Tribune*, September 9, 1949; "Big Crowd Views 'Hot Rod' Races," *Beatrice Daily Sun*, August 29, 1949. Radbruch, in his excellent *Roaring Roadsters*, mistakenly reports the races were held in Hastings. They were actually held in Beatrice. Speedy Bill Smith, the owner of a Lincoln, Nebraska, Speed Shop, took a second in the consolation race and sixth in the main event, winning $39.44. Looking back, Smith remembers thinking "this was reasonably good money for an afternoon's effort."

7. "Three Crashes Feature Hot Rod Races on Sunday," *Missouri Valley Times*, September 5, 1949.

8. Tommy Moore, "Vern Kolb Cops 20-Lap Feature Run," *Argus Leader*, September 6, 1949, p. 9; "Harlan Hot-Rods Win Frequently," *Harlan Tribune*, September 9, 1949.

9. "Flying Wheel Seriously Injures Spectator at Hot Rod Races," *Harlan Advertiser*, October 25, 1949, p. 1.

10. Dallas Havick interview.

Chapter 5. Odd Man Out

1. Bloys Britt and Bill France, *The Racing Flag* (New York: Pocket Books, 1965), p. 40.

2. Parker attended Dana College in Blair, Nebraska, for two and half years, but once the racing began, he stopped attending. He kept some of his ties with the Blair community when a local businessman, who owned a semi-pro football team, asked him play. Parker recruited Lund to play also. The team was roundly drubbed in one event at Des Moines, Iowa.

3. Ollie Pash interview.

4. Ollie Pash interview; Ron Jensen interview. Either Oscar Abraham or Pete Bailey was the promoter.

5. Robert Phipps, "There's Gold in Traffic Jams," *Omaha World-Herald Magazine*, August 27, 1950, p. 6-C.

6. Ron Jensen interview.

7. Opal Bertsch interview.

8. Tom Lund interview.

9. The incident occurred in study hall. Lund several times broke his pencil lead and asked to go to the pencil sharpener. On one of these requests, the male study hall teacher pulled out his knife and sharpened the Lund pencil. He then gave Tiny a little cuff and told him to stop breaking his pencil lead. At that instant, the violence began.

10. Ron Jensen interview.

11. Ollie Pash interview. The legend is that Tiny Lund took the car out on the Harlan track without his parents' permission. Ollie Pash says, "I was right there in the kitchen when the issue of whether Tiny could drive the family car in the races was discussed. His mother overruled his father. The parents knew he was racing the car."

12. Tiny also owned a hot rod that his father, Chris, a race driver himself before World War II and a mechanic with the Iowa Highway Commission, helped work on. Tiny, as the driver of the hot rod, estimated he had entered between thirty-five and forty hot rod events, which meant he had attended eleven sessions, racing in about three contests in each of the eleven sessions. His record was mixed.

13. Smokey Yunick labeled Smith one of the five best mechanics he had ever known. Smokey Yunick, *Best Damn Garage in Town: My Life and Adventures* (Holly Hill, Florida: Carbon Press, 2003), p. 175.

14. "Tiny Lund Killed in Racing Crash," *Harlan Tribune*, August 21, 1975.

15. Sanda Beauchamp Sindt interview.

16. Phipps, "There's Gold in Traffic Jams," p. 6-C.

17. "Wins Rod Race," *Harlan News Advertiser*, May 10, 1950.

Chapter 6. The Racing Capital

1. The day was May 14, 1950.

2. Richard Warner, *Council Bluffs Business Journal*, May 1, 2003, p. 9.

3. "Vana Uninjured in Two Mishaps," *Nonpareil*, May 15, 1950, p. 8; "Larger Stock Car Race Entry Seen," *Nonpareil*, May 18, 1950, p. 11.

4. "Good Crowd for Hot Rod Races," *Harlan Tribune*, June 30, 1950.

5. "2 Iowas Top Bluffs' Races," *Omaha World-Herald*, June 25, 1950, p. B-5.

6. Fred Miller interview.

7. "Tiny Lund Is Driver to Watch in Stock Car Races," *Nonpareil*, July 4, 1950, p. 3; "Lund Notches Third Straight Win," *Nonpareil*, July 15, 1950, p. 5.

8. "Christensen Leads Harlan Invasion at Playland Races," *Nonpareil*, July 22, 1950, p. 5.

9. Robert Phipps, "There's Gold in Traffic Jams," *Omaha World Herald Magazine*, August 27, 1950, p. 6-C.

10. Phipps, "There's Gold in Traffice Jams."

11. Fred Miller interview.

12. Phipps, "There's Gold in Traffic Jams."

13. "Lund Is Double Loser, Playland," *Nonpareil*, July 29, 1950, p. 5.

14. "Tiny Finds Midget That Fits," *Harlan Tribune*, July 21, 1950.

15. "Tiny Finds Midget That Fits."

16. "Local Race Drivers Leading the Field in Southwest Iowa," *Harlan Tribune*, June 30, 1950.

17. "Lund Ends Up 12th in 100 Mile Race Despite Collision," *Harlan Tribune*, July 7, 1950.

18. DeWayne Tiny Lund, "My Topper," *Nonpareil*, August 27, 1950, p. 24.

19. "Lund Rolls Midget at Sioux City; Not Seriously Injured," *Harlan Tribune*, August 11, 1950; Lund, "My Topper," p. 24.

20. "Tiny Lund Will Seek Revenge," *Nonpareil*, July 26, 1950, p. 8.

21. "Lund Is Double Loser," p. 5.

22. "Harlan Drivers Corner Cash at Playland Stadium," *Nonpareil*, August 6, 1950, p. 23.

23. "Christensen Leads Harlan Invasion at Playland Races," *Nonpareil*, July 22, 1950, p. 5.

24. "Harlan Drivers Corner Cash," p. 23.

25. "Harlan Drivers Corner Cash."

26. "Harlan Drivers Corner Cash."

27. "Tiny Finds Midget That Fits."

28. Phipps, "There's Gold in Traffic Jams."

29. "Popular Stock Car Runs Two Days at Fair," *Harlan Tribune*, August 18, 1950.

30. The auto shop was owned by Corky Abel.

31. "Chris Nelson Tops Stock Car Field," *Harlan Tribune*, August 25, 1950.

32. "John White Takes Second Feature," *Nonpareil*, August 26, 1950, p. 5.

33. "Tiny Lund Back with Winning Set," *Harlan Tribune*, September 8, 1950.

34. "Playland Leaders on Deck Friday," *Nonpareil*, September 8, 1950, p. 12.

35. "Lund and No. 55 Ready to Go Sunday," *Nonpareil*, May 1951. This article reported that Lund won 15 out of 28 races. A reasonably careful study of the

paper's reporting shows Lund winning 11 of 27 features. Unless races other than Playland features were counted, it is not likely Lund won 15 features at Playland.

36. "Big Shoes to Fill," *Harlan Tribune*, May 4, 1951.

Chapter 7. Big Shoes to Fill

1. Playland Stadium, "Rules and Regulations of Playland Stadium for Stock Car Racing." This document is one legal-size piece of paper, printed on both sides, with the track rules and regulations.

2. "Lund and No 55 Ready to Go Sunday," *Nonpareil*, May 1951.

3. My personal observation.

4. Hooky Christensen interview.

5. "Beauchamp Racing Atlantic's Lilienthal to Settle Grudges," *Harlan Tribune*, June 22, 1951.

6. Bill Smith interview. Fifteen years later, Smith had a conversation with Swanson in which he (Swanson) admitted and explained in detail how he used the spider gear to get around the track rule prohibiting locked rear ends.

7. "Beauchamp Cleared in Stock Dispute," *Nonpareil*, June 1951; "Beauchamp's Car Must Be Checked," *Omaha World-Herald*, June 1951; "No Decision in Stock Car Dispute," *Nonpareil*, June 1951.

8. Bud Burdick interview; confirmed in Hooky Christensen interview.

9. Cylinder heads, through which intake air and fuel flow and exhaust gases exit, help seal the combustion chambers and cylinders to permit the most efficient controlled explosion to push the pistons. Aluminum heads are lighter than cast iron heads, making less weight for the car engine to pull along. In addition, because aluminum heads dissipate heat better than cast iron, a high compression in the chamber can be achieved before detonation. Another characteristic of the aluminum heads adding power to the engine could be a slightly different shape and size of the heads. In any event, track rules usually mandate that the part be manufactured by the factory. In other words, if it's a Ford, then Ford should have manufactured the part. See http://www.jegs.com/s/tech-articles/cylinder-heads.html and http://www.ehow.com/info_8004042_advantages-heads-ovr-cast-iron.html.

10. Dale Swanson Jr. interview; Bill Smith interview.

11. Robert Phipps, "There's Gold in Traffic Jams."

12. Robert Phipps, "There's Gold in Traffic Jams."

13. "Swanson Motors Dominate Playland," *Nonpareil*, August 1952.

14. "Callia Catches Up With Bobby Slater," *Nonpareil*, June 27, 1951.

15. Robert Beauchamp interview.

16. "Hooky Christensen Wins Four in Row at Council Bluffs," *Harlan Tribune*, July 20, 1951.

17. Robey was still driving race cars in 2006.

18. After his suspension, Beauchamp returned for the August 31 event and became embroiled in a feverish battle with Glenn Robey in the 10-lap fifth heat race. He passed Robey on one corner and then Robey passed him on the next. In the feature, he used the additional laps to his advantage, catching and passing Bud Aitkenhead for the lead on the 20th lap.

19. Marlene Renfeld interview.

20. Donna Beauchamp interview.

21. "Clausen Takes Playland Feature," *Nonpareil*, September 3, 1951.

22. Dale Swanson Jr. interview.

23. I rode with Beauchamp on the track one night.

24. "Swanson Entry in Four Wins," *Nonpareil*, September 1951.

25. Bud Burdick interview.

26. Dale Swanson interview and review of Swanson's scrapbook.

Chapter 8. Lilienthal's Revenge

1. "Swanson Motors Dominate Playland," *Nonpareil*, August 1952.

2. Swanson sold number 5 to Claire Harder from Sioux City and sold 55 to Don Pash from Avoca. Harder, a top driver at the Riverside track in Sioux City, was a strong competitor at Playland.

3. Omaha drivers Keith "Porky" Rachwitz and Tex Gilmore bought motors, and both won features during the season.

4. "Swanson Motors Dominate Playland," *Nonpareil*, August 1952.

5. "Swanson Motors Dominate Playland."

6. Robert Beauchamp interview.

7. "Beauchamp Center of Incident at Playland Following Bud Drake Roll," *Nonpareil*, June 2, 1952.

8. Bud Drake interview.

Chapter 9. The Lost Season

1. "Hot Tempers, Big Accidents Spice Playland Stock Car Races," *Omaha World-Herald*, May 22, 1953.

2. A sum of 125 points was awarded for a feature win, 25 for a speed dash, and 25 for a heat race.

3. "Rival Track Won't Conflict with Good Fellow Races," *Omaha World-Herald*, May 8, 1953.

4. "Officials Have Exacting Duties," *Playland Track News*, vol. 2, no. 4, 1954.

5. "Racing Plum for Barkdoll," *Omaha World-Herald*, September 8, 1951.

6. "Beauchamp Wins Playland Feature," *Nonpareil*, June 6, 1953.

7. "Harlan Stock Car Drivers Make More Headlines," *News Advertiser*, July 28, 1953; Gussie Maloney interview.

8. Gussie Maloney interview.

Chapter 10. The Invasion

1. Elaine Rachwitz interview; Bobby Parker interview.

2. "Father's Day at Playland," *Omaha World-Herald*, June 20, 1954.

3. "Tiny Finds Midget That Fits."

4. "Stock Driver Pockets $9500 in Winning Darlington Race," *Omaha World-Herald*, September 2, 1952.

5. In the first months of 1953, Behnken brought a race car to Daytona Beach and West Palm Beach.

6. "Krueger Drives Many Circuits," *Nonpareil*, June 27, 1954.

7. "Southwest Iowans against the Nation," *Nonpareil*, July 22, 1953.

8. "Southwest Iowans against the Nation."

9. Mike Cochran, "Fort Worth Bounty Hunter Clashes with U.S. Government Agents," April 21, 1997, *Abilene Reporter-News*, April 27, 1997; Stan Kalwasinski, "Bob Pronger—Biography," at http://www.kalracing.com/Autoracing/Bob_Pronger_Biography.htm; personal communication with Stan Kalwasinski.

10. "Southwest Iowans against the Nation," *Nonpareil*, July 22, 1953; "SAFE Pilots Bid Tonight," *Omaha World-Herald*, July 23, 1953; "4923 Watch Bluffs Races," *Omaha World-Herald*, July 24, 1953; "Kirkwood Wins Playland Feature," *Nonpareil*, July 24, 1953.

11. Chris Economaki, *Let 'Em All Go* (Fishers, Indiana: Dave Argabright Publisher, 2006), p. 105.

12. *Rapid City Daily Journal*, July 22, 1953. For a retrospective of the event, see Jim Holland, "Fifty Years Ago, NASCAR's Heavy Hitters Visited Rapid Valley Race Track," *Rapid City Journal*, July 21, 2003.

13. Bill Hockstedler, "Thomas Holds NASCAR Lead, Nips Rathman in GNC Race," *Rapid City Daily Journal*, July 23, 1953, p. 24.

14. Mel Krueger interview.

15. Keith Blackledge interview. Blackledge, the author of most of the newspaper stories, recalled that the reason for the large number was that Ed O'Boyle was a nice fellow and a friend.

16. Economaki, *Let 'Em All Go*, pp. 105–106.

17. Keith Blackledge, "100-Mile Race Provides Brilliant Driving Display, Surprise Finish," *North Platte Telegraph Bulletin*, July 27, 1953.

18. Keith Blackledge, "Dots . . and Dashes," *North Platte Telegraph Bulletin*, July 28, 1953, p. 8.

19. "Grand National 100-Mile Race Starts at 2:30 Today," *Davenport Morning Democrat*, August 2, 1953, p. 40.

20. Another car kept breaking down, then reentering the race, ultimately completing 143 laps.

21. Jerry Jurgens, "Herb Thomas Wins 100-Mile," *Davenport Daily Times*, August 3, 1953, p. 5A; Greg Fielden, *Forty Years of Stock Car Racing*, vol. 1 (Surfside Beach, South Carolina: Galfield Press, 1992), pp. 127–128.

22. Beauchamp could not have visited Darlington in September of either 1953 or 1954 because he was racing at Playland.

Chapter 11. The Ghost of Playland Park

1. Late in the 1953 season, Beauchamp raced the new Swanson car to test and prepare it for a full 1954 season of competition. "Bob Kendall Annexes Feature Win," *Nonpareil*, September 14, 1953, p. 8.

2. "Older Models Okayed for Playland Racing," *Omaha World-Herald*, ca. June 4, 1953.

3. Bud Burdick interview.

4. Robert Beauchamp interview.

5. "Playland Track News," 2, no. 10, August 1954. This source is a one-page insert in *Official Centennial Program* sold at the track to spectators.

6. Bobby Parker interview. Roy Burdick, Bud's brother, was friends with another Harlan mechanic, Gene Parker, whose son, Bobby, came within one broken axle of defeating Bud for the 1953 track championship at Playland Park. The Parkers and Burdicks always pulled their cars up next to each other in the pit area.

7. Bud Burdick interview.

8. "Playland Track News," 2, no. 10, August 1954.

9. "Beauchamp Is Hero at Playland, *Nonpareil*, May 22, 1954.

10. Dan Short interview.

11. Robert Beauchamp interview.

12. Robert Beauchamp interview.

13. "Harlan Serviceman Present When Atomic Bomb Is Exploded," *Harlan News Advertiser*, April 29, 1952.

14. "Main Event Won by Lund," *Omaha World-Herald*, August 28, 1954; "Lund Takes Goodfellow at Playland," *Nonpareil*, August 28, 1954.

15. Hooky Christensen interview.

16. Sonny Morgan interview.

17. Christensen did so well Swanson let him drive the car in a postseason race.

Chapter 12. IMCA

1. "Banker Top Stock Car Driver," *Topeka Daily Capital*, July 1, 1956, p. 2C.

2. Ray Erickson Speed Service was located at 3049 W. Irving Park Road in Chicago.

3. Robert McKee interview; Speedy Bill Smith interview.

4. Junior Brunick interview.

5. Junior Brunick interview.

6. Junior Brunick interview.

7. Dan Short interview; Junior Brunick interview. It was the Short car that Beauchamp rolled on July 4. When Playland changed the rules to permit modified motors, Al Haden, an Omaha race man who eventually owned Sunset Speedway in Omaha, built a new, souped-up motor for the Short old model car that Beauchamp drove. "Racing Changes in Effect Tonight," *Omaha World-Herald*, July 16, 1955, p. 9; "Pash Makes New Bid at Playland," *Omaha World-Herald*, July 23, 1955, p. 10.

8. Mike Mueller, *Chevy Small-Block V-8* (St. Paul, Minnesota: Motorbooks, 2005). This book is a good place to begin understanding the Chevy 55, particularly pp. 32–81. See also Andrew Montgomery, *On the Road* (St. Paul, Minnesota: MBI Publishing Company, 2004), pp. 88–89. Those interested in slipper piston construction may find the following Web site helpful: http://commons .wikimedia.org/wiki/Category:Slipper_pistons.

9. E. M. Christensen Auto Company.

10. Tom McGeehan interview.

11. Frank Winkley, "An Open Letter on IMCA," *Speed Age*, July 1956, pp. 42, 43, 88; Tom McGeehan interview. Indeed, the NASCAR event of 1953 in Nebraska suggested a bit of hippodrome and a noncompetitive outcome.

12. Tom McGeehan interview.

13. See Joe Scallop, "The Shreveport Incident: Gus Schrader and the IMCA," *Automobile Quarterly*, First Quarter, 18, no. 1, 1980, especially p. 10.

14. Laura Hillenbrand, *Seabiscuit* (New York: Ballantine Books 2002), pp. 6–9.

15. "International Motor Contest Association," at http://en.wikipedia.org /wiki/International_Motor_Contest_Association#History.

16. The first NASCAR late model race was on June 19, 1949, in Charlotte.

17. "Stock Car Races Make Auto Men Take Notice," *Des Moines Register*, August 7, 1949, p. S-3.

18. "Stock Car Races Make Auto Men Take Notice."

19. The 1956 yearbook was titled *1957 IMCA Yearbook* because it was in 1957 about the 1956 season.

Chapter 13. The Flying Frenchman

1. Dale Swanson Jr. interview.

2. IMCA press release, *Harlan News Advertiser*, August 30, 1955.

3. "Beauchamp Wins 100-Lap Feature; 'Bugs Out of Car,'" *Harlan Tribune*, August 26, 1955.

4. One might speculate that Swanson may have learned of the half-ton pickup rear end from Lund, who had won an IMCA race a few weeks earlier.

5. Dale Swanson Jr. interview.

6. Sonny Morgan interview.

7. Lloyd Jorgensen interview.

8. The track at LeHi was fourteen miles from Memphis, Tennessee.

9. Greg Fielden, *Forty Years of Stock Car Racing*, vol. 1 (Surfside Beach, South Carolina: Galfield Press, 1992), p. 279.

10. Fielden, *Forty Years of Stock Car Racing*, p. 231.

11. The advertised $12,950 purse attracted other drivers. Lee Petty, one of the regulars who rarely missed a race, was competing, as was Buck Baker, Curtis Turner, Herb Thomas, and Joe Weatherly. Others from farther away were Marvin Panch, Chuck Stevenson, and Johnny Mantz, all from California, and Jim Reed from New York. Mantz and Stevenson had raced in the Indianapolis 500. Tiny Lund's pending appearance was without media fanfare or notice. Lund, running his Chevrolet, did his time trial in 61.26 seconds, approximately eight seconds slower than the time trial winner, Fonty Flock, at 53.79, who drove a Chrysler 300. Lund's twenty-third in the time trials did nothing to suggest he was much of a threat.

12. Fielden, *Forty Years*, vol. 1, pp. 203–204; Photo caption, *Harlan News-Advertiser*, November 1, 1955; "'Speedy' Thompson Wins 300-Mile Stock Car Race in 1956 Ford," *Memphis Commercial Appeal*, October 10, 1955, p. 21.

13. Robert McKee interview.

14. Robert McKee interview.

15. Robert McKee interview.

Chapter 14. Johnny Hoseclamp

1. Gus McDonald interview.

2. Tom McGeehan interview.

3. Two separate and independent sources in my interviews relayed this incident.

4. *IMCA Newsletter*, no, 1, May 2, 1956, p. 3.

5. Sonny Morgan interview.

6. Hotel employee Al Warrender eventually entered IMCA with a car he had bought from Dale Swanson.

7. Dale Swanson Jr. interview.

8. *1957 IMCA Yearbook*, p. 83.

Chapter 15. The Duntov Cam

1. Bradley Dennis, a race mechanic, first informed me of this number. He had it memorized and had never forgotten it. A good review is Martyn L. Schorr, "Show of Force," *Popular Mechanics*, March 2003, pp. 57–63. Sonny Morgan re-

members being able to buy the necessary parts as a power package to convert a regular Chevy engine to one with the cam, creating the added horsepower. Dennis recalls that the parts did not have a number stamped on them, but rather were color coded at the factory with purple paint. It is also listed in the *1957 Chevrolet Stock Car Competition Guide*, p. 2. The IMCA inspectors could have found several unfamiliar parts, all including the cam from the power package conversion kit.

2. Doane Motors was located at 10 East Main.

3. See http://www.meadowdaleraceway.homestead.com/DickDoane.html.

4. Junior Brunick, the driver who bought Swanson's 1934 car in 1955, recalls Dale Swanson telling him that Chevrolet had shipped an experimental cam. Brunick interview.

5. Dale Swanson Jr. interview.

6. Gus McDonald interview; Rex White interview; Sonny Morgan interview.

7. Robert McKee interview.

8. See http://www.lexington-on-line.com/crv.zora.html.

9. Mike Mueller, *Chevy Small Block V-8* (St. Paul, Minnesota: Motorbooks, 2005), p. 115 (the cam was listed as RPO 449); see also Kim Chapin, *Fast as White Lightning* (New York: Three Rivers Press, 1998), pp. 122, 123.

10. "New Stock Car Standard," *Kansas City Times*, December 3, 1956, p. 16.

11. The warehouse was located directly across the Missouri River from the Playland track.

12. Sonny Morgan interview.

13. Gus McDonald interview. A good source to explain further some of these techniques is *Hot Rod Magazine. Horsepower Handbook* (St. Paul, Minnesota: Motorsports, 2004).

Chapter 16. Champion for the Record Books

1. Beauchamp won two in Oskaloosa, Iowa; one in Springfield, Missouri; one in Council Bluffs, Iowa, at Playland Park; one in Fargo, North Dakota; two in Aberdeen, North Dakota; and one in Jamestown, North Dakota. He lost in Springfield when an axle broke and in Hutchinson, Minnesota, when a wheel came off.

2. Dale Swanson Jr. interview; Sonny Morgan interview.

3. Lee Porter, "Hot Words, Wrecks Feature 100 Miler," *Topeka State Journal*, July 5, 1956, p. 15.

4. "Stock, Sports Cars Mingle Today in 200-Lapper Here, White Heads Classy Cast," *Topeka State Journal*, July 4, 1956, p. 13.

5. The half-mile time trial was at the Oskaloosa, Iowa, race.

6. "Workmen Put Finishing Touches on Fair Track," *Topeka State Journal*, July 3, 1956, p. 11.

7. "'Sportsman of the Day' Enters July 4 100 Miler," *Topeka State Journal*, July 2, 1956, p. 10. By this deed, Funk also established his kindness toward Don White. Later in the season, when Funk asked Swanson to build an engine, Swanson at first said yes and then reconsidered and told Funk, "We are in competition with White and we do not want to help anyone who may then help White." Funk interview.

8. Bob Burdick interview.

9. Mel Krueger interview.

10. Dale Swanson Jr. interview.

11. "Beauchamp Loses Brakes, Wins 100-Mile Race Here," *Topeka State Journal*, July 5, 1956, p. 14.

12. Lee Porter, "Hot Words, Wrecks Feature 100-Miler," *Topeka State Journal*, July 5, 1956, p. 15.

13. Porter, "Hot Words, Wrecks Feature 100-Miler."

14. Porter, "Hot Words, Wrecks Feature 100-Miler."

15. Porter, "Hot Words, Wrecks Feature 100-Miler."

16. Dale Swanson Jr. interview; Sonny Morgan interview.

17. Tom McGeehan interview.

18. Dale Swanson Jr. interview.

19. From May 30, Memorial Day, in Topeka, Kansas, to the Des Moines, Iowa, race on July 15, Beauchamp won all the races except two. Darrell Dake and Bob Burdick broke the Beauchamp winning momentum.

20. Beauchamp won at Sioux Falls, South Dakota (July 19 and August 26); Grand Forks, North Dakota (July 22 and July 26); Minot, North Dakota (August 3); Hibbing, Minnesota (two races August 5); Oskaloosa, Iowa (August 8); Mason City, Iowa (August 11); Davenport, Iowa (August 12); Marshalltown, Iowa (August 18); and Cedar Rapids, Iowa (August 19).

21. Sonny Morgan won in Winnipeg, Canada (July 28); Don White won in North Platte, Nebraska, (July 29); and Bob Burdick won at Playland Park in Council Bluffs, Iowa (August 22).

22. Mel Krueger interview.

23. Tom McGeehan interview.

24. Sonny Morgan interview.

25. A short time after The Great Gopher, Schneider entered the Lebanon Valley Open, in which the purse for winning was $1,000.

26. See this work about Panch's career: Kevin Bagwell, *From California to the East Coast: Racing Memories from a NASCAR Legend*, vol. 1 (Port Orange, Florida: Panch Enterprises, 2007), pp. 38–39. Panch actually placed fourth overall rather than third, as stated in this excellent and informative book.

27. Bill Beauchamp interview.

28. Gus McDonald interview.

29. In the second feature Schneider finished seventh, Derr twelfth, and Burdick thirteenth. The IMCA method for determining the overall winner was to add the results of both feature finishes. White was the overall winner, Charles Magnison with two fourth place finishes was second, and Beauchamp was third with a first and fifteenth. Panch was fourth and Morgan ended up fifth. *IMCA Newsletter*, no. 11, October 26, 1956, pp. 8–9; *1957 IMCA Yearbook*, p. 76. See also Lee Ackerman, "Frank Winkley's Marathon on Dirt," November 20, 2009, at http://www.midwestracingarchives.com/2009/11/frank-winkleys-marathon -on-dirt-great.html.

30. Sonny Morgan interview.

31. Dale Swanson Jr. interview.

32. Frank Winkley, "An Open Letter on IMCA," *Speed Age*, July 1956, pp. 42, 43, 88; quotation on p. 88. See also Joe Scalzo, "The Shreveport Incident: Gus Schrader and the IMCA," *Automobile Quarterly*, First Quarter, 1980, pp. 4–17.

33. "Racing Drivers Here," *Kansas City Times*, December 1, 1956, Section K, p. 3; "Awards to Top Drivers," *Kansas City Times*, December 2, 1956, Section A, p. 5.

34. Sonny Morgan interview.

Chapter 17. Building a Beach Car

1. Alamo Plaza was located at 2370 Stewart Avenue SW, today Metropolitan Parkway. Rex White interview.

2. Paul Van Valkenburgh, *Chevrolet—Racing? Fourteen Years of Raucus Silence! 1957–1970* (Warrendale, Pennsylvania: Society of Automotive Engineers, 2000), p. 13. The online Racing Reference Web site indicates Chevrolet won 3 of 56 Grand National races—races 4, 8, and 47. See http://www.racing -reference.info.

3. The address today of what was SEDCO's location is 1244 Central Avenue, East Point, Georgia.

4. Jurelle Schroeder (Hugh Babb's daughter) interview.

5. Bradley Dennis interview.

6. Rex White interview; Rex White, *Gold Thunder* (Jefferson, North Carolina: McFarland and Co., 2005), p. 97.

7. See http://www.MotorsportMemorial.org.

8. Rex White interview.

9. Rex White interview.

10. White, *Gold Thunder*, p. 95. Hapeville was a community a few miles from the Atlanta city center and near what then was known as Hartsfield International Airport. The address was 612 Cofield.

11. White, *Gold Thunder*, p. 97.

12. Stephen K. Anderson. "Pristine Pretender," *Super Rod*, October 2007, pp. 19–23. See also http://www.superchevy.com/features/trifive/0602sc_1957_che vy_bel_air/index.html; http://dcastalley.stores.yahoo.net/hi61chbwirac.html; and http://www.superchevy.com/technical/engines_drivetrain/cams_heads _valvetrain/sucp_0709_chevy_small_block_package/index.html.

13. Smokey Yunick, *Best Damn Garage in Town: My Life and Adventures* (Holly Hill, Florida: Carbon Press, 2003), p. 141.

14. Yunick, *Best Damn Garage in Town*, p. 142.

15. Frank Johnson interview.

16. Yunick, *Best Damn Garage in Town*, p. 143. Wackenhut provided the security.

17. Norman Mayersohn, "Pontiac's Glory Days Recalled," *Atlanta Journal-Constitution*, May 3, 2009, p. 9.

18. Ralph Kramer interview.

19. White, *Gold Thunder*, pp. 93–94.

20. Bradley Dennis drove one of the two Corvettes to Sebring. Betty Skelton made the reservation for their stay at Sebring. According to Dennis, who worked at SEDCO, two additional Corvettes arrived at Sebring: one from Duntov's operation, and a second from Bill Mitchell's GM's Styling Division.

21. Dale Swanson Jr. interview.

22. Sonny Morgan interview; Dale Swanson Jr. interview.

23. *1957 Chevrolet Stock Car Competition Guide.*

24. Aside from IMCA and NASCAR, the *Guide* lists in its narrative two other major sanctioning organizations: USAC and MARC. On the following page is a map of the United States showing the locations where each association holds races; a fifth organization, SCCA, is also displayed on the map. *1957 Chevrolet Stock Car Competition Guide,*" pp. 23–24.

25. Jim Rathman interview. Jim Rathman replaced Delroy as the manager of SEDCO. The precise date is unclear, but it was about the time of the Daytona Beach race. Piggins did not reveal all his plans, but it seems Rathman was considered an interim appointment, and eventually Rathman obtained a Chevrolet dealership in Florida.

26. The original group of drivers consisted of Buck Baker, Possum Jones, Jack Smith, Alfred "Speedy" Thompson, Bob Welborn, Rex White, and Beauchamp; the first six drivers were from NASCAR. Other NASCAR drivers who eventually stopped in at SEDCO were Frankie Schneider and Tom Pistone.

Chapter 18. Corvettes and the Black Widow

1. Auto manufacturer Dusenberg made 36 of these cars in the 1930s; for a time, DePaulo drove for a Dusenberg racing team.

2. "Day by Day in Speed Weeks," *Sunday-News Journal* (Daytona Beach, Florida), February 3, 1957, pp. 1-A, 11-A.

3. Race drivers Paul Goldsmith, Buck Baker, and Speedy Thompson lined up for a beach run during the measured-mile event. Driver Fireball Roberts achieved a 119 mph time in a 1955 Ford.

4. "Walls Wins Prestige Banner," *Daytona Beach Morning Journal*, February 6, 1957, pp. 1, 12.

5. Smokey Yunick, *Best Damn Garage in Town: My Life and Adventures* (Holly Hill, Florida: Carbon Press, 2003), pp. 143–144.

6. Dale Swanson Jr. interview.

7. Betty Skelton interview. She died August 31, 2011.

8. "Norkutt Listed in 'Fair' Condition," *Daytona Beach Morning Journal*, February 9, 1957, p. 1.

9. From a standing start, Paul Goldsmith won at 91.301 mph, Beauchamp was second at 89.79 mph, and Betty Skelton was fifth at 87.4. On the running start, Goldsmith was fourth with 131.91, Skelton was fifth, and Beauchamp was sixth. The above results are from Don O'Reilly, "Daytona Speed Weeks," *Road and Track*, May 1957, p. 33. See also, in the same issue, pp. 23, 32. In addition, see also Karl Ludvigson, *Corvette: America's Star Spangled Sportscar* (New Albany, Indiana: Automobile Quarterly, 1973).

10. Sonny Morgan interview.

11. Robert McKee interview.

12. DePaulo fielded drivers Bill Amick, Ralph Moody, Marvin Panch, Jim Reed, Curtis Turner, and Joe Weatherly.

Chapter 19. Racing in the Sand

1. Speedy Bill Smith interview.

2. Robert Edelstein, *Full Throttle* (New York: The Overlook Press, 2005), pp. 96–97.

3. Bob Deiderio, "Cotton's Strategy for the Race Worked," *Daytona Beach Morning Journal*, February 18, 1957, p. 1; Bernard Kahn, "Averages Record 101.6 in 317hp Pontiac," *Daytona Beach Morning Journal*, February 18, 1957, pp. 1–2. The Kahn article discusses the factory involvement.

4. Marvin Panch interview.

5. Greg Fielden, *Forty Years of Stock Car Racing*, vol. 1 (Surfside Beach, South Carolina: Galfield Press, 1992), p. 261.

6. Peter Golenbock, *American Zoom* (New York: Macmillan, 1996), p. 96.

7. Kevin Bagwell, *From California to the East Coast: Racing Memories from a NASCAR Legend*, vol. 1 (Port Orange, Florida: Panch Enterprises, 2007), pp. 44–45; Kim Chapin, *Fast as White Lightning* (New York: Three Rivers Press,

1998) pp. 60, 61, 62; Rex White, *Gold Thunder* (Jefferson, North Carolina: McFarland and Co., 2005), p. 96.

8. Dale Swanson Jr. interview.

9. Dale Swanson Jr. interview.

10. Dale Swanson Jr. interview.

Chapter 20. Tough Times

1. Clarissa Myrick-Harris, "The Origins of the Civil Rights Movement, 1880–1910," in *Perspectives*, American Historical Association (Washington, D.C.: American Historical Association, 2007). Paper presented at the annual meeting of the American Historical Association in 2007.

2. Greg Fielden, *Forty Years of Stock Car Racing*, vol. 1 (Surfside Beach, South Carolina: Galfield Press, 1992), pp. 257, 258, 265; Paul Van Valkenburgh, *Fourteen Years of Raucus Silence! 1957–1970* (Warrendale, Pennsylvania: Society of Automotive Engineers), pp. 27–28; Tom Cotter and Al Pearce, *Holman Moody: The Legendary Race Team* (St. Paul, Minnesota: MBI Publishing Co., 2002), p. 39.

3. Bud Burdick, the star driver in Omaha, Nebraska, won the 1953 old model season championship at Playland Park, and he competed with Beauchamp with the championship in doubt until the last race of the 1954 season. In 1960, in his first visit at the Daytona 500, Bud finished ninth in his qualifying race and eleventh in the big race. Bud Burdick was a champion over many years in the Omaha area.

4. *1958 IMCA Yearbook*, p. 57.

5. Bob Burdick interview.

6. *1958 IMCA Yearbook*; IMCA newsletters for 1957.

7. William Beauchamp interview.

8. William Beauchamp interview.

9. *1959 IMCA Yearbook*. Another limiting factor to Beauchamp's success was the constant undercurrent of rumor that the auto manufacturers were still helping a few race mechanics and drivers. It is likely that Ford had not completely severed its ties to Burdick, and a few of the Keokuk, Iowa, champions might also still have been receiving help. Beauchamp and Swanson did not have help from Chevrolet.

10. Bob Burdick raced at Pioneer Raceway as Don Quinn from Long Beach, California.

Chapter 21. An Indy Track for Stock Cars

1. The date of the crash was February 3, 1959.

2. Bud Burdick interview.

3. When I visited the Holman-Moody garage, there was little doubt in discussions that Ford was providing some assistance, if only discounted prices on equipment. But in conversations with Bob Burdick, he refused to admit, even decades later, that the Thunderbirds were supplied at any discount.

4. Tom Cotter and Al Pearce, *Holman Moody: The Legendary Race Team* (St. Paul, Minnesota: MBI Publishing Company, 2002), p. 54; Lee Holman interview. Seven T-Birds are listed as entering the race. Fielden indicates eight were built. Lee Holman suggests nine were built.

5. Greg Fielden, *Forty Years of Stock Car Racing*, vol. 2 (Surfside Beach, South Carolina: Galfield Press, 1992), p. 12.

6. According to an Associated Press release dated May 14, 1954, described in "Indianapolis Incident Touched It Off," *Daytona Beach Morning Journal*, February 20, 1959, p. 1.

7. Fielden, *Forty Years*, vol. 2, p. 51.

8. Ann Bruner interview.

9. Morton Paulson, "Track's a Miracle of Engineering," *Daytona Beach Morning Journal*, February 22, 1959, p. 2E.

10. Bill Lazarus, *The Sands of Time* (Champaign, Illinois: Sports Publishing, 2004), p. 138.

11. Paulson, "Track's a Miracle," February 22, 1959, p. 2E.

12. Lazarus, *Sands of Time*, p. 136.

13. Larry Woody, "How the Daytona 500 Works," at http://entertainment .howstuffworks.com/Daytona-500.htm.

14. Judy Judge interview.

15. Barbara Heilman, "A Cool Fireball Named Roberts," *Sports Illustrated*, February 1964. See also Godwin Kelly, *Fireball* (Daytona Beach, Florida: Carbon Press, 2005).

16. "Stock Car Memories Daytona 500, 1958, 1959," (MC-193, TV Magic Memories, Moviecraft Home Video, Orlando Park, Illinois).

17. Bud Burdick interview.

18. Sonny Morgan interview.

19. Godwin Kelly, "Fireball Roberts," *Speedway Illustrated*, August 2006, pp. 31, 32.

20. Peter Golenbock, *American Zoom* (New York: Macmillan, 1993), p. 59.

21. Kevin Bagwell, *From California to the East Coast: Racing Memories from a NASCAR Legend*, vol. 1 (Port Orange, Florida: Panch Enterprises, 2007), p. 59.

22. Bernard Kahn, "On the Mark, Set, Go Today," *Daytona Morning Journal*, February 20, 1959, pp. 1, 2.

Chapter 22. The First Daytona 500

1. Bernard Kahn, "On the Mark, Set, Go Today," *Daytona Morning Journal*, February 20, 1959, pp. 1, 2.

2. Gregory Favre, "'Prophet' Welborn Really Earns Pole," *Atlanta Journal*, February 22, 1959, p. 2D.

3. Fireball Roberts, Curtis Turner, Tim Flock, Jack Smith, and Buck Baker were starting in the back.

4. Gregory Favre, "Fastest U.S. '100' Blazed by Welborn," *Atlanta Journal*, February 21, 1959, p. 5.

5. The misinformation about early NASCAR includes the identity of the person who discovered drafting. Tom Wolfe wrote an excellent article about Junior Johnson that readers might interpret as implying Johnson "discovered" the draft. Tom Wolfe, "The Last American Hero is Junior Johnson. Yes!" *Esquire*, March 1965. Junior Johnson was not the first to discover the draft. The newspapers report many drivers using the "slipstream."

6. Marvin Panch interview; Kevin Bagwell, *From California to the East Coast: Racing Memories from a NASCAR Legend*, vol. 1 (Port Orange, Florida: Panch Enterprises, 2007), pp. 58–61.

7. Tom Brown, "Tires Were a Big Factor in Race," *Daytona Beach Morning Journal*, February 23, 1959, pp. 1, 2. Roy Burdick's pit help included Bud Burdick and Dan Kosiski handling the gas refills; also involved were Holman and Moody employees, assisting all the Thunderbirds. Bill Smith was also in the pit area. Tire changes were not significant, because only one right front tire was changed and, according to Dan Kosiski, it was not even clear that the tire needed changing.

8. In its March 4, 1959, issue, *National Speed Sport News* printed a table with the front-runners, the first five, every five laps of the race. On the day after the race, February 23, 1959, the front page printed a table titled, "Ten Leading Drivers," in 50 mile increments (e.g., 50, 100, 150).

9. "Beauchamp Winner—Or Was It Petty?" *Atlanta Constitution*, February 23, 1959, pp. 7, 9.

10. Lap 70: 1. Pistone, 2. Welborn, 3. Weatherly, 4. Beauchamp, 5. Petty; Lap 75: 1. Pistone, 2. Welborn, 3. Smith, 4. Griffith, 5. Owens; Lap 80: 1. Pistone, 2. Petty, 3. Smith, 4. Griffith, 5. Beauchamp. The *National Speed Sport News*, in its March 4, 1959, issue, printed a table with the front-runners, the first five, every five laps of the race.

11. Al Thomy, "Johnny Says Sho, Petty No," *Atlanta Constitution*, February 23, 1959, p. 9.

12. Al Thomy, "Johnny Says Sho, Petty No."

13. Al Thomy, "Johnny Says Sho, Petty No."

14. Lloyd Jorgensen interview. France also sent telegrams to the Beauchamp and Petty camps. Dan Kosiski interview.

Chapter 23. The Photo Finish Quagmire

1. Several people have made the argument that France's view of the finish line was blocked by Weatherly's car. For this interpretation to hold water, one must believe Bill France would have decided on a winner without accurate knowledge. This is ludicrous. Bill France would not have called a winner unless he believed he knew who won. One must ask why France said Beauchamp won the race.

2. Gregory Favre, "Daytona Quiz: Who Won 500?" *Atlanta Journal*, February 23, 1959, pp. 15–16.

3. Gregory Favre, "Daytona Quiz," p. 15.

4. Gregory Favre, "Daytona Quiz," pp. 15–16.

5. Gregory Favre, "Daytona Quiz," pp. 15–16.

6. Al Thomy, "Suspense? Daytona Outdoes Hitchcock," *Atlanta Journal-Constitution*, February 25, 1959, sports section, p. 2.

7. T. Taylor Warren interview.

8. Rex White interview.

9. Thomy, "Suspense?" sports section, p. 2.

10. Larry Torson interview.

11. Smokey Yunick, *Best Damn Garage in Town: My Life and Adventures* (Holly Hill, Florida: Carbon Press, 2003), p. 101.

12. Bud Burdick interview.

13. Joe Menzer, *The Wildest Ride: A History of Nascar* (New York: Touchstone, 2002), p. 103.

14. Yunick, *Best Damn Garage*, p. 100.

15. Bill Smith interview.

16. Bill Smith interview.

17. T. Taylor Warren interview.

18. I enlisted Batten Communication, Inc., in Atlanta, Georgia, to help analyze the film: "Stock Car Memories Daytona 500 1958, 1959" (MC-193, TV Magic Memories, Moviecraft Home Video).

Chapter 24. Success at Any Cost

1. Frank Mundy interview.

2. Frank Mundy interview.

3. Frank Mundy interview.

4. For further information about this incident, see Peter Golenbock, *Nascar Confidential* (St. Paul, Minnesota: Motorbooks International, 2004), pp. 49–50; Frank Mundy interview.

5. Al Thomy, "Mundy's First Turn Advice Helped Put Johnny on the Spot," *Atlanta Journal-Constitution*, March 23, 1959, p. 12; Frank Mundy interview.

6. Golenbock, *Nascar Confidental*, p. 27.

7. Kim Chapin, *Fast as White Lightning*, (New York: Three Rivers Press, 1998), p. 81.

8. Kim Chapin, *Fast as White Lightning*, p. 81. Brian Donovan, in his *Hard Driving* (Hanover, New Hampshire: Steerforth Press, 2008), describes at great length the struggles of the first black NASCAR driver, Wendell Scott. Scott faced discrimination, but disentangling Bill France's typical treatment of everyone from discrimination is complicated. Scott's son said that France's attitude toward his father was "a business arrangement" (p. 115).

9. Neal Thompson, *Driving with the Devil* (New York: Crown Publishers, 2006), p. 231.

10. Neal Thompson, *Driving with the Devil*, p. 235.

11. Neal Thompson, *Driving with the Devil*, p. 239.

12. Peter Golenbock, *American Zoom* (New York: Macmillan, 1993), p. 57.

13. Chapin, *Fast as White Lightning*, p. 24; Golenbock, *American Zoom*, p. 28.

14. Ed Hinton, *Daytona* (New York: Warner Books, 2001), p. 88.

15. Mark Stewart, *The Pettys* (Brookfield, Connecticut: Millbrook Press, 2001), p. 7.

16. Golenbock, *American Zoom*, p. 28.

17. Greg Fielden, *Forty Years of Stock Car Racing*, vol. 1 (Surfside Beach, South Carolina: Galfield Press, 1992), p. 336.

18. "NASCAR Lee Petty Mechanic of Year," *Atlanta Journal-Constitution*, February 19, 1959, p. 34.

Chapter 25. Covering Up and Rewriting History

1. Bloys Britt and Bill France, *The Racing Flag* (New York: Pocket Books, 1965).

2. Greg Fielden, *Forty Years of Stock Car Racing*, vol. 2 (Surfside Beach, South Carolina: Galfield Press, 1992); Bob Desiderio, "Beauchamp Wins—Unofficially," *Daytona Beach Morning Journal*, February 23, 1959, pp. 1, 2; Bernard Kahn, "Fastest Stock Car Race Ends in Controversy," *Daytona Beach Morning Journal*, February 23, 1959, pp. 1, 2; Tom Brown, "Tires Were Big Factor in Race," *Daytona Beach Morning Journal*, February 23, 1959, pp. 1, 2; "Ten Leading Drivers: Average Speed at 50 Mile Posts," *Daytona Beach Morning Journal*, February 23, 1959, p. 2; "The Daytona 500—Lap-by-Lap," *National Speed Sport News*, March 4, 1959.

3. Britt and France, *Racing Flag*, p. 27.

4. Marshall McLuhan, *Understanding Media* (New York: New American Library, 1964), p. 32. McLuhan used this phrase when writing about the mass media.

Chapter 26. Scoring

1. Bob Desiderio, "Had Him Like This — Says Beauchamp," *Illustrated Speedway News*, February 24, 1959.

2. Howard DeHart interview. DeHart was an important employee of the Holman-Moody race shop, the major garage for Ford racing initiatives, and DeHart was in the Beauchamp pits in 1959.

3. Paul Hudson interview.

4. Ray Chaike interview.

5. Dick Bergen, "How NASCAR Controls the Show," *Speedway Illustrated*, July 2006, p. 30.

6. Jim Reed interview.

7. Helen Hudson interview.

8. In an investigation, no evidence was found that Morris Metcalf was dishonest in the scoring. He was a counter. He supervised the counting of laps. If anything dishonest occurred, it was not done by Morris Metcalf.

9. Morris Metcalf interview; Greg Fielden, *Forty Years of Stock Car Racing*, vol. 1 (Surfside Beach, South Carolina: Galfield Press, 1992), p. 175.

Chapter 27. Connecting the Dots

1. Greg Fielden, *Forty Years of Stock Car Racing*, vol. 1, (Surfside Beach, South Carolina: Galfield Press, 1992), p. 303.

2. Robert Edelstein, *Full Throttle* (New York: Overlook Press, 2005), p. 114.

3. Fielden, *Forty Years*, vol. 1, p. 303. This story and quotation appear in several publications. I have added italics to the Thompson quotation.

4. Donna Beauchamp interview.

5. Al Thomy, "Papa Petty Wants Son to Win — But Richard Must Earn It," *Atlanta Constitution*, June 5, 1959, p. 9.

6. Al Thomy, "Papa Petty Wants Son to Win."

7. Al Thomy, "Papa Petty Wants Son to Win."

8. Greg Fielden, *Forty Years of Stock Car Racing*, vol. 2 (Surfside Beach, South Carolina: Galfield Press, 1992), p. 67.

9. Jim Reed interview.

10. Lee Holman interview.

11. Interview, name withheld.

12. Eddie Samples interview.

13. Wanda Lund interview.

14. William Beauchamp interview.

15. There may be various versions of Friel's exact words at the driver meeting, particularly the words about whether a violation of the "no cut through the infield" rule was an automatic disqualification from the race. In the days after the

race, various claims were made, but it is clear the Pettys did not believe a violation would automatically lead to disqualification, and NASCAR officials allowed the disqualified drivers to stay on the track and complete the event rather than flagging them off the track.

16. Greg Fielden, *Charlotte Motor Speedway* (St. Paul, Minnesota: MBI Publishing Company, 2000), p. 26. See also George Cunningham, "Joe Lee Johnson Wins Thrill-filled World 600," *Charlotte Observer*, June 20, 1960, p. 4-B; and George Cunningham, "Pettys, 4 Others Disqualified from 600," *Charlotte Observer*, June 21, 1960, p. 4-B; Fielden, *Forty Years*, vol. 2, pp. 72–73.

17. One might speculate that after the recent Weaverville race with its lap-counting issues and the other past incidents raising scoring concerns, Bill France might have borrowed from the Holman-Moody example (it had hired Price-Waterhouse to count for a few races) and stationed several other people to count the Petty cars' laps. If these special France-appointed scorers had found that the Pettys did not finish with as many laps as appeared on Elizabeth Petty's scorecards, this would have confirmed the rumor that Wanda Lund had heard to the effect that NASCAR caught the Pettys cheating at some point. In any event, in this race the punishment for cutting across the infield was harsh.

18. Furman Bisher, "Some Petty Differences," *Atlanta Journal*, July 29, 1960, p. 15.

19. Annette Gordon-Reed, law and history professor, faced this problem in her research prior to the time when DNA evidence could have provided more conclusive evidence.

20. Rosalind Bentley, "Rewriting Jefferson," *Atlanta Journal-Constitution*, September 28, 2008, p. K10.

21. Beauchamp told this to several people, including his children and his wife, Donna. They mentioned it when interviewed.

Chapter 28. Out of the Air

1. Gregory Favre, "'Must Catch Lee': Johnny," *Atlanta Journal*, March 21, 1951, p. 6; "Beauchamp Winner—Or Was It Petty?" *Atlanta Constitution*, February 23, 1959, pp. 7, 9.

2. Bob Burdick interview. Beauchamp attempted to convince Roy Burdick to remain in the South after the 1959 Daytona 500, continuing to race the Thunderbird. Burdick had been away from his auto garage business in South Omaha for more than three weeks. He had talked to a Daytona lawyer about bringing suit against NASCAR. The lawyer told him NASCAR would win, and Burdick packed up and left. His brother, Bud, and Dan Kosiski had already left Daytona with the Thunderbird. Dan Kosiski interview. The Kosiski family had a prominent South Omaha racing garage. Dan's brother Bob had challenged Beauchamp and Burdick for the Playland track championship in 1954.

3. Accounts of and statistics for the owner of Beauchamp's Lakewood T-Bird are incorrect. Most list Roy Burdick as the owner. Beauchamp was the owner. The Atlanta press coverage of the race accurately reported Beauchamp's ownership of the car.

4. It was difficult for NASCAR drivers to travel the long distance to New York, so a number of drivers received some incentive money. Rex White received $100 to make the trip and race. Rex White interview.

5. Jim Reed interview.

6. Frank M. Blunk, "15,000 See Reed Take Auto Grind," *New York Times*, April 26, 1959, p. S-1.

7. Frank M. Blunk, "15,000 See Reed Take Auto Grind," p. S-5.

8. The online source http://www.racing-reference.info lists the car Beauchamp drove at Reading as owned by Lee Petty. However, Jim Reed was the owner, not Lee Petty. In several personal interviews, Jim Reed has told the story of Beauchamp taking the car to Reading, Pennsylvania. The local newspaper does not list Beauchamp driving a Petty car. The above-mentioned racing reference was informed but has refused to correct this factual error. Aside from the documentation that the racing reference is incorrect, the fact of Beauchamp driving a Lee Petty car does not make sense.

9. Dale Swanson was also at the 1960 Daytona 500, not as an owner, but as the paid mechanic for Bob Potter. A capable but not exceptional driver, Potter was based in Minnesota and had driven in the IMCA circuit. He came away with tenth in the qualifying event and fifteenth in the Daytona 500.

10. Greg Fielden, *Forty Years of Stock Car Racing*, vol. 2 (Surfside Beach, South Carolina: Galfield Press, 1992), p. 44.

11. This race was held February 12 between the two 40-lap qualifying races.

12. Ned Jarrett interview; Reb Wickersham interview.

13. Dale Swanson Jr. interview. He watched the taping of the program.

14. Dale Swanson Jr. interview.

15. Richard Peers interview.

16. Lee Holman Jr. interview.

17. Bud Burdick interview.

18. Ann Bruner interview.

19. Dale Swanson Jr. interview.

20. Dale Swanson Jr. interview.

21. Fred Miller interview.

22. *Harlan News-Advertiser*, March 17, 1969, p. 8. http://hrn.stparchive.com/Archive/HRN/HRN03171969P08.php

23. Randy Rath interview.

24. Chatburn Avenue.

25. Dick Archibald interview.

Chapter 29. The Hard Charger Wins Slow

1. Robert McKee interview; Speedy Bill Smith interview. The racing records fail to reflect that Lund began his NASCAR season as driver and owner.

2. Gus Holzmueller Jr. interview.

3. Rex White interview.

4. Rex White interview. Many people close to racing are familiar with Lund's connection to this expression.

5. The fish camp was at Monck's Corner, Cross, South Carolina.

6. Kim Chapin, *Fast as White Lightning* (New York: Three Rivers Press, 1998), p. 21; Larry Frank interview.

7. Larry Frank interview. Frank and Lund used plastic milk cartons on their fishing lines. Also, Rex White described Lund's method of fishing in White's *Gold Thunder* (Jefferson, North Carolina: McFarland and Co., 2005), p. 88.

8. Marvin Panch interview.

9. Speedy Bill Smith interview. The sequence of events is unclear. Ruthie seems to have left Tiny in 1963, yet she appears in photographs after Tiny won the Daytona.

10. Marvin Panch interview.

11. Kevin Bagwell, *From California to the East Coast: Racing Memories from a NASCAR Legend*, vol. 2 (Port Orange, Florida: Panch Enterprises, 2007), pp. 18–22; Marvin Panch interview.

12. Larry Frank interview.

13. Greg Fielden, *Forty Years of Stock Car Racing*, vol. 2 (Surfside Beach, South Carolina: Galfield Press, 1992), pp. 194–195; Marvin Panch interview; Ed Hinton, *Daytona* (New York: Warner Books, 2001), p. 120.

14. Wanda Lund interview.

15. The years were 1968, 1970, and 1971.

16. In 1968 and 1969 the division was called the Grand Touring division. Then NASCAR, under financial pressure, reshuffled the events and called the circuit Grand American Central. In 1971 Lund was the champion, but the circuit only held eleven races.

17. During his career, Lund won five or fewer Grand National races. The total depends on how the records are counted. At this time, for certain races, Grand National cars raced in the same event and on the same track with Grand American cars. Occasionally, on short tracks, the Grand American cars won. Tiny won several events that were also cross-listed as Grand National races, but he was credited with a Grand American victory. Lund's accomplishments in the Grand American division cemented his fame.

Epilogue

1. Condo building is planned for the space.

2. Kim Chapin, *Fast as White Lightning* (New York: Three Rivers Press, 1998), p. 12. One can speculate that Lund's exposure to radiation during the twenty years he had served in the military was finally affecting his health.

3. Kim Chapin, *Fast as White Lightning*.

4. Roger Byers interview.

5. Interview with Kenny Myler's stepdaughter; interview with Maurice Petty's wife. Kenny "Red" Myler, who had come South in 1956 with Lund, was at Talladega that day. Those in the car with Myler recall an eerie silence in the drive back to Randleman after the race.

6. The funeral was on August 19, 1975.

7. Randy Rath interview.

8. Randy Rath interview.

9. Dale Swanson Jr. interview.

10. Dale Swanson Jr. interview.

11. One place where this axiom is followed is in the film *The Man Who Shot Liberty Valance* (1962). Jimmy Stewart's character was credited with killing Liberty Valance, but it was actually the man played by John Wayne who killed Liberty. Years later, when the Stewart character was a U.S. senator and the truth was known, a reporter had to decide what to print.

12. Fans watched races at local tracks everywhere in the United States. Auto racing was not exclusively a southeastern phenomenon. Three factors were characteristic of southern racing: a warm weather climate, impoverished communities, and driver training through moonshine runs. Stock car racing became the sport of the lower class, in part because it required fewer resources to participate and offered a small amount of cash to the winner. What gave NASCAR a big boost is that cable television needed more programming and that portable video equipment became available, facilitating the filming of sporting events, including races. Bill France could not have anticipated the video revolution that made them rich.

13. This was widely reported. For example, see Ed Hinton, *Daytona* (New York: Warner Books, 2001), pp. 90–93.

14. Scott Shults, *The First 25 Years of Stock Car Racing* (Peoria, Illinois: Oldtimers Racing Club, n.d.).

15. Glenn Robey, who competed fiercely and sometimes successfully against him at the beginning in 1950, still was racing in the twenty-first century.

16. Paul Malcom interview.

17. Donna Beauchamp interview; also, Norma Brix interview.

18. Norma Brix interview.

19. "Occupation: Race Driver, Hobby: Collecting Things," 1962 newspaper article from Leslie family scrapbook.

20. Norma Brix interview.

21. Bob Beauchamp interview.

22. Bob Beauchamp interview; Donna Beauchamp interview.

23. John Beauchamp's funeral was in Atlantic, Iowa, with many people attending. Dale Swanson sent flowers in the shape of a 55.

INDEX

racing dangers, 10–11, 15, 17, 23, 48,
58, 73, 74, 102, 109, 115, 118, 152–53,
160
racing maneuvers: banging, xiii, 22,
35, 36, 40, 41, 48, 58, 62, 70, 133,
149, 156, 159; blocking, 23, 30, 36,
40, 62, 111, 123; braking, 22–23, 24,
54, 87, 91, 149, 152; bumping, 24,
30, 43, 48, 59, 70, 133; drafting, 120,
137, 157, 186n5; spinning out, xii,
xiii, 22, 23–24, 30–31, 34–35, 40,
61–62, 111, 124
Raduenz, Art, 75
Rapid City (Nebraska), 52–53
Rathman, Dick, 52, 53–54
Rayburn, Jerry, 156
Richter, Donna, *photos 7, 19*
Riley, Chuck, 58–59
Roberts, Fireball, 95, 104, 116, 119,
120–21, 123, 125, 132, 135, 143,
182n3, 185n3
Robey, Glenn, 22, 36–37, 173n17,
174n18, 193n15
Rose, Mauri, 95, 108
Ross, Curtis "Cyclone," 11

St. Paul-Minneapolis Fair, 75
Scharf, Chuck, 50
Scott, Wendell, 188n8
SEDCO garage, ix, 94–99, 101, 103,
107, 108–10, 181n3, 182n20, 182n25,
182n26; banquet, *photo 19*
Selser, Wayne, 6, 8, 27
Shaffer, Norman, 13
Shelby County Fair, 2–4, 6, 26–27
Shenandoah (Iowa), 36
Short, George, *photo 15*
Short, Merle, 65–66
Short, Mrs. George, *photo 15*
Shuck, Gordon, 13

Sioux Falls (South Dakota), 14, 70, 72,
78, 79, 90, 180n20
Skelton, Betty, 101–2, 182n20, 183n7,
183n9, *photo 19*
Sloan, Alex, 67
Sloboth, Tom, 36, 61–62
Slusky, Abe, 8–9, 11, 22, 29, 32, 44–46,
50, 159
Slusky, Louis, 8, 11
Smith, Bill "Speedy," 19, 32, 65, 72,
74, 104, 153, 170n6, 171n14, 173n6,
186n7
Smith, Jack, 121–23, 135, 137, 143,
182n26, 185n3, 186n10, *photo 19*
Society for Autosports, Fellowship,
and Education (SAFE), 49–51,
59
Southern Engineering Development
Company. *See* SEDCO
Southern 500, 49
speedway cars, 67, 92
Spencer (Iowa), 72, 78
spider gear, 32–33, 173n6
sprint cars. *See* speedway cars
state fairs, 31, 89, 90
Swanson, Dale: partnership with
John Beauchamp, ix, xiii, 4, 5–6,
9, 12, 13–14, 19–20, 29–30, 34–35,
39, 40, 54, 56–57, 58–59, 61–62,
65, 69, 71, 73, 75–79, 85–87, 90–91,
100, 104, 110, 111, 151–53, 176n1,
191n9, 193n23; partnership with
Dwayne "Tiny" Lund, ix, 10, 16,
18–20, 21–22, 23, 25, 26–28, 29–30,
37–39, 46, 61, 62, 64–65, 77, 156,
159, 178n4; *photos 4, 7, 9, 15, 17, 19,
20*; relationship with Phyllis Kohls,
3, 46, 70, 88, 108
Swanson, Dale, Jr., *photo 20*
Swanson, Phyllis, *photos 7, 19*

Teague, Marshall, 118
teardown inspections, 32–34, 35, 57, 79–80, 84
Terry, Chuck, 40
Thomas, Herb, 52, 53–54, 138, 178n11
Thompson, Speedy, 106, 142, 146, 149, 183n3, 182n26
Thompson, Wally, 32
Topeka (Kansas), 78, 79, 85–88, 89, 180n19,
Turko Motors, 25
Turner, Curtis, 104, 120, 142–43, 146, 151, 178n11, 183n12, 185n3

United States Auto Club (USAC), 92, 182n24

Vogt, Red, 129, 131

Wainwright, Tiny, 25
Wausau (Wisconsin), 71, 75

Weatherly, Joe, 104, 119–20, 122–24, 125, 137, 178n11, 183n12, 187n1, 186n10
Welborn, Bob, *photo 19*
White, Don, 70, 72, 75, 76–79, 86–90, 91, 112, 179n7, 180n21, 180n29
White, Rex, ix, 95, 96–97, 99, 106, 119, 126, 149, 155, 182n26, 191n4, 192n7, *photo 19*
Wimble, Bill, 156
Winkley, Frank, 67, 88, 90, 92
Womochil, Bob, 58
Wyatt, Roxine "Socky," 22–23

Yetter (Iowa), 16
Yunick, Smokey, 97–98, 101, 103, 117, 127, 131, 161, 171n13

Zenchuck, George, 40, *photo 7*
Zenchuck, Mrs. George, *photo 7*